PRAISE FOR *THE ROAD TO Z*

'*The Road to Zero Emissions* is a timely reminder of the hurdles that need to be overcome in a sector that is currently high risk and low margin. Alternative power source options need to be considered and this will require significant investment.'
Richard Burnett, Chief Executive, Road Haulage Association

'Future change, improving road transport and helping improve our environment are at the heart of *The Road to Zero Emissions*. While there is a lot of government and media messaging about climate change and protecting the environment, there are few publications, if any, that address these issues so comprehensively and clearly as this book. It is especially important in providing the way forward to achieve the necessary changes required to protect our planet and I am happy to endorse this book wholeheartedly.'
Martin Port, CEO, BigChange

'This book provides a critical examination of how global vehicle manufacturers, transport and logistic organizations and governments are tackling the threat of climate change. The world is engaged in a digital, electronic revolution that will challenge and disrupt many of the organizations featured in this book. How they respond and who will survive are covered on this journey.'
Professor Tim Baines, Operations and Information Management Department, Aston Business School

'Details a clear pathway to the future of road transport and its important relationship with the environment. The success of zero emissions technology requires more efficient, shorter product development times. Rapid technology delivery has been accelerated through successful collaboration between manufacturers who are busy developing products for the wider market and product specialists such as Electra. I am delighted that this important book has been written and that the work of Electra Commercial Vehicles has been included.'
Sid Sadique, Chairman/Owner, Electra Trucks Ltd

'A concise narrative of the issues and hurdles that manufacturers, transport operators and their supply chains need to face.'
Steve Hobson, Editor, *Motor Transport*

'The challenge of achieving zero emissions will not only require new products, energy systems and infrastructure investment; it also needs to provide training and support for all levels of management in a very complex supply chain. Business model innovation will be a key driver of change and this book highlights many possible solutions.'
Thomas van Mouric, CEO, Culina Group

'*The Road to Zero Emissions* provides a comprehensive and insightful view of the important issues which will drive the reduction in energy consumption and the environmental impact.'
Bob Harbey, Executive Director, Microlise

'Having been responsible for the operation and management of many transport companies and thousands of vehicles over the last 50 years, I am well aware of the challenges to achieving zero emissions. This comprehensive analysis of the future will provide many transport operators with a guidebook through the maze of options.'
Glyn Davies, Chairman, Landex Holdings

'Fossil fuel emissions have significantly contributed towards the climate change challenge that is arguably the biggest crisis facing the world today. This book critically examines the choices that industry and governments must make to reduce the threat of climate change, which in turn will have profound consequences for many of the world's leading business units.'
Professor Malcom McDonald, Cranfield University

The Road to Zero Emissions

*The future of trucks, transport and
automotive industry supply chains*

Dennis Evans

Des Evans

Alistair Williamson

KoganPage

First published in Great Britain and the United States in 2020 by Kogan Page Limited

2nd Floor, 45 Gee Street
London
EC1V 3RS
United Kingdom
www.koganpage.com

122 W 27th St, 10th Floor
New York, NY 10001
USA

4737/23 Ansari Road
Daryaganj
New Delhi 110002
India

Kogan Page books are printed on paper from sustainable forests.

ISBNs

Hardback   978 1 78966 562 8
Paperback   978 1 78966 560 4
Ebook   978 1 78966 561 1

British Library Cataloguing-in-Publication Data

A CIP record for this book is available from the British Library.

Library of Congress Cataloging-in-Publication Number

2020941849

Typeset by Integra Software Services, Pondicherry
Print production managed by Jellyfish
Printed and bound by CPI Group (UK) Ltd, Croydon CR0 4YY

CONTENTS

ABOUT THE AUTHORS

The co-authors have spent over 120 years in the automotive and transport business and have been closely involved with the commercial success of several truck manufacturing operations since 1975. Most recently they have over 50 years between them with MAN Truck & Bus Ltd, a division of Traton AG (the commercial vehicle division of VW AG).

Dennis Evans

Dennis Evans served as Head of Aftersales Business Development and Strategic Projects for MAN Truck & Bus UK Ltd in the period from 2005–2016, following a successful career in the automotive industry working for several major manufacturers and Tier 1 suppliers in 23 countries since 1975. These included original equipment manufacturers (OEMs) such as Ford Motor Company, Unipart, Rover, Land Rover, Mini, BMW, and body builder Mayflower Ltd. Mayflower was a Tier 1 supplier to Rover, MG, Ford, Aston Martin, Chrysler, Mercedes and Alexanders – a UK bus manufacturer. Dennis Evans has specialized in the development of market representation strategies and innovative customer relationship and retention programmes.

Des Evans OBE

Des Evans OBE was recognized in the 2016 Queen's Birthday Honours List for services to industry. He served as CEO for a decade at MAN Truck & Bus UK Ltd and successfully built the VW-owned UK operation from a £50 million turnover business to one delivering over £500 million in the period from 1993–2013. Following Des's retirement from MAN in 2015, he became an Honorary Professor at Aston University and continued to share his experience with MBA students on Business Model concepts that have the power to re-imagine established business practices. This is a role also shared with Cranfield University and as a valued adviser to many industry trade associations. Des's legacy is rooted in the development of innovative and disruptive business models that have changed the basis of competition in the industry.

Alistair Williamson MBA

Alistair Williamson MBA started his working life as a development engineer with Bedford Trucks and graduated through engineering, sales, business development and marketing roles at Scania (Great Britain) Limited. He became Marketing Director for MAN Truck & Bus UK Limited in a period of rapid development, where he introduced the word 'trucknology' into the commercial vehicle lexicon and launched the MAN TGA range in the UK market. Alistair subsequently became Vice President Worldwide Marketing for MAN Truck & Bus AG based in Munich, where he was responsible for the worldwide launches of the D20 engine and the TGL/TGM truck ranges. He has operated his own successful marketing consultancy for 15 years, during which time he has carried out many significant projects for other automotive companies. Additionally, he has developed an innovative web portal, www.truckepedia.com, which provides the commercial vehicle, distribution, transport and logistics industries with an innovative 'business intelligence service' aimed at developing commercial relationships through knowledge management and business development projects.

PREFACE

A letter to the future

The Arctic is warming rapidly and is on the front line of climate change. As our world warms, the region's glaciers weep. Iceland's 400-plus glaciers have been melting steadily, now losing roughly 11 billion tonnes of ice every year. Scientists fear that by 2200, Iceland will no longer be a land of ice. All the country's glaciers will have disappeared.

A century ago, the Okjökull glacier covered 15 square kilometres (5.8 square miles), measuring some 50 metres thick. But ravaged by warming temperatures, it has now shrunk to barely one square kilometre of ice less than 15 metres deep, meaning it is no longer classified as a glacier. It is now seen as 'dead ice.'

The plaque to the lost glacier is inscribed in Icelandic and English and is 'a letter to the future' authored by one of Iceland's most prominent writers, Andri Snær Magnason. It was erected by scientists in Iceland in June 2019.

The letter reads:

In the next 200 years all our glaciers are expected to follow the same path. This monument is to acknowledge that we know what is happening and what needs to be done. Only you know if we did it.

The Road to Zero Emissions roadmap

The Road to Zero Emissions will provide a roadmap for those wishing to avoid the disaster of Okjökull in Iceland. This is a road we do not wish to travel; our journey is to gain the knowledge and motivation to make a positive contribution to climate change and deliver on the goals of the Paris Agreement. Think of this book as 'your letter and guide to the future of trucks and transportation'.

FIGURE 0.1   A letter to the future

SOURCE https://news.rice.edu/2019/08/13/memorial-honoring-lost-glacier-to-be-installed-in-iceland-aug-18-2/

ACKNOWLEDGEMENTS

The authors would like to give their sincere thanks to a number of organizations and people who have contributed significantly.

The research we undertook found many answers to the questions raised in reports from the International Energy Agency. The Paris Agreement – a seminal document charting the obligations nearly every country in the world has signed up to – has been expertly detailed on the website of The Centre for Climate and Energy solutions: https://www.c2es.org/content/paris-climate-agreement-qa/

The many white papers and strategy documents issued by the UK Government and the European Commission have enabled the authors to document what budgets and investment criteria will be available to support the strategic projects necessary to deliver the goals of the Paris Agreement. We wish to thank all of these research bodies for their knowledge and expertise.

In particular, we would like to thank a number of senior consultants working for McKinsey & Company for their generous contributions and insight. These include: Alex Matthey at McKinsey's Munich Office; Martin Hattrup-Silberberg at McKinsey's Frankfurt Office; Andreas Cornet, a Senior Partner in McKinsey's Munich office; and Harald Deubener, a Partner in McKinsey's Stuttgart Office.

BCG – Boston Consulting Group – have also provided additional expertise and experience with the results of their numerous research studies on electric vehicles. Our thanks to members of their project teams: Michelle Andersen, Nikolaus Land and Thomas Dauner. The generous access provided to your documents 'Where to Profit as Tech Transforms Mobility' and 'The Future of Battery Production' furnished us with invaluable insights into the trends that will shape the future of the automotive supply chains in the next 50 years.

In addition, the insight and information provided by the BloombergNEF, and in particular Colin McKerracher, has been invaluable.

Our sincere gratitude to The Faraday Institution – the UK's independent body for electrochemical energy storage research and skills development. Matt Howard, in his role as Head of Engagement, has been very generous with his time and sharing of key research data on the threats and opportunities the UK automotive industry faces, and we thank him for his cooperation in supplying facts and ` to enhance our knowledge of key developments in this area.

Roland Berger, a leading European consultancy based in Munich, Germany, have provided insight into the future of the truck aftersales business, the growth of OEM-owned service factories, and trends into aftersales operations over the next 10 years.

Chapter 11 of this book on business innovation and disruptive business models illustrates how changing the basis of competition can be accomplished in mature industries. We are thankful to Professor Tim Baines of Aston Business School and Professor Malcolm McDonald of Cranfield University for their insight and experience that contributed to this chapter.

A special mention for Tony Pain, a recognized and respected transport industry consultant. Tony was a great sounding board for the place that alternative fuels will have in our industry; his insight into the threat from Chinese battery manufacturers has proved prophetic. Our thanks to Tony for sharing his knowledge and experience in this area.

The target audience for this book is served by a number of trade magazines and trade associations including RTM – Road Transport Media. RTM have been central to providing market intelligence and the latest news on key trends in the UK truck and transport business. We have worked closely with key members of the RTM executive team. We would like to thank Will Shiers, editor of *Commercial Motor*, RTM Director Steve Hobson, Divisional Director Vic Bunby and Managing Director Andy Salter for their support in getting the message out to the industry at large.

On a personal note Dennis Evans would like to thank his good friend Lieutenant Colonel (Retd) Kevan Ball for sharing his experiences of managing and implementing significant sustainability projects for the Army and the military commitment to ecological programme management on our daily dog-walking exercises.

Our enormous thanks to the publishing and editing team at Kogan Page, who have been instrumental in getting this story to market; our thanks go to Head of Publishing Julia Swales, and Adam Cox and his editorial team.

Introduction

What do you think the world would be like without the invention of the wheel and the axle? Many jobs would be much harder, and transportation specifically would certainly look much different than it does today in 2020. In many practical ways, the wheel and axle make the world go around, as does transport, which is integral to the functioning of almost all modern economies.

Horse-drawn wheeled transport has since been replaced by the internal combustion engine (ICE), which became the motive force of transport in 1896 when Rudolf Diesel successfully patented the diesel engine. In modern times, there has been an increased push beyond this technology towards electric vehicles for much the same reasons as the horse-drawn carriage was replaced – efficiency and effectiveness. However, at the same time the internal combustion engine was being adopted, Nikola Tesla invented and patented an alternating current electric motor. Unfortunately, this failed to establish itself. In hindsight it is interesting to speculate whether the existential environmental threat we face today could have been averted had the electric motor prevailed over the fossil fuel energy source that has dominated our transport industry since its adoption.

Was this a missed opportunity?

The main driver for writing this book was rooted in helping readers to understand the global, industrial, sociological and economic revolution the world is being challenged by in 2020, but also the development of alternative energy sources for transport and how to make sense of the changes and challenges ahead.

Book contents summary

In this book we will cover in detail how we can avoid missing significant opportunities in the future. Together we will explore the following:

- **Chapter 1**: an overview of the threats and challenges posed by climate change and the future of the fossil fuel industry subject to a decline in petrol and diesel demand.

- **Chapter 2**: the rise and fall of diesel as a dominant fuel source, the impact of 'Dieselgate' and how original equipment manufacturers (OEMs) have responded to environmental regulations.

- **Chapter 3**: the goals, impact and long-term ambitions of the Paris Agreement.

- **Chapter 4**: the climate change challenge – the impact of greenhouse gases and CO_2 – and how the global community of nations agreed a programme of activity to address the threat of global warming.

- **Chapter 5**: the infrastructure challenge and the role of government in supporting a zero-emission transport system through the innovative development of a concept we describe as 'freight-ports'.

- **Chapter 6**: the impact of new battery technology on future employment in the automotive industry and the critical importance of the sustainable sourcing of rare earth materials (REMs).

- **Chapter 7**: EV (electrical vehicle) charging infrastructure, energy pricing, carbon taxation and the impact on the national grid.

- **Chapter 8**: the world's 'Top 10' OEMs – truck manufacturers – and their product development plans to provide alternative fuel-powered vehicles.

- **Chapter 9**: 'new entrants' into the developing EV market space.

- **Chapter 10**: alternative fuels – is hydrogen the fuel of the future for heavy-duty trucks?

- **Chapter 11**: business innovation, disruptive business models and changing the basis of competition.

- **Chapter 12**: the shift in the centre of gravity for the global automotive industry from the United States and Western Europe to Asia and particularly China.

- **Chapter 13**: a summary of the journey to zero-emission vehicles (ZEVs) so far.

- **Chapter 14**: the future of trucks and transport – 2050 and beyond: the future OEM distribution model including dealer franchising; the massive investment in future freight management and technology-driven maintenance services; the reinvention of truck stops.

What is net-zero emissions and how will it be achieved?

The state of net-zero emissions will be achieved when any remaining human-caused greenhouse gas emissions (GHGs) are balanced out. Net-zero emissions means that harmful human-made emissions are balanced out by removing GHGs from the atmosphere (a process known as carbon removal). The initial challenge is to address human-caused emissions. Such emissions include those from fossil-fuelled vehicles and factories – these should be reduced to close to zero as quickly as possible. Any remaining GHGs must be reduced by a corresponding amount of carbon removal. Examples of how this can be implemented are by restoring forests or through direct air capture and storage (DACS) technology. The concept of net-zero emissions could be described as that of 'climate neutrality' (Levin and Davis, 2019).

The IPCC demonstrates in its most recent report of 2018 that net emissions must be reduced to zero in order to stabilize global temperatures. The report also states that any scenario that does not involve a reduction to zero will not stop climate change. This objective has been ratified by Switzerland, the EU and many other countries, under the Paris Agreement (IPCC, 2019).

To reach net-zero emissions and limit global warming to 1.5°C, it is necessary to remove and permanently store CO_2 from the atmosphere. As noted by MyClimate:

> This is called Carbon Dioxide Removal (CDR). As it is the opposite of emissions, these practices or technologies are often described as achieving 'negative emissions' or 'sinks'. There is a direct link between zero-net emissions and CDR: The earlier zero-net emissions are achieved, the less CDR is necessary. However, it should be noted: the later this goal is reached, the higher the negative emissions need to be (MyClimate, nd).

Since Earth already reacts strongly to small changes in the amount of CO_2, methane and other greenhouse gases in the atmosphere, emissions of these gases must be reduced until the whole system is back in balance again. Net-zero emissions means that all man-made greenhouse gas emissions must be removed from the atmosphere through reduction measures, thus reducing the Earth's net climate balance, after removal via natural and artificial sink, to zero. This way humankind would be carbon neutral and the global temperature would stabilize (MyClimate, nd).

Global greenhouse gas emissions by economic sector

Global greenhouse gas emissions can be broken down by economic activities that lead to their production. As shown in Figure 0.1, electricity and heat production is the largest contributor and accounts for 25 per cent of global greenhouse gas (GHG) emissions. Agriculture, forestry and other land use produce 24 per cent, and industry accounts for 21 per cent of GHGs. In contrast, transportation accounts for only 14 per cent of global greenhouse gas emissions (EPA, 2020).

GHGs from this sector primarily involve fossil fuels burned for road, rail, air and marine transportation. Almost all (95 per cent) of the world's transportation energy comes from petroleum-based fuels, largely gasoline and diesel (EPA, 2020).

The suitability of alternative fuels to petroleum products varies across the transport sector and reflects the diverse nature of the global transportation

FIGURE 0.1 Global greenhouse gas emissions by economic sector

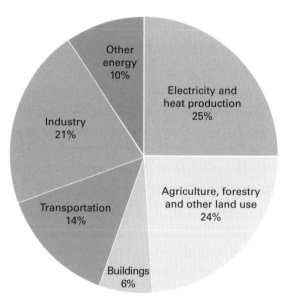

SOURCE EPA, 2020

FIGURE 0.2 Global greenhouse gas emissions within the transport sector

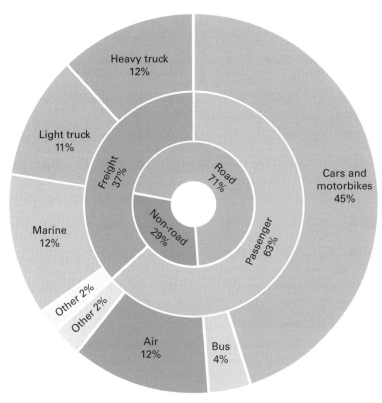

SOURCE EIA, 2020

system. When we consider Figure 0.2, cars and motorbikes make up nearly 50 per cent of GHGs from all transportation modes and nearly two thirds (63 per cent) of all road transportation GHGs. Meanwhile freight transportation makes up just over one third (37 per cent) of global GHGs. Light truck accounts for 11 per cent of road freight and heavy truck makes up 12 per cent. The balance of freight movement is 12 per cent marine and other (2 per cent) is primarily rail and air (EIA, 2017).

Achieving significant emission reductions in passenger car transportation

There are a variety of opportunities to reduce GHGs associated with passenger car transportation:

- Alternative fuels: using fuels that emit less CO_2 than fuels currently being used. Alternative sources can include biofuels, hydrogen, electricity from renewable sources such as wind and solar, or fossil fuels that are less CO_2-intensive than the fuels they replace.

- Improving fuel efficiency with advanced design, materials and technologies.
- Improving operating practices: adopting practices that minimize fuel use; improving driving practices and vehicle maintenance.
- Reducing travel demand: employing urban planning to reduce the number of miles that people drive each day. Reducing the need for driving through travel efficiency measures such as commuter, biking, 'work from home' and pedestrian programmes.

Achieving significant emission reductions in light and heavy-duty road transport

Achieving significant emission reductions in light and heavy-duty road transport requires either the use of alternative low-carbon fuels within internal combustion engines, or a shift to electric drivetrains with energy storage in battery (BEVs) or hydrogen (FCEVs) form. Electric drivetrains deliver the advantage of far greater in-vehicle energy efficiency, but the key technical issue is whether energy storage densities and charging rates can be sufficient to make them a feasible alternative to diesel or gasoline trucks for long distances.

Improvements in internal combustion engine design, in aerodynamics and in tyre design have and will continue to produce increases in the overall energy and thus carbon efficiency (ie grams of CO_2 per tonne kilometre) of diesel and gasoline trucks. Given the great heterogeneity of the truck fleet, it is difficult to establish an overall measure of the pace of efficiency improvement, but available data suggests slower improvement in the heavy-duty vehicle fleet than in the light-duty vehicle fleet. Whereas over the last 20 years European vans and passenger cars have achieved an average emission per kilometre reduction of 2 per cent and 3 per cent per annum respectively, the trucking industry went through a period of efficiency improvements until the 1990s, but has stagnated in recent decades, with, for instance, the fuel consumption of UK heavy goods vehicles decreasing from 8.8 miles per gallon in 2004 to 8.5 miles per gallon in 2016 (Department of Transport (UK), 2019).

While there is significant potential to increase energy efficiency through incremental improvements to internal combustion engines and vehicle

FIGURE 0.3   Energy demand forecast for transport by region and mode

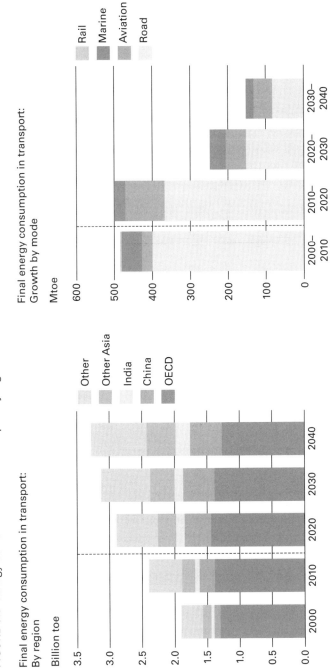

Final energy consumption in transport:
By region

Billion toe

Final energy consumption in transport:
Growth by mode

Mtoe

Other
Other Asia
India
China
OECD

Rail
Marine
Aviation
Road

SOURCE   BP Energy Economics, 2019

design, actual emissions reduction – as against a slower pace of growth – requires a shift to either alternative fuels or an electric drivetrain. The latter route will and should dominate, since the use of electric drivetrains (whether battery or hydrogen powered) will be increasingly technically feasible, will achieve the greatest carbon emissions reductions, and will become a lower-cost option for an increasingly wide range of bus and truck sizes and distances during the course of the 2020s.

Meanwhile, the global energy demand in transportation is forecast to increase. Despite the fact that there have been and continue to be improvements in vehicle efficiency, continued population growth and forecast trends in road traffic counteract the benefits that arise through vehicles being less fuel consuming. CO_2 emissions of any fuel that contains carbon are proportionately linked to the amount of fuel usage. This means that only decreases in the volume of diesel used will reduce greenhouse gas emissions in the transport industry. Decreases in the volume of diesel used can be achieved in one of three ways:

- using fuel more efficiently;
- reducing the need for fuel use; or
- substituting a fuel for diesel that produces proportionately lower CO_2 emissions than diesel fuel on a well-to-wheels basis. Figure 0.3 shows the projected increases in energy demands for transport by region and modes to 2040 (BP Energy Economics, 2019).

The journey ahead

A big part of the journey to zero emissions to 2050 and beyond will be the success, or otherwise, of government initiatives to develop relevant infrastructure that can cope with the transition from a fossil-fuelled economy to an alternative energy green technology economy. Government regulation and policy initiatives will loom large in the shaping of the future of the transport business. This will include the impact of regulation on the infrastructure changes that will enable the application of alternative energies to replace environmentally damaging fossil fuels. A significant feature of any future infrastructure strategy will have to take account of government regulation of cities and the drive to reduce air pollution.

In order to understand the next 50 years of transportation, we need to realize that the direction of travel we take will also be profoundly influenced by many factors including:

- geopolitical cooperation;
- OEMs ability to manage two opposing forces: fossil fuel vs electrification or alternative fuels;
- adapting to the threat of alternative fuels and the required investment in new production methods;
- investor communities, eg hedge funds and sovereign wealth funds;
- power generation companies;
- harnessing innovation and new technologies;
- intellectual property management and data security;
- digitization services such as the new 5G – an advanced wireless telecommunications technology;
- sourcing of rare earth materials (REMs);
- development of relevant infrastructure to manage 'last mile' freight movement and the introduction of urban consolidation centres in the form of freight-ports to regenerate redundant ICE manufacturing plants on the edges of major cities.

References

BP Energy Economics (2019) BP Energy Outlook 2019 Edition. Retrieved from: https://www.bp.com/content/dam/bp/business-sites/en/global/corporate/pdfs/energy-economics/energy-outlook/bp-energy-outlook-2019.pdf (archived at https://perma.cc/KC3Y-QUQV)

Department of Transport (UK) (2019) Energy and environment: data tables (ENV). Retrieved from: https://www.gov.uk/government/statistical-data-sets/energy-and-environment-data-tables-env (archived at https://perma.cc/9EFE-CH5K)

EIA (2017) International Energy Outlook 2017. Retrieved from: https://www.eia.gov/outlooks/archive/ieo17/ (archived at https://perma.cc/2H23-L43R) (2017).pdf

EPA (2020) Global Greenhouse Gas Emissions Data. Retrieved from: https://www.epa.gov/ghgemissions/global-greenhouse-gas-emissions-data (archived at https://perma.cc/AZT8-9JTQ)

IPCC (2019) Global Warming of 1.5°C. Retrieved from: https://www.ipcc.ch/site/assets/uploads/sites/2/2019/06/SR15_Summary_Volume_Low_Res.pdf (archived at https://perma.cc/2SBX-XPZJ)

Levin, K and Davis, C (2019) What does 'net-zero emissions' mean? 6 common questions, Answered, *WRI*. Retrieved from: https://www.wri.org/blog/2019/09/what-does-net-zero-emissions-mean-6-common-questions-answered (archived at https://perma.cc/TK3J-2T9E)

My Climate (nd) What are 'negative emissions'?, *My Climate*. Retrieved from: https://www.myclimate.org/information/faq/faq-detail/what-are-negative-emissions/ (archived at https://perma.cc/CBA5-HV4G)

01

The road to zero emissions

This chapter will familiarize the reader with:

- The threat posed by 'global warming' and climate change.
- Environmental traffic zones.
- Development of urban consolidation centres/last-mile 'freight-ports'.
- The potential impact of battery electric vehicles (BEVs) on future oil demand.
- The challenge to save 200,000 auto industry jobs.
- Rare earth materials (REMs) and their importance in the development of battery technology.

The threat of global warming and climate change

The threat of global warming and climate change has dominated the geopolitical landscape since 1988 when the Intergovernmental Panel on Climate Change (IPCC) was formed through combined work from the World Meteorological Organization (WMO) and the United Nations Environmental Programme (UNEP) (IPCC, 2020).

The goal of the IPCC is to provide the world with a clear state of knowledge on climate change and its potential environmental and social-economic impacts (IPCC, 2020).

Building on the work of the IPCC, the United Nations established a UN Framework Climate Change Convention (UNFCCC). Annually, the UNFCCC organizes a world conference named Climate of the Parties (COP). The Kyoto

Protocol was agreed in Kyoto, Japan in 1997 at COP3. COP21 took place in 2015 in Paris; negotiations at COP21 led to the Paris Agreement.

The central aim of the Paris Agreement is to reduce greenhouse gas emissions (GHGs) and limit the rise in global average temperature to below 2°C above pre-industrial levels. There is also an overarching 'stretch target' to limit the rise to 1.5°C (Lynn and Zabula, 2016).

Representatives from 196 countries attended the conference and as of 2019, 196 states plus the European Union have signed the Paris Agreement. A further 183 nations and the European Union have ratified the agreement.

Those in 'climate change denial', who are challenging the science, are out to derail the goals of the Paris Agreement. This has put the spotlight on differences between the G8 and G20 alliances on how to regulate the environmental and commercial markets that will impact how the transition from a fossil fuel economy plays out going forward.

First and foremost, human-caused emissions – like those from fossil-fuelled vehicles and factories – should be reduced to as close to zero as possible, and transitioning to emissions-free transport such as electric or hydrogen cars and trucks is currently high on the agenda of all of the developed economies.

Any remaining GHGs would be balanced with an equivalent amount of carbon removal, for example by restoring forests or through direct air capture and storage (DACS) technology. Carbon capture and storage is considered a longer-term and very expensive and capital-intensive solution, and is currently an option pursued by many oil and gas company organizations as their contribution to the climate challenge while wishing to continue investments in fossil fuel and gas production.

The concept of net-zero emissions is akin to 'climate neutrality' (Levin and Davis, 2019).

There are two main variables that control global energy consumption (three counting price): the total number of people in the world and the average per capita energy each person consumes (Figure 1.1). While per capita energy consumption is falling throughout much of the OECD, it is rising everywhere else as countries like China, India and Brazil strive to become like 'us' (Energy Matters, 2018).

The world's population (currently 7.6 billion) is expected to reach 8.6 billion by 2030, 9.8 billion by 2050 and 11.2 billion by 2100, according to a United Nations report (United Nations, 2017).

At the same time, BP and UN data points to global mean per capita energy consumption growing to 2.63 tonnes of oil equivalent (toe) per annum by 2100. That is a further increase of 47 per cent over the 2015 figure (Energy Matters, 2018).

FIGURE 1.1 World per capita energy consumption

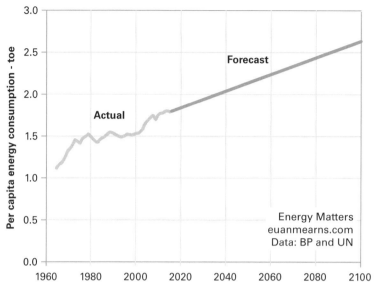

SOURCE Energy Matters, 2018

GHGs unchecked in a 'business as usual' scenario will mean that the 1.5°C target agreed in the Paris Agreement cannot be met. Mitigation techniques and interventions are therefore required to contain the projected growth in GHGs as a consequence of the forecast increase in world population and world per capita energy consumption (Energy Matters, 2018).

The World Resources Institute (WRI) suggests that to meet the Paris Agreement's temperature goals, the world will need to reach net-zero emissions on the following timelines (Levin and Davis, 2019):

- In scenarios that limit warming to 1.5°C, *carbon dioxide* (CO_2) reaches net-zero on average by **2050** (in scenarios with low or no overshoot) to **2052** (in scenarios that have high overshoot, in which temperature rise surpasses 1.5°C for some time before being brought down). *Total GHG emissions* reach net-zero between **2063 and 2068**.

- In 2°C scenarios, CO_2 reaches net-zero on average by **2070** (in scenarios with a greater than 66 per cent likelihood of limiting warming to 2°C) to **2085** (50–66 per cent likelihood). *Total GHG emissions* reach net-zero by 2100.

FIGURE 1.2 How to get to net-zero emissions by 2100

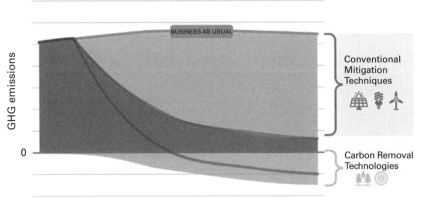

SOURCE Levin and Davis, 2019

FIGURE 1.3 Global timeline to meet net-zero emissions

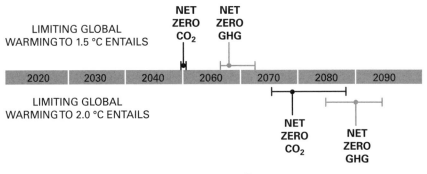

SOURCE Levin and Davis, 2019

The WRI forecasts (Figures 1.2 and 1.3) are for a global overview of possible outcomes over the next 50–100 years, up to 2100. Each individual country will have different targets and timescales (Levin and Davis, 2019).

Government action in the EU has seen the recent introduction of radical regulations. These regulations will create zero-emission and clean air zones in major cities and penalize products that fail to comply with environmental permits for access to urban environments.

The UK has implemented a robust 'industrial clean air strategy', which focuses on the goal of clean air through product compliance. The development of alternative energies, the electrification of transport and the critical issue of infrastructure development will require the government to seriously consider balancing how it invests in energy innovation projects; this could cost significantly less of taxpayers' money than projects such as 'HS2' and a third runway for London Heathrow.

The UK Government strategy is built around a core mission: to put the UK at the forefront of the design and manufacturing of zero-emission vehicles and for all new cars and vans to be effectively zero-emission by 2040 (Department for Transport, 2018).

As set out in the NO_2 plan, the UK Government will end the sale of new conventional petrol and diesel cars and vans by 2040. It is expected that the majority of new cars and vans sold will be 100 per cent zero-emission and by 2050 the UK Government wants almost every car and van to be zero-emission. This level of ambition puts the UK at the forefront of the global transition to cleaner road transport (Department for Transport, 2018).

Many forecasts exist that promote the idea that diesel has a short life and is now considered a pernicious polluting fuel. The most recent report from the International Energy Agency (IEA) predicts that the oil industry may well see a 40 per cent reduction in demand from transport, ie 3 million barrels a day over the next decade by 2030, but also forecasts that 70 per cent of long-haul freight will still be carried using fossil-fuelled powertrains (IEA, 2018).

The future of trucks and transportation and the underlying forces of change will unleash a whole new industry powered by electricity and technology that will usher in an industrial and economic revolution the likes of which the world has yet to see.

Environmental traffic management zones

Environmental and economic forces are gathering that will change the way trucks and transportation are operated and affect the future of millions of people engaged in these industries.

Zero-emission zones will become the norm, an example of which is what happened in London in 2019 (Mayor of London, 2019).

Despite forecasts that diesel as a transport fuel is on its way out, we certainly believe that it will have a long future for heavy trucks (HTs), but many existing automotive manufacturing operations, currently residing on the edge of half-planned zero-emission zones, are already almost obsolete and will become redundant in the near future.

Witness the closure of Ford factories in Southampton and Bridgend, and the announcement by Honda UK in April 2019 of the closure of its car plant; 3,500 jobs will be lost, where once it assembled over 200,000 cars a year (Chapman, 2019).

The UK Government is committed to supporting policies that comply with the Paris Agreement and deliver not only on the climate change goals of restricting temperature rise to 1.5°C but also a bold and 'integrated industrial strategy' designed to build a high-growth economy across the UK. Infrastructure planning will be key to sustaining a successful transition and it will take more than penalizing owners of non-compliant cars and trucks to deliver the Paris Agreement goals. The development of 'urban freight consolidation centres' or 'freight-ports' is potentially a critical future investment requirement.

The potential impact of battery electric vehicles (BEVs)

In the United States, the first successful electric car made its debut in around 1890 thanks to William Morrison. His six-passenger vehicle, capable of a top speed of 14 miles per hour, was little more than an electrified wagon, but it helped spark interest in electric vehicles (Energy.Gov, 2014).

The US Department of Energy notes:

> The first turning point, many have suggested, was the introduction of the Toyota Prius. Released in Japan in 1997, the Prius became the world's first mass-produced hybrid electric vehicle. In 2000, the Prius was released worldwide, and it became an instant success. To make the Prius a reality, Toyota used a nickel metal hydride battery – a technology that was supported by the Energy Department's research. Since then, rising gasoline prices and growing concern about carbon pollution have helped make the Prius the best-selling hybrid worldwide during the past decade (Energy.Gov, 2014).

The progressive development of modern electric cars can be traced to the launch of the Toyota Prius in 1997. It has taken 20 years for the Prius to gain full market acceptance. In 2020 the Toyota Prius is in its fourth generation of development and is a familiar sight, utilized as a taxi by fleet buyers and as a private motor vehicle.

Commercial vehicles in the light and medium sectors are now getting serious attention, with many existing OEMs and new entrants exploring BEV technology. There is a trade-off here due to:

- limited recharging facilities;
- cost of BEV vs ICE;
- reduced payload due to the additional weight of batteries when compared to an equivalent diesel engine vehicle;
- reduced range of BEVs compared to ICE;
- different operational requirements of commercial vehicles.

Heavy trucks need an entirely different approach to light and medium trucks. Heavy trucks carry more payload over longer distances and therefore would need an alternative fuel to diesel to achieve net-zero emissions. Net-zero emissions could be achieved using alternative fuels such as biomethane compressed natural gas (Bio-CNG) with minor modifications to existing ICE (internal combustion engine) diesel engine heavy trucks. However, again the biggest problem is the limited refuelling infrastructure. The Bio-CNG refuelling infrastructure lends itself to local operations such as waste collection, buses, and short distribution journeys made by larger fleets such as for supermarkets.

The full-scale deployment of clean fuels such as Bio-CNG has been held back by three main barriers:

- the higher retail cost of vehicles;
- a low level of consumer acceptance; and
- the lack of infrastructure for recharging and refuelling.

At the moment there is a potential vicious circle where investors do not invest in alternative fuel infrastructure as there are not enough vehicles. The manufacturing industry does not offer alternative fuel vehicles at competitive prices as there is insufficient consumer demand. And consumers do not purchase the vehicles due to the lack of dedicated infrastructure.

The availability of recharging/refuelling stations is not only a technical prerequisite for the functioning of alternative fuel vehicles, but also one of the most critical components of consumer acceptance. It is unlikely therefore that Bio-CNG will be the commercial vehicle fuel of the future to replace diesel.

SAE Mobilus note:

One alternative energy source for heavy trucks receiving renewed interest
is hydrogen. Conventional internal combustion engines can be modified to
run on pure hydrogen ('HICEs') and could see early deployment as they are
substantially cheaper than fuel cells. However, hydrogen combustion is less
efficient than a fuel cell and releases NO_x, hence is not expected to play a
significant long-term role in heavy transport.

Hydrogen fuel cell electric vehicles (FCEVs) have analogous powertrains to BEVs.
Both leverage batteries to power electric motors driving the wheels. However, the
difference remains in the source of recharging the cells. BEVs require an external
energy source for recharging power while hydrogen fuel cells utilize the fuel
on the vehicle. This duality in power sources is not new to the road transport
industry but is recognized as a necessity moving forward (Borst, 2019).

The future fuel source choice for heavy trucks demands very different action
from manufacturers and regulatory authorities. This will lead to changes in
production and supply chain development. Because of the pressure to develop
BEVs and HCEVs this book will look at who might emerge as winners
and losers.

It is forecast that the potential impact from the existing automotive
OEMs failing to invest in the UK for their BEV production makes it likely
that almost 200,000 jobs will be lost (Figure 1.4) (Faraday Insitution, 2019).

FIGURE 1.4   ICE and EV employment 2017 to 2040

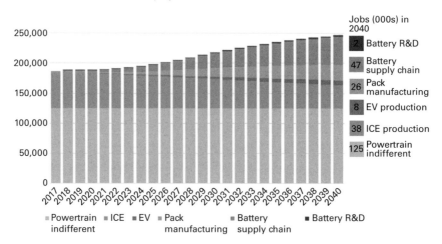

SOURCE Faraday Institution, 2019

The global transition from producing ICE vehicles to producing BEVs and HCEVs will have a considerable impact on the UK labour market. Job creation will outpace job losses in the UK only if the UK secures BEV, HCEV and battery manufacturing and effectively competes with the likes of Tesla and BYD who are leaders in battery capacity through their investment in battery gigafactories in the United States, Germany and Asia.

The Faraday Institution, which has been supported by significant UK Government funding of around £250 million, has undertaken detailed research of the emerging battery market supporting the electrification of transport and have reached significant conclusions in their reports and findings, which can be found on their website https://faraday.ac.uk/ (Faraday Insitution, 2019).

The Faraday Institution suggests that 'battery pack, battery cell and electrode manufacturing will all be located in the UK. In this base scenario, the overall industry workforce of the EV and EV battery ecosystem would grow by 32 per cent from 186,000 to 246,000 employees by 2040.' Please refer to Figure 1.4 (Faraday Insitution, 2019).

Oil demand has increased by 30 per cent since 2000. Barclays Investment Bank suggests, 'The next 20 years are likely to prove crucial, with reliance on oil expected to peak between 2030 and 2035 if countries stick to their current low-carbon pledges, although that peak could come as soon as 2025 if the world was to increase its focus on reducing emissions.' Based on current policies the more likely outcome is that oil demand stagnates out to 2050, as increased use of petrochemicals offsets the electrification of transport (Barclays Investment Bank, 2019).

Rare earth material sourcing

Another key factor that also needs to be considered from an environmental impact point of view is the ethical sourcing of lithium batteries, whose primary source of rare earth materials is African, Asian and South American markets where employee conditions and health and safety considerations will need to be subject to effective regulation. China is leading the way in monopolizing the sourcing of lithium and cobalt. Europe and the United States need to raise their game in the development of battery technology and material sourcing. Solid-state batteries are in development, and the primary material to support this development is zinc.

Statista notes:

Total global reserves of zinc are estimated to be some 230 million metric tonnes (Figure 1.5). Because of the heavy consumption of this metal, zinc reserves are expected to last only for the next 17 years. Australia owns the largest zinc reserves worldwide – an estimated 64 million metric tonnes. Other countries with significant reserves include China, Peru, and Mexico. The United States has zinc reserves that are estimated at about 11 million metric tonnes. China is the global top producer of zinc from mines. In 2018, Chinese zinc mine production came to some 4.3 million metric tonnes. That was more than one-third of the total global mine production, which was approximately 13 million metric tonnes (Statista, nd).

It is also interesting to note that the person credited as the inventor of lithium-ion battery technology is Professor John Bannister Goodenough, who is also the man behind the development of solid-state technology. This is a key area where disruptive technology will play a part in defining the transport era we are entering.

FIGURE 1.5 Global zinc reserves as of 2019, by country (millions of metric tonnes)

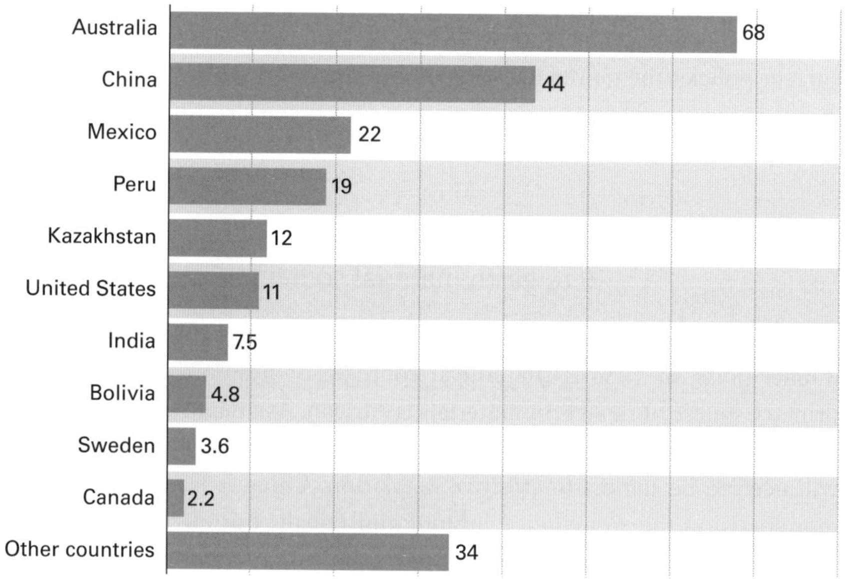

Australia	68
China	44
Mexico	22
Peru	19
Kazakhstan	12
United States	11
India	7.5
Bolivia	4.8
Sweden	3.6
Canada	2.2
Other countries	34

SOURCE Statista, nd

Disruptive technologies and business models are trends we have seen make dramatic changes in other business sectors, and in the period from 2020 to 2040 we will witness the acceleration of changes to traditional markets. Already we have experienced dramatic changes to the taxi (Uber) and home delivery (Amazon) markets due to the use of technology. The digitization of commercial vehicles and the growth of telematics has seen significant improvements in transport efficiencies and workshop maintenance performance.

The Internet of Things (IoT) is a significant challenge to OEMs, suppliers, and transport and logistics providers, who need to master the demands of improved productivity and customer expectations driven by vast amounts of intelligence generated by integrated systems embedded in today's products.

The emergence of electric trucks will pose new challenges for dealerships and workshops as they embrace new business models to offset the reduction in maintenance required of BEVs.

What is certain is that we are witnessing a major shift in the concept of transportation and the technologies needed to build an environmentally, economically and ethically sustainable future.

The International Energy Agency in its 2018 report does claim that the future of trucks will see a 40 per cent decline in the daily fossil fuel demand by 2050, but it does not see the end of fossil fuel demand by transport, and long-haul distribution will still be operating using diesel and consuming more than 50 per cent of today's demand (IEA, 2017).

However, the infrastructure challenge remains the key to accelerating the change required to deliver on the principal aims of the journey to net-zero emissions by 2050, and the future of the planet.

Summary

- The threat of global warming and climate change has dominated the geopolitical landscape for most of the second decade of the 21st century.
- The conflict between the world's two largest economies, the United States and China, is rooted in trade wars, escalation of tariffs and competition for the dominance of intellectual property that will impact the future of transport, mobility and the shape of city and urban life in the next century.
- Government action in the EU has seen the recent introduction of radical regulations. These regulations will create zero-emission and clean air zones

in major cities and penalize products that fail to comply with environmental permits for access to urban environments.

- The UK has implemented a robust 'industrial clean air strategy', which focuses on the goal of clean air through product compliance.

- Zero-emission zones will become the norm in 20 major cities, and the development of 'last mile' urban consolidation centres or 'freight-ports' will be crucial to sustain the pollution goals of the government's 'Clean Air Industrial Policy'.

- The global transition from producing ICE vehicles to producing BEVs will have a considerable impact on the UK labour market unless there is a significant investment in battery technologies and the development of UK gigafactories to secure a future auto industry manufacturing base.

- China is leading the way in monopolizing the sourcing of REMs such as lithium and cobalt. Europe and the United States need to raise their game in the development of battery technology and material sourcing.

References

Barclays Investment Bank (2019) Oil in 3D: the demand outlook to 2050. Retrieved from: https://www.investmentbank.barclays.com/content/dam/barclaysmicrosites/ibpublic/documents/our-insights/oil/oil-in-3d.pdf (archived at https://perma.cc/BL8J-MKL6)

Borst, M (2019) Is hydrogen the future for trucking? *SAE Mobilus*. Retrieved from: https://saemobilus.sae.org/power/feature/2019/06/hydrogen-fuel-cell-trucks (archived at https://perma.cc/SG4U-9X82)

Chapman, B (2019) Honda to close Swindon plant by 2021 with loss of 3,500 jobs, *Independent*. Retrieved from: https://www.independent.co.uk/news/business/honda-swindon-manufacturing-plant-closure-jobs-employees-latest-a8911766.html (archived at https://perma.cc/2Y2B-A2GQ)

Department for Transport (2018) *The Road to Zero*, Department for Transport, London

Energy Matters (2018) Global Energy Forecast to 2100. Retrieved from: http://euanmearns.com/global-energy-forecast-to-2100/ (archived at https://perma.cc/6D4N-W7CZ)

Energy.Gov (2014) The History of the Electric Car. Retrieved from: https://www.energy.gov/articles/history-electric-car (archived at https://perma.cc/P2CZ-HWRC)

Faraday Institution (2019) *UK Electric Vehicle and Battery Production Potential to 2040*, Faraday Institution, Cambridge

IEA (2017) *The Future of Trucks*, IEA, Paris

IEA (2018) *Energy Report*, IEA, Paris

IPCC (2020) Intergovernmental Panel on Climate Change. Retrieved from: https://report.ipcc.ch/ (archived at https://perma.cc/E94M-SC22)

Levin, K and Davis, C (2019) What does 'net-zero emission' mean? *WRI*. Retrieved from: https://www.wri.org/blog/2019/09/what-does-net-zero-emissions-mean-6-common-questions-answered (archived at https://perma.cc/S5YH-L2QJ)

Lynn, J and Zabula, W (2016) Outcomes of COP21 and the IPCC, *WMO*. Retrieved from: https://public.wmo.int/en/resources/bulletin/outcomes-of-cop21-and-ipcc (archived at https://perma.cc/Q42N-YQQY)

Mayor of London (2019) The mayor's ultra low emission zone for London. Retrieved from: https://www.london.gov.uk/what-we-do/environment/pollution-and-air-quality/mayors-ultra-low-emission-zone-london (archived at https://perma.cc/RG2D-NPB5)

Statista (nd) Global zinc reserves as of 2019, by country. Retrieved from: https://www.statista.com/statistics/273639/global-zinc-reserves-by-country/ (archived at https://perma.cc/6K2Y-LYEX)

United Nations (2017) World population projected to reach 9.8 billion in 2050, and 11.2 billion in 2100. Retrieved from: https://www.un.org/development/desa/en/news/population/world-population-prospects-2017.html (archived at https://perma.cc/U9HX-CS5J)

02

The fall of the diesel engine and the rise of the electric motor

This chapter will familiarize the reader with:

- The death of Rudolf Diesel and the demise of the diesel engine due to the 'Dieselgate' scandal.
- Testing, compliance and the impact of environmental regulation and taxes on engine technology in the 1970s and '80s.
- The shift towards low-carbon transport.
- Fuel economy vs 'clean air'.
- The impact of Nikola Tesla and the invention of AC power.
- The rise of Tesla Motors, Elon Musk and the challenge to the conventional auto OEMs

Introduction

In 1913, a German engineer travelled to the UK to attend a meeting with an organization called the Consolidated Diesel Manufacturing Company.

This man was Rudolf Diesel, the person credited as the inventor of the eponymous 'diesel engine'. In 1896, Diesel was contracted by MAN AG (now owned by VW Group under Traton AG) to develop his patented diesel engine platform that would eventually power modern trucks, trains and shipping around the world.

Unfortunately, Diesel did not survive his journey to the UK and was announced missing at sea on 29 September 1913 (MAN Museum, nd).

The death of Rudolf Diesel could effectively be labelled the first 'Dieselgate' moment. In 2020, years after this tragedy, we face the prospect of the potential 'death of the diesel engine' from gathering environmental and economic forces that will change the way trucks and transportation are operated and affect the future of millions of people engaged in these industries.

'Dieselgate' and the potential demise of the diesel engine

Diesel fuel as an energy source has been with us since 1893, but in 2015 diesel suddenly became a 'dirty word' and not just a perceived 'dirty fuel'.

The actions of VW from 2013 to 2015 and the subsequent 'Dieselgate' scandal led to consequences that have potentially hastened the demise of diesel as a fuel for the future. To the authors the timing of these events represented not just a comedy of errors, but potentially the biggest corporate suicide attempt ever. In the face of current environmental pressure, VW created the situation where not only is the company under siege but the very future of diesel is under threat.

In 2015 many VW media reports declared that 'several rogue software engineers' were to blame for the company's emission-test cheating scandal. Many lawmakers in the United States declared it would take years to fix the half a million vehicles impacted by this scandal. It was more than just an attempt to defeat environmental testing; it was to ultimately undermine the reputation and credibility of an automotive giant. At this time VW had just replaced Toyota as the world's largest-selling brand.

John German, a US automotive engineer, was thrust into the global spotlight in 2015 after he and his colleagues were credited with helping uncover one of the biggest ever corporate scandals. 'We really didn't expect to find anything,' German said of his research. He and his team discovered that Volkswagen had installed sophisticated software, designed to evade strict emission tests across the world (Neate, 2015).

German's simple test – checking the car's emissions on real roads rather than in lab test conditions – led to the resignation of VW's chief executive Martin Winterkorn after the company was forced to admit it installed 'defeat devices' in 11 million cars (Bryant and Sharman, 2015).

The scandal has wiped more than €24 billion ($26.8 billion) off VW's market value, in addition to fines from regulatory authorities approaching another €30 billion (Bryant and Sharman, 2015). How did we get to this point? Would any of us imagine that any major multinational companies could or would be involved in such a scandal?

The fuel crisis in the 1970s

In 1970, world events were shaping the future of environmental legislation that focused on a car's fuel economy. The geopolitical events that have shaped markets for transport and trucks in the 20th century are rooted in the oil crisis of the 1970s that kick-started the drive for smaller and more fuel-efficient cars.

The National Highway Traffic Safety Administration (NHTSA) in the United States, and California in particular, developed a law known as the CAFE – Corporate Average Fuel Economy – standard (NHTSA, 2019). Companies whose products were not fuel efficient were exposed to significant penalties, which could be described as an early foray into carbon taxing. All manufacturers with ambitions to succeed in the United States had to seriously review their design and development plans. This led some companies to accelerate their product planning through merger and acquisition in order to fill technology gaps and shorten the time to market.

At the same time, government regulation for fuel efficiency and environmental targets focused on noise and air pollution. The automotive industry generally resisted government attempts to impose product performance standards until the 1980s.

The decision by the US Environmental Protection Agency (EPA) to focus attention on clean air and emissions targets saw car and truck manufacturers pay attention to future vehicle design and manufacture that would shape the future of markets for transport and services.

It also saw a period of consolidation in cars and commercial vehicles (CVs) to extract synergies from research and development (R&D) and engine and body design, using lightweight materials and the implementation of innovative 'platform engineering' manufacturing strategies that saw the emergence of integrated global tier-supply chains.

CASE STUDY
Regulation compliance through successful M&A

An interesting case study from this period is the BMW–Rover acquisition in 1994 that had some interesting outcomes and benefits to one party in terms of how they were able to take advantage of the new regulatory environment through the development of a new product.

In 1994 BMW announced the successful takeover of Rover Group, and in the process acquired the brands of Mini, Land Rover and MG sports cars in addition to the Rover brand that had worked closely with Honda on joint venture programmes in Europe and the United States.

This takeover was much more than BMW wishing to take out a rival to its 3 Series and 5 Series. There were also problems that arose from this, for example the integration problems with Rover/BMW, which led to the sale of Rover to the Phoenix Group in 2000 and Land Rover to Ford. However, the outcome for the BMW Group was very positive, mainly due to the probably unintended consequences for the company in terms of it being able to be compliant with the emerging strict environment regulations operating in the United States, where to compete successfully required a focus on environmentally optimized vehicles and compliance with the EPA fuel economy regulations (Chapman, 2019).

Consider this for a moment:

1 BMW purchased Rover from BAE for £800 million in 1994 to strike a blow to Rover's decade-long joint venture (JV) partner Honda, thus the 15-year link with Honda was brutally severed (O'Grady, 2005).

2 In addition to Rover, BMW took control of the Land Rover, Mini and MG brands (O'Grady, 2005).

3 In 2000 BMW sold Land Rover to Ford for £1.8 billion and MG/Rover to the Phoenix Group for £10 (yes, a tenner!) (Chapman, 2019).

4 The Mini brand became a massive success following the launch of Mini One and Mini Cooper in 2001. In 2008, seven years after its launch, Mini sales in the United States were almost a quarter of total BMW sales there – 54,000 Minis were sold compared to total US BMW sales of 243,000 (Carsalesbase, nd).

5 By 2008, years following the initial purchase of Rover, BMW had recovered the initial cost of acquiring Rover Group and also secured the future of the Mini brand. Equally, BMW learned a great deal about 4x4 technology through the capture of Land Rover technology, which assisted BMW in the development of BMW X series.

The other major factor rarely mentioned by 'industry experts' is the contribution made by future Mini sales in the US to the achievement of 'CAFE'. Mini was not just a significant product for the Munich manufacturer, it was also a significant tax break when you view its contribution to complying with environmental regulation in the market (NHTSA, 2019).

While BMW and Rover are a million miles away from the subject of trucks and transportation this is an interesting case study to highlight how OEMs have responded to competitive and regulatory pressures to shape the market for products and services.

It is doubtful that in the 21st century we will see OEMs profiting from the unintended positive consequences realized by BMW when they acquired the Mini brand.

The pressure on all automotive manufacturers to deliver a carbon-neutral, zero-emission future, focused on energy efficiencies, fuel economy and environmental sustainability, remains a key driver of change in the market sectors for trucks and transportation, but simply adopting innovative merger and acquisition strategies will not be enough to survive in the future markets for trucks and transportation services.

The dash for diesel

The story of how diesel became a dominant engine technology long before John German and his team discovered VW's falsifying emissions data from test conditions, started after the 1992 Kyoto Protocol required governments to reduce CO_2 emissions by 8 per cent by 2013 (United Nations, 2008).

At the time of this policy announcement the global warming impact of greenhouse gas emissions (GHGs) was well known. The means of reduction, however, were not stipulated, and as a result in Europe it led to widespread adoption of diesel vehicles. Due to its relative fuel efficiency, diesel can produce 15 per cent less CO_2 than petrol engines (Vidal, 2015).

Vehicle manufacturers effectively lobbied the European Commission to promote diesel with the result that most EU countries introduced tax incentives to promote diesel over petrol engines and the impact of these policies saw a massive increase in diesel car sales (Vidal, 2015).

In 1995 diesel sales made up less than 10 per cent of annual sales in Europe; by 2012 this was over 50 per cent. In Norway, from 2001 to 2010 diesel sales rose from 13.3 per cent to 73.9 per cent; in Ireland it rose from 12 per cent to 62.3 per cent. It is interesting to know that Norway has recently announced that diesel cars will no longer be legally allowed to be sold from 2025 (Smedley, 2019).

Low-carbon transport – policy choices

One of the significant issues arising from government policies of the 1980s and 1990s is that the focus on CO_2 reduction obscured the fact that even the most efficient diesel cars emitted over three times more NO_2 per kilometre and 10 times more PM (particulate matter) than petrol engines.

It was evident that policy makers had made a conscious trade-off to accept ill health as a result of increasing air pollution in order to meet CO_2

targets. In 2015 a press report from the *Guardian* highlighted evidence from the Clean Air London action group that:

> Even though the European Commission, national governments, and the vehicle manufacturers knew how dangerous diesel is, together they incentivized it, and deliberately engineered a massive switch away from petrol (Vidal, 2015).

The Department of the Environment has invested in various research on the quality of air, and in 1993 a report stated that diesel emissions were a health hazard, containing compounds known to be carcinogenic that may cause impairment to respiratory function and lead to morbidity and mortality. Research of this nature continues to highlight the fact that fine particles from diesel emissions were responsible for increases in death due to respiratory reasons and lung cancer (HM Government – EPA, 1992).

Government ministers and civil servants have been aware of the dangers of diesel emissions being bad for air quality but focused more on the impact of climate change reduction and lower CO_2 targets rather than air quality infringements due to NO_2 and PM levels. Figure 2.1 shows that in order for the UK to meet its 20% reduction in CO_2 emissions by 2020, reducing transport emissions is a significant factor. This will place a strong focus on diesel emissions in particular.

FIGURE 2.1 UK greenhouse gas emissions, by sector

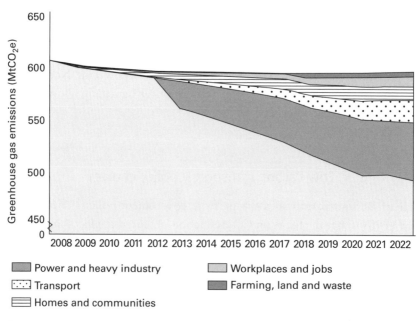

SOURCE HM Government DoEE, 2009

The rise and fall of the diesel engine

It was particularly owing to rapid advances in engine technology that the diesel passenger car market grew substantially in the 1990s, and this growth phenomenon was particularly apparent in Europe. While diesel cars were more expensive than their petrol equivalents, drivers liked the fuel efficiency of diesel engines, which reduced running costs over the long term.

Governments became very concerned about rising carbon emissions and began advising citizens to switch to diesels, which were thought to emit less CO_2 than their petrol counterparts. Adam Forrest at the *Guardian* wrote: 'Diesel's biggest moment in the UK was probably in 2001, when Gordon Brown, then chancellor of the Labour government, cut fuel duty on diesel vehicles as a deliberate effort to encourage people to switch' (Forrest, 2017).

The problems with diesel engine emissions took a long time to surface but when they did, they revealed the error of the CO_2 reduction argument. In 2012 came the first major evidence of some truly dreadful health impacts. Nitrogen oxides and dioxides (NO_x) and particulate matter (PM) emitted by diesel exhausts were identified as 'silent killers'. The studies multiplied rapidly and produced damning evidence. Research by the European Environment Agency (EEA) found that nitrogen dioxide (NO_2) from diesel fumes had caused around 71,000 premature deaths across the continent in a single year. It said the UK experienced 11,940 annual premature deaths from NO_2, the second highest in Europe behind Italy. Adam Forrest states: 'The World Health Organization declared diesel exhaust a carcinogenic, a cause of lung cancer in the same category as asbestos and mustard gas' (Forrest, 2017).

Then, in 2015, came Dieselgate. In September 2015, Volkswagen, which vies with Toyota for top spot in the list of world's biggest car companies and a firm that had for years been running its own marketing campaign in favour of 'clean diesel', rocked the industry by admitting that it had cheated on its emission tests. David King, the UK government's former chief scientific adviser on climate change, admitted that ministers had made a huge mistake by promoting diesel. They had trusted the car industry when it said the fuel was clean. 'It turns out we were wrong,' he said (Forrest, 2017).

The number of diesel vehicles – all legally emitting several times more NO_x and PM than the petrol vehicles they replaced – rose from under 2 million in the UK to 12 million (Smedley, 2019).

Since the VW scandal broke in 2015, there have been many who have spoken out against diesel technology and the failure of regulators and manufacturers to be truthful about its impact on the environment.

'ClientEarth', an influential environmental lobby group, has consistently called for incentives to move people away from diesel vehicles towards leaner forms of transport. The environmental law group stated it was still vitally important for people to let the government know what they thought of their draft plans (ClientEarth, 2017)

CEO James Thornton added:

> We are challenging on two fronts because of the urgency of this public health crisis. We're asking the High Court to consider the problems with the plans and consultation. That is now in the court's hands. In the meantime, it is important for as many people as possible to tell Defra that the plans don't make sense and won't tackle illegal air quality in our towns and cities (ClientEarth, 2017).

Despite the concerns of action groups such as ClientEarth, the government is determined to tackle the challenge of developing effective policies to deliver a low-carbon economy and a future less dependent on fossil-fuelled transportation.

The fall and rise of the electric motor

While Rudolf Diesel gained fame and fortune at the turn of the 20th century, a little-known Serbian scientist/inventor named Nikola Tesla, who was born in 1856, two years before Diesel, was making a name for himself through the invention of the alternating current (AC) electrical system, which remains the predominant electrical system that powers the globe today. Tesla had many highs and lows throughout his life yet his impact on modern-day technology is very apparent. He died on 7th January 1943, but the legacy of his life and works did not die with him. The world's first fully electric-powered car company, named after Tesla, was founded in 2003 by a group of engineers led by South African entrepreneur and engineer Elon Musk.

Central to Tesla's breakthrough as a high-performance sports vehicle that changed the perception of what electric vehicles could be was the role of alternating current motors. Tesla demonstrated that an electric car could have the same performance as fossil fuel-powered sports cars such as BMW and Porsche.

Tesla and Elon Musk have become the Rudolf Diesel and Ford Motor Company of the 21st century. Tesla aims to build a million cars per annum and dominate the electric car market for many years to come (Lambert, 2016).

Tesla also is redefining the automotive 'Factory of the Future'. Through its vertically integrated supply chain for the sourcing and manufacture of future EV powertrains it is challenging the historical giants of the US and German car industries to compete with its design strategy for EVs vs conventional ICE manufacturing and design platforms.

In Chapter 6 we detail how Tesla is leading the way in competing with China and other major US and European OEMs.

Low-carbon transport – UK Government

The UK Government is now accelerating the shift to low-carbon transport – key actions are summarized below (Department for Transport, 2018):

- End the sale of new conventional petrol and diesel cars and vans by 2040.
- Spend £1 billion supporting the take-up of ultra-low-emission vehicles (ULEVs), including helping consumers to overcome the upfront cost of an electric car.
- Develop one of the best electric vehicle charging networks in the world by:
  - investing an additional £80 million, alongside £15 million from Highways England, to support charging infrastructure deployment;
  - taking new powers under the Automated and Electric Vehicles Bill, allowing the government to set requirements for the provision of charging points (HM Government, 2018).
- Accelerate the uptake of low-emission taxis and buses by:
  - providing £50 million for the Plug-in Taxi programme, which gives taxi drivers up to £7,500 off the purchase price of a new ULEV taxi, alongside £14 million to support 10 local areas to deliver dedicated charge points for taxis;
  - providing £100 million for a national programme of support for retrofitting and new low-emission buses in England and Wales.

- Work with industry as they develop an automotive sector deal to accelerate the transition to zero-emission vehicles.

- Announce plans for the public sector to lead the way in transitioning to zero-emission vehicles.

- Invest £1.2 billion to make cycling and walking the natural choice for shorter journeys.

- Work to enable cost-effective options for shifting more freight from road to rail, including using low-emission rail freight for deliveries into urban areas, with zero-emission last-mile deliveries.

- Position the UK at the forefront of research, development and demonstration of connected and autonomous vehicle technologies, including through the establishment of the Centre for Connected and Autonomous Vehicles and investment of over £250 million, matched by industry (HM Government, 2019).

- Innovation: invest around £841 million of public funds in innovation in low-carbon transport technology and fuels, including ensuring the UK builds on its strengths and leads the world in the design, development and manufacture of electric batteries through investment of up to £246 million in the Faraday Challenge.

While this government declaration may sound like it is committed to noble plans, the fact remains that the legacy of the 'Dieselgate' events still hangs over the future of diesel as a fuel with a future.

In his book *Clearing the Air*, Tim Smedley reports how much we have to thank VW for raising the diesel emissions so high on the political agenda and into the public consciousness (Smedley, 2019).

He suggests the VW scandal will go down in history as the single biggest contribution to improvements in air quality in Europe. The proposed 2040 ban on petrol and diesel cars became a reality in 2019, and this would never have happened without the VW scandal. VW has been hit very hard by the fallout from its cheating. In the United States it has pleaded to three felony accounts and agreed to pay fines totalling $2.8 billion plus a civil resolution of $1.5 billion (Smedley, 2019).

Oliver Schmidt, head of VW's US environmental and engineering office, was sentenced to seven years in prison by US Courts. In 2018 it was reported that VW had been fined $25 billion in the US for the sale of 580,000 vehicles that didn't meet the emission standards (Parloff, 2018).

In May 2018, Martin Winterkorn, the former CEO of VW at the time of 'Dieselgate', was indicted by US authorities for 'conspiracy to defraud' and a warrant for his arrest was issued. The intense scrutiny of VW led to investigation of other transport sectors (Ewing, 2018)

It is interesting that the tag 'Dieselgate' stuck, and not 'VWgate', and as we enter 2020 it is no longer just about VW, it's now about the future of diesel fuel itself.

While the VW situation exposed the problem in millions of cars across the United States and Europe, spot checks of HGVs in the UK between August and November 2017 found that almost 8 per cent of trucks carried some sort of emissions defeat device. Out of 4,709 trucks checked, 327 had been modified to switch off emission controls (Smedley, 2019).

If that level was applied across the current HGV truck population then it is possible that more than 35,000 illegally polluting trucks are operating across the UK every day. Trucks in the UK that are currently operating at the Euro 6 level of compliance are excluded from any penalties applied in cities running Clean Air Zones. In London, from April 2019 any non-compliant truck is subject to a daily £100 fine (Pickup, 2018).

Unfortunately, over 70 per cent of the UK's truck population are non-compliant, ie operating at Euro 3 and below. This is currently an active population of over 250,000 air-polluting trucks in the UK that should be eligible for a scrappage programme, backed by the government, similar to one actioned for cars in early 2000 (SMMT, nd).

Such an initiative would also lend itself to supporting innovative regeneration and employment opportunities in the recycling industry. It would also be an integral part of relevant infrastructure regeneration plans the government should be seriously considering.

Details of how the issues arising from the demise of diesel as an energy source may be mitigated by more effective government policy and action are covered in Chapter 5.

The power and influence of lobby groups

One can only speculate now, had different voices prevailed and the electrification of transport succeeded instead of fossil fuel motoring, how different the environmental crisis we are witnessing today might have been. This raises the spectre of how powerful lobby groups really can influence the direction in which nations travel. The oil companies in the early 20th century were powerful voices and forces of influence that helped shape the industrial-military complexes of the 20th century.

We need to ensure that the power of influence from industry does not impose malignant and undemocratic change on society that can have impacts on future generations the like of which we are experiencing today.

Tomorrow's government and industry challenges

The challenge facing governments and industry across the globe is rooted in three strategically important areas:

1 sourcing of rare earth materials (REMs);

2 communication networks, eg 5G networks – the next generation of mobile internet connection, which offers much faster data download and upload speeds;

3 intellectual property (IP) and data protection.

In 2020, the ownership and exploitation of mineral resource such as lithium, cobalt, zinc and copper – rare earth materials – are a strategic asset dominated by China in the race to monopolize the production of batteries. In the future, zinc looks likely to be the competitive resource to support the development of solid-state battery technology and the major existing reserves of this material are in China and Australia – please refer to Chapter 1 (Statista, nd).

Decisions being made on how we connect and communicate, and the ownership and use of data/intellectual property are vital to government control. Again, we can see the spectre of powerful lobby groups emerging to influence how the world's population co-exists. China and the United States are locked in disputes over the use of 5G telecoms networks and the potential security conflicts that may exist.

The Internet of Things (IoT) will include such future visions as self-driving vehicles; the future promise of these autonomous vehicles can only be fully delivered through the implementation of superfast 5G mobile networks. By 2024, as a result of these networks, global mobile data traffic is expected to be at least five times greater than in 2020. In highly populated areas with high urban density, the current 4G networks simply won't be fast enough – 5G networks will be as much as 100 times faster than the existing 4G networks.

When 5G commercial networks are fully implemented, the first practical uses will include: enhanced mobile broadband, which will bring better experiences for smartphone users; and fixed wireless access, providing superfast fibre speeds without the need for fibre to the premises (FTTP). 5G smartphones started to become available at the beginning of 2019 (Ericsson, 2019).

Apple is expected to launch the iPhone 12 with 5G capability in 2020; all previous iPhones will only achieve 4G speeds (Eadicicco, 2020).

The main benefits of 5G devices will be considerably faster speeds when accessing large data sources such as downloading and streaming content – an HD movie will download in seven minutes via 5G as opposed to 48 minutes via a 4G network (Holmes, 2019).

5G devices will provide increased computing power and faster response times and will thus deliver virtually instantaneous connections to the network, as well as greater connectivity for mobile users.

The commercial value of 5G is by far the most significant opportunity and offers great business potential. People and businesses will be more connected, enabling smarter and more sustainable networks with a competitive advantage.

5G has not been without its detractors and critics because of its high implementation cost and the requirement to replace existing 4G devices with 5G. Nonetheless, there's wide support for the increased reliability and speed 5G offers, including the extra bandwidth needed to create the IoT – a network that links not just phones and computers but also robots, cars, trucks, transportation and all manner of sensor-equipped consumer products and infrastructure.

5G could equally provide the platform for a new generation of 'smart cities' in which energy grids, traffic signals and emergency services are connected together (Campanaro, 2018).

We do not appear to have in place the institutions to act as the multilateral powerbrokers required to ensure we avoid the mistakes that were made last century around the exploitation of energy resources, as witnessed by the fortunes of Rudolf Diesel and Nikola Tesla.

The missed opportunity in the selection and use of energy choices in the early part of the 20th century is something we now ponder in hindsight. We must learn from this accident of history when dealing with the crisis of material sourcing, communication and digital services innovation, and avoid making similar mistakes that will be regrettable 100 years from now.

Summary

- The death of Diesel and the decline of diesel engines due to the 'Dieselgate' scandal.

- The 'dash for diesel' and the seeds of its decline.

- Testing, compliance and the impact of environmental regulation and taxes on engine technology since 1980.

- The UK Government is now accelerating the shift to low-carbon transport – key actions aim to end the sale of new conventional petrol and diesel cars and vans by 2040.

- In London, from April 2019 any non-compliant truck became subject to a daily £100 fine. Unfortunately, over 70 per cent of the UK's trucks are non-compliant, ie operating at Euro 3 and below.

- Climate vs clean air – both are critical, policy makers take sides.

- The impact of Nikola Tesla and the invention of AC power in 1915. The missed opportunity a century ago to leverage the potential of the electric motor. The failure to commercialize innovation and invention and the consequences for the environment.

- The rise of the Tesla car brand in 2015. Elon Musk has challenged the conventional automotive OEMs. Tesla and Musk have become the Rudolf Diesel and Ford Motor Company of the 21st century.

- We need to ensure that the power of influence from industry does not impose malignant and undemocratic change on society that can have impacts for future generations.

- Decisions being made on how we connect and communicate, and the ownership and use of data/intellectual property are vital to government control.

References

Bryant, C and Sharman, A (2015) Martin Winterkorn resigns as VW boss over emissions scandal, *Financial Times*. Retrieved from: https://www.ft.com/content/d2288862-61d1-11e5-97e9-7f0bf5e7177b (archived at https://perma.cc/L9EE-29VD)

Campanaro, A (2018) What is 5G? The next wireless revolution explained, *NBC News*. Retrieved from: https://www.nbcnews.com/mach/tech/what-5g-next-wireless-revolution-explained-ncna855816 (archived at https://perma.cc/47Q5-Z6XY)

Carsalesbase (nd) US Car Sales. Retrieved from: http://carsalesbase.com/us-car-sales-data (archived at https://perma.cc/3FSN-FC69)

Chapman, B (2019) Honda to close Swindon plant by 2021 with loss of 3,500 jobs, *Independent*. Retrieved from: https://www.independent.co.uk/news/business/honda-swindon-manufacturing-plant-closure-jobs-employees-latest-a8911766.html (archived at https://perma.cc/952P-Y3WW)

ClientEarth (2017) ClientEarth challenges UK government's air pollution consultation. Retrieved from: https://www.clientearth.org/clientearth-challenges-uk-governments-air-pollution-consultation/ (archived at https://perma.cc/WN93-5FXV)

Department for Transport (2018) *The Road to Zero*, Department for Transport, London

Eadicicco, L (2020) Apple's iPhone 12 is expected to bring major changes like a new design, 5G, and 3D cameras – here's everything we know about it so far, *Business Insider*. Retrieved from: https://www.businessinsider.com/apple-iphone-12-rumors-5g-release-camera-specs-2019-6?r=US&IR=T (archived at https://perma.cc/L4CP-XRPS)

Ericsson (2019) Gearing up for 5G. Retrieved from: https://www.ericsson.com/en/5g/what-is-5g?gclid=Cj0KCQiAk7TuBRDQARIsAMRrfUZkM8h8BA5CeSVpTIDFzB3ij5auy_kc8S9yFy2PWVvYnu4YD8R5L7waArEOEALw_wcB (archived at https://perma.cc/7LSN-FXSJ)

Ewing, J (2018) Ex-Volkswagen CEO charged with fraud over diesel emissions, *New York Times*. Retrieved from: https://www.nytimes.com/2018/05/03/business/volkswagen-ceo-diesel-fraud.html (archived at https://perma.cc/8MQ3-AVMX)

Forrest, A (2017) The death of diesel: has the one-time wonder fuel become the new asbestos? *Guardian*. Retrieved from: https://www.theguardian.com/cities/2017/apr/13/death-of-diesel-wonder-fuel-new-asbestos (archived at https://perma.cc/S2DY-S4RU)

HM Government – EPA (1992) Environmental Protection Agency Act, 1992, HM Government, London

HM Government (2018) Automated and Electric Vehicles Act 2018, HM Government, London

HM Government (2019) Centre for Connected and Autonomous Vehicles. Retrieved from: https://www.gov.uk/government/organisations/centre-for-connected-and-autonomous-vehicles (archived at https://perma.cc/394X-C8AR)

HM Government DoEE (2009) The UK low carbon transition plan, HM Government, London

Holmes, C (2019) 5G vs 4G: how much time the new technology saves you. *Let's Talk*. Retrieved from: https://www.letstalk.com/cellphones/guides/5g-vs-4g/ (archived at https://perma.cc/UGB3-ZHXP)

Lambert, F (2016) Tesla's Fremont factory could manufacture up to 1 million vehicles per year, says Musk, *Electrek*. Retrieved from: https://electrek.co/2016/05/05/teslas-fremont-factory-1-million-vehicles-per-year-musk/ (archived at https://perma.cc/DC4A-XD8H)

MAN Museum (nd) Rudolf Diesel's tragic end. Retrieved from: https://museum.man-es.com/en/historical-figures/rudolf-diesel/the-tragic-end (archived at https://perma.cc/3YKY-ATXP)

Neate, R (2015) Meet John German: the man who helped expose Volkswagen's emissions scandal, *Guardian*. Retrieved from: https://www.theguardian.com/business/2015/sep/26/volkswagen-scandal-emissions-tests-john-german-research (archived at https://perma.cc/8DR9-UZJN)

NHTSA (2019) Corporate average fuel economy. Retrieved from: https://www.nhtsa.gov/laws-regulations/corporate-average-fuel-economy (archived at https://perma.cc/ZKQ9-XT69)

O'Grady, S (2005) So who killed MG Rover? *Independent*. Retrieved from: https://www.independent.co.uk/life-style/motoring/features/so-who-killed-mg-rover-518885.html (archived at https://perma.cc/68BC-VQ68)

Parloff, R (2018) How VW paid $25 billion for 'Dieselgate' – and got off easy, *Fortune*. Retrieved from: https://fortune.com/2018/02/06/volkswagen-vw-emissions-scandal-penalties/ (archived at https://perma.cc/M88D-GT9G)

Pickup, O (2018) How businesses can avoid London's ultra-low emission zone charge, *Telegraph*. Retrieved from: https://www.telegraph.co.uk/business/advice-for-smes/avoid-london-ulez-charge/ (archived at https://perma.cc/9FHP-5R9A)

Smedley, T (2019) *Clearing the Air: The beginning and the end of air pollution*, Bloomsbury

SMMT (nd) Heavy goods vehicle registrations. Retrieved from: https://www.smmt.co.uk/vehicle-data/heavy-goods-vehicle-registrations/ (archived at https://perma.cc/8BU3-GCBL)

Statista (nd) Global zinc reserves as of 2019, by country (in millions of tonnes). Retrieved from: https://www.statista.com/statistics/273639/global-zinc-reserves-by-country/ (archived at https://perma.cc/8GE8-MYN5)

United Nations (2008) Kyoto Protocol to the UN Framework Convention on Climate Change, UN, New York

Vidal, J (2015) The rise of diesel in Europe: the impact on health and pollution, *Guardian*. Retrieved from: https://www.theguardian.com/environment/2015/sep/22/the-rise-diesel-in-europe-impact-on-health-pollution (archived at https://perma.cc/B748-7X2Z)

03

Climate change action and the Paris Agreement

This chapter will familiarize the reader with:

- The primary goals of the Paris Agreement.
- Current country status with regard to greenhouse gas and CO_2 generation.
- How involvement in the Paris Agreement affects transport policies – what are nations doing, especially about fuel taxing?
- How climate change actions are measured, monitored and reported.
- What external bodies other than the United Nations exist to watch and monitor activity and success in reducing emissions?
- The Paris Agreement and the United States – is it important that they re-engage?

Introduction

It is possible that 2019 will have proven to be a pivotal year for the subject of global warming and the impact of climate change on the future of the planet. The images on every news story from September to December showed Australia on fire, Indonesia under water and North American states devastated by extreme weather caused by tornadoes and hurricanes.

The Intergovernmental Panel on Climate Change (IPCC) released a startling press release calling for urgent measures to combat melting glaciers and ice sheets:

> 'The open sea, the Arctic, the Antarctic and the high mountains may seem far away to many people,' said Hoesung Lee, Chair of the IPCC. 'But we depend on them and are influenced by them directly and indirectly in many ways – for weather and climate, for food and water, for energy, trade, transport, recreation and tourism, for health and wellbeing, for culture and identity' (IPCC, 2019).

Equally, an article in *New Scientist* highlighted the concern over the melting of the glaciers in Greenland; rightly so – the consequence of the disappearance of ice in Greenland as a significant contributor to the rise in sea levels in the future was highlighted (Marshall, 2019).

New Scientist predicts that global sea levels could rise by 52 to 98 centimetres by 2100. They also state that this is partly due to ice loss from Greenland, underscoring that action is required now (Marshall, 2019). This report may have been the trigger for US President Donald Trump to register an interest in potentially acquiring Greenland, primarily for the potential sourcing of rare earth materials (REMs) that are believed exist in vast quantities under the ice (Pengelly, 2019) and that the erosion of the Arctic's glaciers is a serious threat to the planet that cannot be ignored (Marshall, 2019).

The last decade (2010–2019) has also officially been reported in the news as the hottest ever (WMO, 2020). At the World Economic Forum held in Davos in January 2020, the agenda was dominated by whether the countries that are signed up to the Paris Agreement were doing enough to address climate change. This involves support for one of the core principles of the Paris Agreement of restricting temperature rises to below 2°C.

This chapter will explore which regions and countries in the world are the ones most responsible for CO_2 emissions and highlight what action is being taken, at a governmental level but equally important at a corporate level.

Different regions will inevitably adopt different approaches due to the nature of their economy, the maturity of specific industries and dependencies on chosen energy systems. For example, France has a bigger investment in nuclear energy than China, which is heavily invested in coal-fired energy generation; this has a significant impact on CO_2 emissions per capita, which will be lower in France and higher in China. In fact, China's CO_2 per capita footprint is 6.98 tonnes per annum vs France at 5.48 tonnes (Ritchie and Roser, 2017).

Interestingly, the worst performer on a per capita basis is Saudi Arabia, emitting 19.28 tonnes per capita, followed closely by Australia at 16.9 tonnes and the United States at 16.24 tonnes. Russia at 11.76 tonnes per capita is worse than Iran at 8.28 tonnes. Finally, the UK generates 5.8 tonnes per capita, which compares favourably to Germany at 8.01 tonnes (Ritchie and Roser, 2017).

The important issues to consider now are: does everyone know what their individual country or company contribution is to solving the climate problem? Have you been made aware of your company or individual carbon footprint? Do you know how to calculate your carbon footprint? And what action can be undertaken to take steps to improve it?

Answering some of these questions and directing readers to sources of information and case studies that will provide if not an answer then certainly food for thought is the aim of the rest of this chapter.

The first thing we need to do is fully grasp what the Paris Agreement, reached in 2015, set out to deliver.

The Paris Agreement

The ultimate ambition of the Paris Agreement is to achieve net zero-emissions and climate resilience by 2050 through a series of progressive measures. The goal is to keep global temperature rise by 2100 to well below 2°C above pre-industrial levels and to implement measures that will limit the temperature increase to less than 1.5°C – see Figure 3.1.

In 2015, every country in the world except Syria and Nicaragua signed the multilateral Paris Agreement, which commits nations to a programme of activity to reduce the amount of carbon dioxide generated in the world. In 2017 the United States decided it would no longer be a part of this agreement and announced its intention to withdraw from it. However, the United States became a 'lone-star' in November 2017 when both Nicaragua and Syria announced they would be joining the agreement.

President Trump declared this was in line with his administration's policy of 'America First'; the world's press described it as 'America Alone'. Any declaration of notice takes 12 months to take effect and any nation could not evoke notice for three years after the initial signing of the agreement, so in effect the United States cannot technically issue notice to withdraw from the Paris Agreement until 4 November 2020. The irony of this is that 4 November 2020 is the first day after the next Presidential

FIGURE 3.1   Ambition mechanism within the Paris Agreement

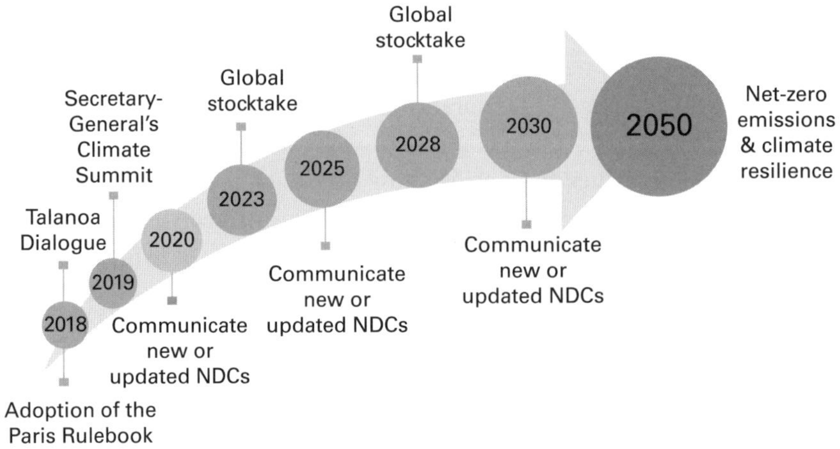

SOURCE   Fransen *et al*, 2017

election and in theory, should a different administration be elected, then the potential for the United States to change its mind is very real – so watch this space. As the greatest western power, with vast resources and technical know-how, the US clearly has an important role to play in climate change, not least of which being that it has tremendous influence on smaller countries that follow its actions.

As outlined in the introduction, the aim of this chapter is to shine a light on those activities deemed to have the biggest impact on achieving the goal by 2050 to be carbon neutral.

The first question to ask is, 'How big is the problem?' Table 3.1 below illustrates the size of the problem we face.

From this data some key trends can be observed:

- Annually *c.*36 billion tonnes of CO_2 are emitted into the earth's atmosphere and this figure continues to rise.

- China is the world's largest emitter of CO_2 – accounting for more than 25 per cent of global emissions. They are followed by the United States at 15 per cent, EU-28 at 10 per cent, India at 7 per cent and Russia at 5 per cent).

- The UK generates *c.*1.3 per cent of CO_2 and Germany *c.*2.5 per cent as a proportion of the global total (Ritchie and Roser, 2017).

TABLE 3.1 Tax breaks for fossil fuel in road transport

Region	Tonnes of CO_2	% of global total
Asia	19 billion	53%
North America	6.5 billion	18%
Europe	6.1 billion	17%
Africa	1.3 billion	3.7%
South America	1.1 billion	3.2%
Oceana (Australia/N Zealand)	0.5 billion	1.3%
International aviation and shipping	1.15 billion	3.2%

SOURCE Ritchie and Roser, 2017

As we enter the new decade in 2020, it will be interesting to see what outcomes result from the first meeting of members of the G20 nations attending the World Economic Forum in Davos following the November UN Climate Change meeting in Madrid.

It will also be very interesting to see the outcome of the crucial UN climate talks at COP26, which is being hosted by the UK in November 2021 (postponed from November 2020 due to the Covid-19 pandemic) (Harvey, 2020).

President Donald Trump announced his intention in 2017 to take the United States out of the Paris Agreement. In his keynote speech at the January 2020 Davos Economic Summit he reiterated his belief that climate change is a 'hoax' and denounced the activists as 'Prophets of doom' (*Guardian*, 2020).

Trump's remarks prompted Greta Thunberg, a young Swedish activist who has addressed the UN Conference on climate change, to remind the political and corporate elite of their obligation to future generations to save the planet and demonstrate a commitment to action now. It is in this polarized political and environmental context that the world waits to see who can progress effective action to deliver on the goals of the Paris Agreement (*Guardian*, 2020).

The role of transport in increasing global emissions

Global CO_2 emissions will reach *c*.36 billion tonnes in 2020 and are forecast to rise to *c*.40 billion tonnes by 2040. Transportation (including road, rail, marine and air) is estimated to be the fastest-growing global source of emissions. Globally, transport generates *c.*20 per cent of greenhouse gas emissions (GHEs) per year and is estimated to generate approximately 7.6 billion tonnes of CO_2 annually (Climate Watch, nd)

There are significant variations when one considers the transportation component of CO_2 emissions by country. The top 10 countries with the largest transportation emissions – ranked highest to lowest emitters – in 2014 were:

1 United States – *c.*22.8%

2 China – 10.3%

3 Russia – 3.1%

4 India – 3.1%

5 Brazil – 2.8%

6 Japan – 2.7%

7 Canada – 2.3%

8 Germany – 2.0%

9 Mexico – 2.0%

10 Iran – 1.8%

Collectively the countries above produced 53 per cent of global transport emissions in 2014. By comparison the UK produces only 1.5 per cent of global transport emissions (Wang and Ge, 2019).

Transportation is therefore a key target area to reduce global CO_2 emissions. Government transport legislation can shape and drive changes in CO_2 output.

How involvement in the Paris Agreement affects transport policy

There are some key issues that government transport departments and original equipment manufacturers (OEMs) will have to focus on addressing in the next few years. For example, all European truck manufacturers and regulators are going to have to review their support for certain types of alternative fuels. Some types of gas fuel are still considered fossil fuel and should be subject to any duty imposed by governments on petrol and diesel, not given any preferential treatment, as they are proven to be detrimental to air quality.

The priority, especially for light commercial vehicles (LCVs), will be to focus on the promotion of zero-emission electric vehicles for urban delivery

TABLE 3.2 Tax breaks for fossil fuel in road transport

Member State		Diesel duty rate per unit of energy € (nat currency)	Gas duty rate per unit of energy € (nat currency)	Potential tax revenue gain if diesel rate is applied to gas (in € million)
	Austria	11.42	1.66	7.80
	Belgium	16.74	0.00	6.75
	France	16.56	1.53	50.37
	Germany	13.12	3.86	61.59
	Italy	17.22	0.09	674.92
	Netherlands	14.05	4.68	20.00
	Portugal	13.54	1.86	7.98
	Spain	10.57	1.15	142.95
	Sweden	12.73 (SEK 131.52)	6.09 (SEK 62.9)	5.69 (SEK 58.8)
	United Kingdom	18.14 (GBP 16.16)	6.37 (GBP 5.67)	data not available
	Poland	9.57 (PLN 40.96)	4.53 (PLN 19.38)	2.61 (PLN 11.17)
	Romania	11.34 (RON 52.87)	2.73 (RON 12.71)	data not available

Sources: CE Delft (2017), European Commission Excise Duty Tables (2019), Eurostat (2019)

Notes: Calculated revenues are based on 2017 final gas consumption in road transport (excl. VAT)

TRANSPORT & ENVIRONMENT   @transenv @transenv transportenvironment.org

SOURCE Bannon, 2017

and halt any incentives for resources into gas infrastructure and incentives for liquid natural gas (LNG) trucks. Table 3.2 demonstrates the tax implications and government income opportunities available through applying a fair duty rate on energy products.

The priority, especially for LCVs, is to focus on the promotion of zero-emission electric vehicles for urban delivery and halt any incentives for resources into gas infrastructure and incentives for LNG trucks.

In road tests conducted by the Dutch government utilizing three LNG-powered vehicles, it was revealed that trucks powered by LNG emit between two and five times as much NO_x as equivalent diesel-powered trucks (Figure 3.2). NO_x is very poisonous and when released into the atmosphere contributes heavily to acid rain and suffocating smog. Manufacturers have claimed that LNG-powered trucks emit 30 per cent less NO_x than diesel-powered equivalents, but the results of the tests conducted clearly challenge this. Additionally, a number of countries offer subsidies and tax breaks for operators choosing to use LNG fuel (Table 3.2) (Bannon, 2018).

FIGURE 3.2 LNG trucks emit up to five times more NO$_x$ pollution than diesel

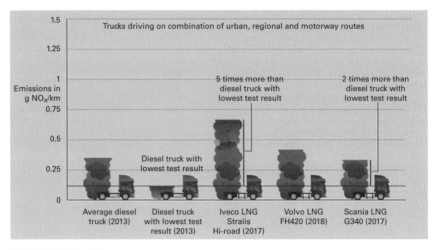

SOURCE Bannon, 2018

FIGURE 3.3 Gas trucks do not eliminate particle emissions

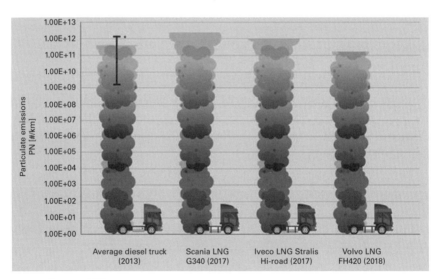

SOURCE Bannon, 2018

The on-road tests also showed that all three gas trucks tested produced levels of particulate emissions (PEs) comparable to diesel trucks (Figure 3.3). Particulates are solid particles caused by unburned carbons from fossil fuel combustion. These particles can penetrate deep into the lungs and be absorbed into the blood, causing heart disease, strokes and lung cancer. These findings are in sharp contrast to truckmakers' advertisements claiming that with LNG trucks particle emissions are almost completely eliminated (Bannon, 2018).

The case for rethinking how LNG gas should be treated due to its harmful emissions of pollutants is outlined in Figure 3.2 (Bannon, 2018).

Emission targets for trucks and buses

Emission and consumption targets are methods frequently used by governments to direct and possibly incentivize OEMs and tier suppliers to produce cleaner and more efficient vehicles. There are no agreed global standards for emissions, with each world region setting its own standards. On occasion there are even different standards within countries or states, such as the case of California in the United States.

The Paris Agreement obligates participant countries to complete a National Declared Contribution (NDC) to be reported at agreed intervals to monitor progress and individual company achievements that are influenced by regulation targets such as that mentioned above, and will be a significant contribution to individual country achievements in reducing emissions.

United States

In the United States, both the Environmental Protection Agency (EPA) and the National Highway Traffic Safety Administration (NHTSA) are taking coordinated steps to enable the production of a new generation of clean vehicles, through reduced GHG emissions and improved fuel use from on-road vehicles and engines (EPA, nd). As the EPA notes:

> In August 2011, in response to a Presidential Memorandum issued in May 2010, the EPA in coordination with NHSTA issued greenhouse gas emissions and fuel economy standards for medium and heavy-duty trucks manufactured in model years 2014–2018. The agencies estimate that the combined standards will reduce CO_2 emissions by about 270 million metric tonnes and save about 530 million barrels of oil over the life of vehicles built for the 2014 to 2018 model years, providing $49 billion in net program benefits. The reduced fuel use alone would enable $50 billion in fuel savings to accrue to vehicle owners, or $42 billion in net savings (EPA, nd).

While these figures sound impressive it is important to note that these US emission standards will only reduce their current transportation emissions by around 15 per cent. This is a far cry from the zero-emission standards sought in other countries. In effect the Trump administration is only planning 'lip service measures' in comparison with the lofty aims of the Paris Agreement.

Canada

In Canada the responsibility for the regulation of internal combustion engine (ICE) powered vehicles lies with Environment and Climate Change Canada (ECCC) and Transport Canada (TC). As noted in DieselNet:

> Canada has the authority to regulate emissions from on-road engines, as well as from most categories of off-road engines. Authority to regulate emissions from aircraft, railway locomotives and commercial marine vessels remains with Transport Canada (TC). Regulations have been adopted to control emissions of criteria air contaminants (CACs) as well as greenhouse gases (GHGs) (DieselNet, nda).

In general Canada has adapted to setting vehicle emission standards by harmonizing their regulations with those of the US EPA federal standards. In 1988, on-road vehicle emission standards were first aligned with the US federal standards. As noted in Canadian Regulation of Air Pollution: Canada:

> In February 2001, the Minister of the Environment in the Federal Agenda on Cleaner Vehicles, Engines and Fuels set out a number of policy measures that continued the harmonization of on-road emission standards, as well as expanded this harmonization by developing emission standards for off-road engines and standards for fuels that are aligned with the federal US requirements (Library of Congress, 2018).

In following the legislation in the United States, Canada will not make any significant steps to reducing global GHGs. A reduction of 15 per cent is all that will be achieved, as in the United States.

Asia and China

Asia has many emission standards and regulations and they are very complex. China is the world's largest automobile market and the second-largest emitter of vehicle-related emissions at 10 per cent, second only to the

United States. Many of China's cities have had serious air quality issues over recent years (Howard and Zhu, 2019).

Sources of pollution are predominantly:

- Mobile/automotive sources:
  - Pollutant exhaust gases created by the combustion of fossil fuels such as gasoline and diesel. Water and CO_2 are not included in this category, but CO, NO_x and hydrocarbons are and are thus subject to legislative control.
  - CO, NO_x and hydrocarbons are emitted by gasoline engines while diesel engines also emit particulates that are regulated.
- Stationary sources:
  - Local authorities control the sulphur content of heavy fuel oils used in such applications; these have been a major source of pollution.

Howard and Zhu detail:

> The Chinese government is tackling the pollution problem and significantly improving air quality. A series of emission legislation upgrades have been introduced, which have largely followed European standards. The next upgrade, known as China 6, is due for implementation from July 2020. This will put China right at the top of the list of countries with the most challenging vehicle emissions standards. By doing this many thousands of tonnes of serious pollutants such as particulate matter (PM) and oxides of nitrogen (NO_x) will be removed from China's air.

> Whilst China 6a limits (to be introduced in July 2020) will largely equate to Euro 6 ones, there are some key differences in application. The most significant is the application of particulate number (PN) limits to all gasoline-powered cars, not just gasoline direct injection (GDI) versions as in Europe. This will mean a far wider adoption of gasoline particulate filters (GPFs). Even hybrids, traditionally seen as very low emission vehicles, face the prospect of needing GPFs as their frequent stop/start cycles produce an output of particulates with every engine start. Things will get tougher still when China 6a is replaced by 6b in July 2023, with revised limits significantly lower than European equivalents (Howard and Zhu, 2019).

China is also developing fuel standards for heavy-duty commercial vehicles to start in 2021, with the overall goal of reducing fuel consumption from these vehicles by 15 per cent below 2015 levels. When fully implemented, these standards will be in line with standards in the United States, Canada, Japan and the EU. These emissions standards apply to atmospheric pollutants like NO_x and particulate matter, but do not regulate CO_2 specifically.

Japan

Japan introduced its first new engine emissions standards for on-road light-duty vehicles (LDVs) and heavy-duty engines (HD) in the late 1980s. Nevertheless, Japanese standards remained very relaxed throughout the 1990s (DieselNet, ndb). DieselNet outlines:

> In 2003 the Ministry of Ecology & Environment (MOEE) finalized very stringent 2005 emission standards for both light and heavy vehicles. At the time they came to power, the 2005 heavy-duty emission standards (NO_x = 2 g/kWh, PM = 0.027 g/kWh) were the most stringent diesel emission regulation in the world. Effective 2009, these limits were further tightened to a level in-between the US 2010 and Euro V requirements, and the 2016 limits are comparable in stringency to the US 2010 and Euro VI standards.

> Most categories of on-road vehicles, including passenger cars and heavy-duty trucks and buses, are also subject to mandatory fuel efficiency targets. The Japanese fuel efficiency requirements for heavy trucks and buses were the world's first fuel economy regulation for heavy vehicles (DieselNet, ndb).

Japan's targeted NDCs, agreed as part of the commitment to the Paris Agreement, have been described as 'highly insufficient' or 'totally inadequate' (Climate Action Tracker, nd).

As such, Japan's current transport legislation will not achieve zero emissions by 2050. Climate Action Tracker states:

> One major positive policy development is in the Japanese transport sector, where the government, together with all major car manufacturing companies, is planning to set a long-term target of reducing tank-to-wheel CO_2 emissions by 90 per cent below 2010 levels by 2050 for new passenger vehicles, assuming a near 100 per cent share of electric vehicles (Climate Action Tracker, nd).

EU

The European Union has never placed targets for CO_2 emissions on trucks and buses. The United States, China, Japan and Canada have imposed targets on their commercial vehicle population. On 1 January 2019 the European Commission introduced, for the first time, targets and measures covering fuel economy and CO_2 emissions for trucks.

As a result of the new CO_2 legislation, all new trucks going on the road must achieve 15 per cent lower CO_2 emissions by 2025 compared with those of 2019. By 2030 emissions must be a minimum of 30 per cent lower, although this target is subject to further review in 2022. Lower targets will be placed on electric, hybrid and other alternatives such as hydrogen, which is forecast to be a significant fuel of the future (Muzi, 2019)

The European truck industry is now being challenged for the first time in almost 20 years to be active in supporting the goals of the Paris Agreement but still many commentators believe that it will not be enough to deliver on the goal to reduce sea temperature rise to 1.5°C.

Probably the single most talked about topic in the commercial vehicle industry in 2019 (besides preparation for Brexit) has been the electrification of the fleet. In the latest EU Commission directive, OEMs are encouraged to go electric through a form of offsetting. This would support the goal of a CO_2 reduction of 15 per cent in 2025 compared to 1990 levels, and 30 per cent by 2030.

The commission has agreed a form of offset if a certain level of BEV sales is achieved, which would reduce the target of 15 and 30 per cent by 2–3 per cent. By selling new BEVs and delivering 2 per cent of sales that are electric there will be an offset that effectively assists the achievement of the 2025 and 2030 targets (International Transport Forum, 2018).

Truck makers can take advantage of the zero counting of all electric trucks into their fleet CO_2 emissions. From September 2020 onwards, truck manufacturers will also benefit from the additional metre of cab space allowed in design to accommodate space requirements for batteries and hydrogen fuel stacks. This change to design criteria is also favourable to aerodynamic performance and ultimately fuel economy. The EU also announced that all electric trucks would also be exempt from road toll charges.

While many of these new regulations will accelerate the transition to emission-free and low-emission product, they will fall short of the 2030 and 2050 targets. In 2019, forecasts from the European Environment Agency (EEA) estimated that EU truck emissions will fall by perhaps 13.5 per cent by 2030, well short of the 30 per cent target when compared to 1990. Many of the European manufacturers will be focusing on improved diesel efficiency, ie Euro 6.2e or Euro 7, and the electrification of their light duty ranges and vans (EEA, 2019).

A €20,000 per truck reduction in fuel costs over the initial five years of operation could be achieved if the 2025 standards are successfully applied.

This will result in a huge saving for haulage, logistics and distribution operators. Full application of the 2030 standards would save up to €60,000 per truck over the initial five years (Yang, 2018).

The UK's dependence on imported oil and the European economy will be substantially reduced as a direct result of these standards. In turn this will also create 80,000 additional jobs through to 2030. This is what a greener economy can look like in the future.

The 'holy grail' of a decarbonized transport industry is a prize on the horizon that both environmentalists and industry operators can see emerging as a result of new regulations being accepted and implemented going forward.

How is the investment in a carbon-neutral transport system being paid for?

The late 1980s and early 1990s witnessed what has been described as the 'Dash for Diesel'. Government action on how duty was applied to petrol and diesel clearly created an advantage not just for the sale of diesel passenger cars but also for the truck and van producers.

Unfortunately, the downside of increased pollutants did not deter governments at the time from delivering tax advantages for diesel in support of the haulage industry.

The manner in which most nations collect some form of carbon tax to generate revenue that can ultimately be used to support transport and environmental projects is down to the following:

- duty on fuel and therefore diesel and petrol pricing;
- infrastructure congestion control – charges such as road tolls;
- emissions control – introduction of city congestion zones and zero- or low-emission zones with daily penalties/fines for non-compliant vehicles.

Fuel duties

All governments in Europe need to review the carbon tax on fuel and come to some sensible arrangements that deliver a balance between economic and commercial need and environmental imperatives that support the climate change goal of the Paris Agreement.

The UK and Belgium are the only two EU markets that have come close to taxing petrol and diesel with a common duty; in all other EU markets diesel has a distinct advantage over petrol. A report by Transport & Environment calculates this is costing European governments €24 billion in lost tax revenue every year (Bannon, 2015).

Theoretically this represents a €24 billion missed opportunity to invest in some meaningful transport infrastructure activity led by green technology business initiatives, for example the building of battery gigafactories (a term coined by Elon Musk for his planned Tesla battery and electric vehicle factories – see Chapter 6) or exploring the potential for innovative urban consolidation centres on the edges of cities where redundant car and truck production facilities are closed or being mothballed.

Significant differences remain in force in key EU markets between petrol and diesel taxing across Europe. In Germany the diesel tax was €0.47 per litre compared to €0.65 on petrol – almost a 40 per cent difference. This translated into a €7.3 billion shortfall for the German exchequer (Bannon, 2017).

While Belgium is recognized as having acted in 2019 to equalize the tax on diesel and petrol due to the 3 cents difference in 2018 tax policy, the cost to the Belgian exchequer was €225 million (Bannon, 2017).

Spain faced an even greater discrepancy due to its fuel tax policy and it was estimated that the cost to its exchequer was around €3 billion in lost tax receipts. Just consider for a moment how green technology business could have benefited from an energy or infrastructure innovation fund established from a windfall of this magnitude (Bannon, 2017).

In Greece the backlash from applying almost 30 cents difference per litre between diesel and petrol has incentivized greater use of diesel cars in the cities, and contributed to a pollution crisis that culminated in the Mayor of Athens planning to ban all diesel cars from Athens City from 2025; a similar pledge has been made by the Mayor of Madrid (Bannon, 2015).

A product of the EU-wide variation in taxes applied to fuel is a phenomenon known as 'Fuel Tourism' or more precisely 'Tank Tourism'. The EU originally adopted a minimum tax level set at 33 cents per litre. Luxembourg has operated at almost the lowest level with a €0.33 per litre tax applied up to May 2019 and as a result it exports almost 80 per cent of its fuel consumed to foreign motorists and truck drivers. However, this is a loophole that will be closed soon, as countries demand a fuel rebate from the EU to compensate for this blatant error in how the EU plans and implements environment and transport policy.

Eight countries – Belgium, France, Hungary, Ireland, Italy, Romania, Slovenia and Spain – have successfully applied for compensation and around €4 billion was returned to truck operations in 2018, up from nothing in at the turn of the century (Muzi, 2014).

Infrastructure Charges

An increasing form of carbon tax collection has been from the design and implementation of motorway tolls, congestion charges and more recently zero- and low-emission zones. They vary from country to country in terms of the conditions and times under which they operate but the primary goals remain reducing congestion, improving road safety and reducing urban pollution.

The outcome from the congestion and emission zone planners has resulted in a number of common deliverables.

For example:

- Improvement of cycle paths in cities to encourage people to use bikes not cars.

- Experiments with the development of mobility hubs where the public can rent electric vehicles by the hour or use public transport to travel into city centres.

- Separate intracity requirements from intercity requirements – they are very different. This reinforces the idea to rethink the role of innovative urban consolidation centres, details of which are explored in Chapter 5.

While it's important to recognize what policies are being pursued by regulatory authorities it's also necessary to know how any progress is being monitored and reported.

How are climate change actions monitored and measured?

Before we get too carried away on a tide of goodwill generated by regulation and acceleration of the adoption of electric vans and trucks, it is useful to become familiar with just how progress on decarbonization is being monitored, analysed and most importantly reported upon.

The Paris Agreement defined the use of NDCs as the mechanism for recording and reporting individual country obligations that were agreed, and how individual countries define these targets has been extensively reported by the International Transport Forum (ITF).

The ITF is an intergovernmental organization and currently includes 60 member countries. Core responsibilities undertaken by the ITF include acting as a collective body of experts to develop world transport policy, and organizing the Annual Summit of the International Transport Forum.

The Annual Forum attracts transport ministers from around the world to meet with business and subject matter experts. The ITF is politically autonomous and administratively integrated with the OECD. It is unique in that it is the only world organization that encompasses all transport methods.

The declared mission of the ITF is to promote a deeper understanding of the role of transport in driving:

- economic growth;
- environmental sustainability and social inclusion;
- the public profile of transport policy (ITF, 2018).

As we have established, 5 per cent of the 190 countries signed up to the Paris Agreement generate almost 80 per cent of annual global CO_2 emissions. Therefore, it's not difficult to see that there will be 'widespread different targets' set for every country. The most important goal initially was to establish the base from which everyone was operating and then to agree the ambition to factor into the milestones on 2025 and 2030.

The UNFCCC did not provide any specific template, structure or content requirements for the development of NDCs, so as a result, several guidance documents for the preparation of NDCs were developed by other institutions. The International Transport Forum website has probably the best analysis and reporting on how NDCs have been developed (ITF, 2018).

EU Commission national emission reduction targets 2021–2030

Legislation in support of climate action geared to delivering the goals of the Paris Agreement was developed by members of the EU Parliament in 2016 and became known as the Effort Sharing Regulation (ESR). The ESR covers 60 per cent of the EU's greenhouse gas emissions, and has set binding national emission reduction targets for the 2021–2030 period for sectors such as transport, buildings, agriculture and waste (Carbon Market Watch, nd).

FIGURE 3.4 EU Climate Leader Board

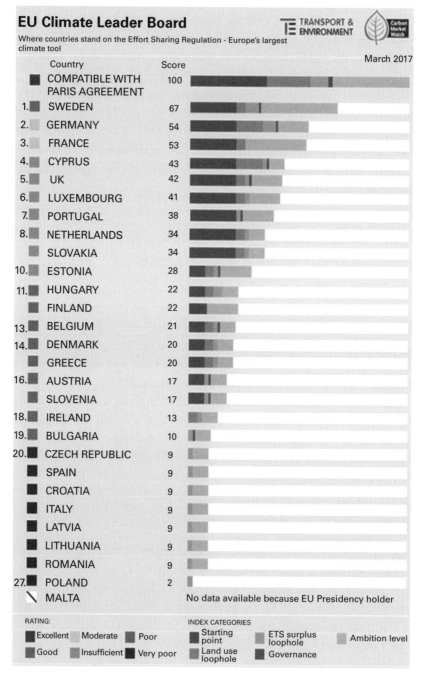

SOURCE Bannon, 2017

The outcome from various meetings in 2016 was to agree five principles on which target setting would be based:

1 Starting point for emissions reduction goal.

2 Avoidance of loopholes such as credits based on land use.

3 Avoidance of loopholes based on any emissions credits from Emissions Trading Systems.

4 Governance – agreement on five-year compliance reviews.

5 Levels of ambition compared to 1990 base – 45 per cent reduction by 2025, 95 per cent reduction by 2030.

For each category, points are awarded based on country positions in relation to the Commission proposal.

The outcome from the work undertaken by Carbon Market Watch and the Transport and Environment organization was an EU Climate Leader Board that illustrates to all EU citizens the progress being made by their respective governments – see Figure 3.4.

Initial performance of EU countries participating in the ESR monitor

Sweden scored the highest among all EU countries because it was very assertive in its advocacy for closing loopholes and ambitious in setting emission reduction targets. It was too early to say Sweden benefited from any 'Greta Thunberg effect' as she had not started any school rebellion at this stage. Sadly, only three countries in Europe were seen to be energetically and ambitiously pushing to deliver on the Paris Agreement commitments (Laville, 2019).

Poland, Italy, Spain and the Czech Republic appear to weaken the Commission proposals, countering Europe's efforts to comply with the Paris Agreement. Austria and Finland seem to suffer from a poverty of ambition and were actively pushing for using additional forestry credits to offset poor emissions levels in other areas (Bannon, 2017).

Ireland also performs poorly. It only needs to reduce its emissions by 1 per cent by 2030 compared to its 2005 levels, when taking the different flexibilities into account. Nevertheless, the country is still trying to stall reduction efforts for another decade by pushing to further weaken the Commission proposal. The country can achieve a better score by advocating for a better starting point from which the emission reductions targets are applied.

Slovakia, Germany and France have an average score on this leader board and the UK is rated insufficient and must do better. Perhaps when regular order is restored post Brexit then the UK Government will see its way forward with a relevant and more ambitious set of actions in support of the Paris Agreement obligations.

While this work by two leading think-tanks on the subject of climate change action and sustainable transport has developed methods and approaches to analysing, monitoring and reporting progress on all nations' support for the Paris Agreement, it is very likely that the goal to limit rising temperature to 1.5°C remains out of reach for many nations. This reflects a sense of pessimism that was a feature of both the Madrid November 2019 UN Climate Summit and the January 2020 Davos Economic Forum; at both events delegates left with a feeling that the world was still not doing enough to meet the ambition of the Paris Agreement.

How can corporations develop effective sustainable emission reduction plans?

Despite the gloom and general pessimism about the ability of nations to deliver on the goals of the Paris Agreement, and the collective sigh of disapproval from the United Nations at the retreat by the United States in 2017, there are a number of initiatives that support and promote best practice in developing corporate carbon reduction plans.

One of the most recognized and successful initiatives is the Science-Based Targets initiative (SBTi). A collection of not-for-profit organizations came together in 2002 and formed the Carbon Disclosure Project (CDP), whose aim was to help companies transition to low-carbon business models with a dedicated focus on emissions reduction and energy-efficiency projects.

The CDP is a collaborative association of several not-for-profit organizations including the World Resources Institute (WRI), World Wildlife Fund for nature (WWF), and the United Nations Global Compact (UNGC).

The CDP champions the development and implementation of science-based target setting and has made its aim in 2020 that SBTi will be recognized as the global best practice standard for reducing greenhouse gas emissions. Science-based targeting is rooted in the GHG Protocol Corporate Standard that classifies a company's GHG emissions into three scopes:

- Scope 1 emissions are direct emissions from owned or controlled sources.
- Scope 2 emissions are indirect emissions from generation of purchased energy sources.
- Scope 3 emissions are all direct emissions not purchased in Scope 2 that occur in the value chain of the reporting company, both upstream and downstream emissions.

The SBTi methodology has been universally recognized as a best practice model, based on the following key factors:

- The organization is expected to create credible targets and have a leadership culture determined to invest in appropriate resource to engage and motivate all stakeholders involved in the management of scope 1 and 2 emissions.
- The organization recognizes there are direct and indirect areas to investigate, monitor and measure and that an effective roadmap for internal and external partners needs to be effectively coordinated over time and the early identification of emission hotspots must be a priority.
- The organization recognizes that the biggest challenge will be the collection and validation of scope 3 third-party partners' emissions and carbon footprint and measures to drive the improvements necessary to deliver the emission reduction target.
- An organization's climate change target can only be described as science based if it is aligned with the goal of limiting global warming to no more than 2.0°C above pre-industrial levels.

The CDP organization is a leading practitioner of best practice in carbon reduction action plans, business model innovation and risk management, and for those wishing to know more about how to embark on this target-setting exercise the website to review is www.cdp.net.

There is no silver bullet or universal common cure for the emissions challenge we face. Every nation, every company, every individual will have to make decisions on how they can influence their carbon footprint and make a positive contribution to the goal of limiting global warming within the thresholds defined by the Paris Agreement.

However, for the benefit of readers of this book we would like to illustrate an example of a complex corporate challenge to define, measure, monitor and improve the end-to-end carbon footprint of one of the world's largest retail organizations, Tesco PLC, which has 6,000 stores worldwide.

This is an organization that will be pursued for business by most of the major commercial vehicle manufacturers. It is essential that all potential truck suppliers to Tesco not only understand this company's emissions reduction plans but should also be prepared to align themselves with Tesco's company objectives, and demonstrate how their truck-related products and services could make a positive contribution.

CASE STUDY
What science-based targets are important to Tesco?

In the case study, Tesco declared their commitment to the following goals (Science Based Targets, nd):

- A reduction of scope 1 and scope 2 greenhouse gas emissions by 60 per cent by 2025 using 2015 as a base year.
- Reduction of scope 3 GHG emissions of 17 per cent by 2030.

Scope 3 emissions cover those emitted by supply chain partners and requires Tesco to validate and report emissions from third-party logistics partners, transport providers, fuel and energy services, and waste and recycling operations. Scope 3 activity is the most challenging for companies to deliver.

Tesco became a member of the Renewable Energy 100 coalition (RE100) in 2017 – a global corporate leadership initiative bringing together influential businesses committed to 100 per cent renewable electricity. Led by the Climate Group in partnership with CDP Worldwide, RE100's purpose is to accelerate change towards zero-carbon grids at global scale (RE100, nd). Tesco is committed to sourcing 100 per cent of its electricity from renewable sources by 2030 with an interim target of 65 per cent by 2025 (Umeasiegbu, 2017).

Tesco put great emphasis on demonstrating how serious it was about tackling climate change and improving its reputation in this area, and recognized that it needed to meet the following challenges:

- Science-based targets (SBTs) were a new methodology to become familiar with. Tesco management recognized the importance of awareness, education and communication, and securing buy-in across the company and along the extended enterprise became a critical success factor to be managed.

- Setting realistic goals in support of the emission reduction goals required the involvement of many functions from supply chain and logistics integration to complex property portfolio management.

- Agricultural emissions represented 70 per cent of total supply chain greenhouse gases and the Tesco leadership group incorporated agriculture emissions into a stand-alone target with specific reduction targets separate from other scope 3 contributions in recognition of the unique challenge necessary to deliver agriculture emission reductions.

In addition to joining the RE100 coalition and a commitment to switching to 100 per cent renewable electricity by 2030, Tesco invested £8 million in Asia in onsite generation. Over £700 million has been invested in energy and refrigeration improvements, which has resulted in a 41 per cent reduction per square foot in emissions at stores and distribution centres when compared to the baseline levels established in 2006 (Science Based Targets, nd).

Tesco's leadership team recognize the importance of having science-based targets that can be seen as credible and realistic goals that are clearly aligned with the aims of the Paris Agreement.

Summary and conclusions

There is no question that in 2015 the decision of almost all the world's nations, except for Syria and Nicaragua, to commit to delivering a programme of climate change action to limit the impact of global warming to below 2°C was a momentous occasion.

While transport is not the major generator of emissions and pollutants it is recognized as a significant industry that needs to seriously address the problem. This chapter has focused specifically on what the vehicle manufacturers, transport, logistics and distribution industry, and government regulators can do to mitigate the impact of carbon emissions, and we are witnessing progress.

Progress on regulation in Europe has seen the introduction, for the first time, of emissions regulations for trucks and buses in 2019. The 15 and 30 per cent reductions in emissions by 2025 and 2030 support the goals of the

Paris Agreement. However, the adoption of low-emission and zero-emission products has yet to make any impact on GHG emissions and most manufacturers did not implement series production plans for electric vans and trucks until the start of the 2020. Indeed, many electric vans and light commercial vehicles will not be available until late 2020–2021.

The forecasts for the adoption of electric commercial vehicles have focused on the van and light commercial vehicle sector. Globally, it is estimated that 30–40 per cent of the world's commercial vehicle sales will be electric by 2030 (IEA, 2017). This is an estimate for about a million vehicles, many of which will be operated in Asia, and specifically China. The development of zero-emission or low-emission heavy-duty trucks will not be based on electric platforms but, most likely, improved diesel technology and hydrogen.

This chapter has detailed how government fiscal policy can influence transport fleet purchase decisions that can be subject to the impact of differential fuel type taxing. Subsidies for both energy supply and transport products can be very effective in determining the shape of future markets.

China has been very effective in influencing its amazing growth in electric vehicle sales through the availability of government subsidy. This has also applied to the development of solar energy and battery production with the emergence of many gigafactories now producing lithium-ion batteries for electric vehicles.

The UK Government now needs to focus attention on its fuel pricing and renewable energy subsidy support if it is to support job opportunities in the UK automotive industry.

The automotive industry in the UK employs almost 800,000 people and is threatened with significant job losses if the investment in battery production facilities is abandoned. The information released by the Faraday Institution, which is discussed in Chapter 1, details the potential threats to jobs related to battery production investment.

The United States stated in 2017 that it is withdrawing from the Paris Agreement following President Trump's decision. The Trump administration's continued roll-back by the EPA of regulations designed to curb emissions from transport has been rejected by many states, and indicates that US commitment to the Paris Agreement aims would be compromised. Many commentators have highlighted many reasons for the United States to stay involved, citing the opportunity for jobs and the economy, and the positive impact on health and national security as being primary reasons for re-joining the agreement.

However, on the flip side, the downside of their continued rejection of the agreement has seen European politicians raise the idea of placing a carbon pollution tax on products from the United States. Whether this would ever be realized is debatable, but adds to the growing tensions among nations dealing with the various tariff agreement discussions that dominated world economics in 2019.

There is still much to do to reduce the 36 billion tonnes of carbon dioxide generated by the 193 nations on the planet originally involved in the Paris Agreement. Climate activists claim there is no planet B, therefore the rest of our book attempts to outline what potential Plans B, C, D and E might be.

Chapter 8 looks at what the current vehicle manufacturers are planning and Chapter 9 details who the emerging green technology businesses might be that could succeed in creating the sustainable carbon-neutral transport ecosystem of the future.

References

Bannon, E (2015) Europe's tax deals for diesel, *Transport & Environment*. Retrieved from: https://www.transportenvironment.org/publications/europes-tax-deals-diesel (archived at https://perma.cc/YR3P-CASR)

Bannon, E (2017) The EU Climate Leader Board, *Transport & Environment*. Retrieved from: https://www.transportenvironment.org/publications/eu-climate-leader-board (archived at https://perma.cc/2YSH-Q26M)

Bannon, E (2018) On-road tests show gas trucks up to 5 times worse for air pollution, *Transport & Environment*. Retrieved from: https://www.transport environment.org/press/road-tests-show-gas-trucks-5-times-worse-air-pollution (archived at https://perma.cc/9CXN-BKRD)

Carbon Market Watch (nd) Effort Sharing Regulation. Retrieved from: https://carbonmarketwatch.org/our-work/climate-governance/effort-sharing-regulation/ (archived at https://perma.cc/7LNX-U9ML)

Climate Action Tracker (nd) Country Summary – Japan. Retrieved from: https://climateactiontracker.org/countries/japan/ (archived at https://perma.cc/33DN-SV5W)

Climate Watch (nd) Historical GHG Emissions. Retrieved from: https://www.climatewatchdata.org/ghg-emissions?breakBy=sector&gases=202&regions=NAR&sectors=624%2C614 (archived at https://perma.cc/24PV-F2JU)

DieselNet (nda) Emission Standards – Canada. Retrieved from https://dieselnet.com/standards/ca/ (archived at https://perma.cc/DK6H-KRYH)

DieselNet (ndb) Emission Standards – Japan. Retrieved from: https://dieselnet.com/standards/jp/index.php (archived at https://perma.cc/7W62-EGHJ)

EEA (2019) Total greenhouse gas emission trends and projections in Europe. Retrieved from: https://www.eea.europa.eu/data-and-maps/indicators/greenhouse-gas-emission-trends-6/assessment-3 (archived at https://perma.cc/6AEY-LEKN)

EPA (nd) Regulations for greenhouse gas emissions from commercial trucks & buses. Retrieved from: https://www.epa.gov/regulations-emissions-vehicles-and-engines/regulations-greenhouse-gas-emissions-commercial-trucks (archived at https://perma.cc/U362-VFU4)

Fransen, T et al (2017) Enhancing NDCS by 2020: Achieving the goals of the Paris Agreement, WRI. Retrieved from: https://wriorg.s3.amazonaws.com/s3fs-public/WRI17_NDC.pdf (archived at https://perma.cc/UG8N-GLNE)

Guardian (2020) Trump decries climate 'prophets of doom' in Davos keynote speech – video. Retrieved from: https://www.theguardian.com/us-news/video/2020/jan/21/trump-decries-climate-prophets-of-doom-in-davos-keynote-speech-video (archived at https://perma.cc/5TYV-Z6JW)

Harvey, F (2020) Saving the planet: UK role vital if COP 26 climate talks to succeed, Guardian. Retrieved from: https://www.theguardian.com/environment/2020/feb/03/saving-the-planet-uk-role-vital-if-cop-26-climate-talks-to-succeed (archived at https://perma.cc/4E97-UULL)

Howard, K and Zhu, P (2019) China 6: the world's most challenging emissions standard, Lubrizol Additives 360. Retrieved from: https://www.lubrizoladditives360.com/china-6-worlds-challenging-emissions-standard/ (archived at https://perma.cc/LYC3-PCFS)

IEA (2017) The Future of Trucks. Retrieved from: https://www.iea.org/reports/the-future-of-trucks (archived at https://perma.cc/M7M8-GMS8)

International Transport Forum (2018) Transport CO_2 and the Paris Climate Agreement. Retrieved from: https://www.itf-oecd.org/transport-co2-paris-climate-agreement-ndcs (archived at https://perma.cc/L9ZV-6VRQ)

IPCC (2019) Choices made now are critical for the future of our ocean and cryosphere. Retrieved from: https://www.ipcc.ch/2019/09/25/srocc-press-release/ (archived at https://perma.cc/6RKT-R82T)

Laville, S (2019) 'Greta Thunberg effect' driving growth in carbon offsetting, Guardian, Retrieved from: https://www.theguardian.com/environment/2019/nov/08/greta-thunberg-effect-driving-growth-in-carbon-offsetting (archived at https://perma.cc/2QWE-W9YU)

Library of Congress (2018) Regulation of air pollution: Canada. Retrieved from: https://www.loc.gov/law/help/air-pollution/canada.php (archived at https://perma.cc/X5JE-6QH6)

Marshall, M (2019) Greenland lost almost 4 trillion tonnes of ice in less than 30 years, *New Scientist*. Retrieved from: https://www.newscientist.com/article/2226676-greenland-lost-almost-4-trillion-tonnes-of-ice-in-less-than-30-years/ (archived at https://perma.cc/DKV4-YNAE)

Muzi, N (2014) (2020, February 4). EU agrees on safer, cleaner lorries – but by 2022, *Transport & Environment*. Retrieved from: https://www.transportenvironment.org/press/eu-agrees-safer-cleaner-lorries-2022 (archived at https://perma.cc/U3DH-9S4F)

Muzi, N (2019) EU agrees first-ever CO_2 targets for trucks, delivering a 30% cut in fuel burnt and kick-starting zero-emission vehicles, *Transport & Environment*. Retrieved from: https://www.transportenvironment.org/press/eu-agrees-first-ever-co2-targets-trucks-delivering-30-cut-fuel-burnt-and-kick-starting-zero (archived at https://perma.cc/368V-78JU)

Pengelly, M (2019) Trump confirms he is considering attempt to buy Greenland, *Guardian*. Retrieved from: https://www.theguardian.com/world/2019/aug/18/trump-considering-buying-greenland (archived at https://perma.cc/56TV-MCM6)

RE100 (nd) RE100 Overview. Retrieved from http://re100.org/ (archived at https://perma.cc/MSE3-VN47)

Ritchie, H and Roser, M (2017) Our world in data: CO_2 and greenhouse gas emissions. Retrieved from: https://ourworldindata.org/co2-and-other-greenhouse-gas-emissions (archived at https://perma.cc/TZM6-VBUD)

Science-Based Targets (nd) Case study: Tesco. Retrieved from: https://sciencebasedtargets.org/wp-content/uploads/2018/03/SBT_Tesco_CaseStudy.pdf (archived at https://perma.cc/93U4-TN7F)

Umeasiegbu, K (2017) Tesco commits to use 100% renewable electricity by 2030 *Tesco Plc*. Retrieved from: https://www.tescoplc.com/blog/carbon-renewable-electricity-tesco/ (archived at https://perma.cc/N9SV-8NCE)

Wang, S and Ge, M (2019) Everything you need to know about the fastest-growing source of global emissions: transport, *WRI*. Retrieved from https://www.wri.org/blog/2019/10/everything-you-need-know-about-fastest-growing-source-global-emissions-transport (archived at https://perma.cc/49LM-PU5U)

WMO (2020) WMO confirms 2019 as second hottest year on record. Retrieved from: https://public.wmo.int/en/media/press-release/wmo-confirms-2019-second-hottest-year-record (archived at https://perma.cc/BVG3-GXMZ)

Yang, Z (2018) Overview of global fuel economy policies, *ICCT*. Retrieved from https: https://theicct.org/sites/default/files/Global-Fuel-Economy-Policies-Overview_ICCT_ZYang_20032018.pdf (archived at https://perma.cc/V9NB-5Q5M)

04

The climate change challenge

This chapter will familiarize the reader with:

- Reporting CO_2 levels in the atmosphere.
- Defining a 'greenhouse gas'.
- Industrial processes requiring regulation.
- New standards for heavy-duty truck emissions from 2025 to 2030.
- 'Europe on the Move' – EU emission regulations.
- Funding available to support UK and European actions to reduce emissions.
- The case for a vehicle scrappage programme to accelerate the withdrawal of higher-emitting Euro 3 and lower vehicles.

CO_2 levels in the atmosphere

The level of carbon dioxide (CO_2) released into the atmosphere has increased significantly since the beginning of the industrial era, as noted in research (Global CCS Institute, 2018a).

CO_2 and other greenhouse gases have chemical properties that allow them to absorb infrared (IR) radiation from the sun. CO_2 in the earth's upper atmosphere prevents IR radiation escaping. Thus CO_2 has a critical impact on global warming.

The current raised temperature level we are experiencing, which has surpassed the sustainable threshold, can only be attributed to human activity and human-caused increase in CO_2 levels. Figure 4.1 demonstrates 'The Greenhouse Effect' of increased CO_2.

FIGURE 4.1 'The Greenhouse Effect'

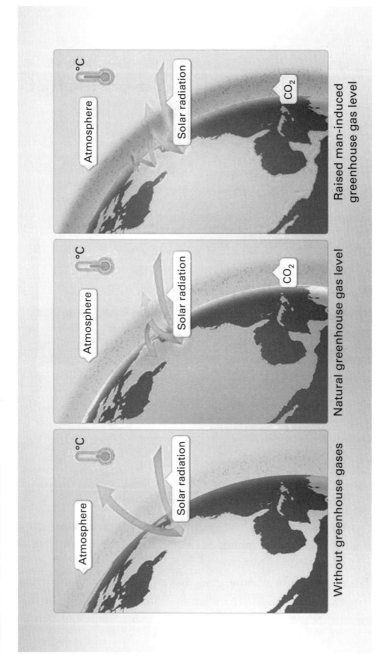

Without greenhouse gases   Natural greenhouse gas level   Raised man-induced greenhouse gas level

SOURCE Global CCS Institute, 2018a

Long-term monitoring has shown that the ramifications of increased CO_2 in the atmosphere is causing the earth to warm and the oceans to become more acidic. But what is being done about this? And what can be done?

Various degrees of activism to force governments and industry to react with immediate policy developments are widely reported, such as Extinction Rebellion. The Intergovernmental Panel on Climate Change (IPCC) has also published a special report entitled 'Global Warming of 1.5°C', which raises awareness on this crucial issue (IPCC, 2018).

Scientists broadly concur that the world temperature has risen by 1°C since pre-industrial times due to human activity.

Scientific evidence for warming of the climate system is unequivocal
(IPCC, 2018).

It is forecast that based on current trends the predicted 1.5°C increase in global temperature will be reached between 2030 and 2052. Global warming is already having a measurable effect on people's lives and on ecosystems, hence the requirement for 'net-zero emissions'. If a 2°C increase is reached, then the impact will be considerable. Heatwaves, droughts and flooding can be expected. Sea levels could rise by 10 cm, which would impact heavily on world population groups living on land close to the current sea level. Farming and fishing would be negatively affected under this scenario, as would human health as the number of mosquitos carrying disease would increase significantly. It is essential therefore that global warming is limited to 1.5°C as stated in the Paris Agreement.

The IPCC report makes clear that this cannot be achieved without the full deployment of effective carbon capture and storage (CCS) (IPCC, 2018). CCS technologies can be considered as 'renewables' technologies, which can keep on working to reduce CO_2 in the future while we still depend on fossil fuels.

The Global CCS Institute summarizes that successful CCS involves three main actions:

1 **Capture:** The separation of CO_2 from other gases produced at large industrial process facilities such as coal and natural gas-fired power plants, steel mills, cement plants and refineries.

2 **Transport:** Once separated, the CO_2 is compressed and transported via pipelines, trucks, ships or other methods to a suitable site for geological storage.

3 **Storage:** CO_2 is injected into deep underground rock formations, usually at depths of one kilometre or more (Global CCS Institute, 2018b).

Because CCS can achieve significant CO_2 emission reductions, it is considered a key option within the portfolio of approaches required to reduce greenhouse gas emissions (Global CCS Institute, 2018b).

Halting climate change demands urgent action by all of us, not just governments. The Global CCS Institute predicts that, without urgent action, the earth's temperature will continue to rise, causing the world climate to change; sea levels will rise significantly, and ocean and land conditions will be adversely affected.

The world must make a change. Those of us working in the transport industry also have a significant role to play with the emissions created by trucks, ships and aeroplanes.

Figure 4.2 shows that average global temperatures have risen markedly in recent decades in comparison with the baseline used (between 1961 and 1990). The chart reveals a sharp 1–1.2°C rise. The issues of global warming and climate change are among the biggest challenges faced by the world (Ritchie and Roser, 2017)

FIGURE 4.2 Global temperature increase 1850 to 2018

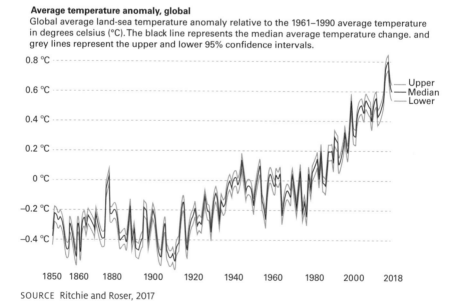

Average temperature anomaly, global
Global average land-sea temperature anomaly relative to the 1961–1990 average temperature in degrees celsius (°C). The black line represents the median average temperature change. and grey lines represent the upper and lower 95% confidence intervals.

SOURCE Ritchie and Roser, 2017

Why managing CO_2 matters

Carbon dioxide is scientifically expressed as one part of carbon and two parts of oxygen. CO_2 is very important as it facilitates plant growth through a process called photosynthesis. All species of life on earth depend on plants for food and timber products for shelter; CO_2 is therefore essential to life on earth. CO_2 is harmless in small quantities, but in global terms, high levels can be harmful to plant, animal and human life, and therefore it is important that global CO_2 levels are managed carefully.

Commonly occurring natural greenhouse gases in the earth's upper atmosphere that can cause IR radiation to be trapped include water vapour, CO_2, methane, nitrous oxide and fluorinated gases (Global CCS Institute, 2018a).

Greenhouse gases present in the earth's atmosphere are as shown in Figure 4.3; CO_2 is clearly the greatest in volume by a considerable margin.

Industrialization and human intervention remain the most substantial contributors to the generation of CO_2 in the atmosphere. This increase in global GHGs has caused the earth's temperature to rise to levels that are unacceptable to the climate change activists who are putting increased pressure on governments to react (Global CCS Institute, 2018a).

Global CO_2 levels began increasing slowly between 1750 and 1850 (Figure 4.4). Since 1850 and the Industrial Revolution, levels have risen

FIGURE 4.3 Human-caused greenhouse gases in the atmosphere

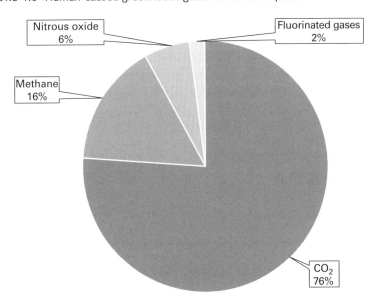

SOURCE EPA, nd

FIGURE 4.4 Annual global total CO_2 emissions by region

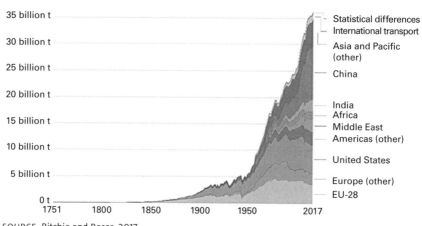

SOURCE Ritchie and Roser, 2017

sharply and by 2017, human-caused CO_2 emissions reached around 36 billion tonnes per annum. The increase in CO_2 began in Europe and then the United States. Since 1950, China and Asia have become the largest emitters of CO_2 on the planet (Ritchie and Roser, 2017).

The global average atmospheric carbon dioxide in 2018 was 407.4 parts per million (ppm for short), with a range of uncertainty of plus or minus 0.1 ppm. Carbon dioxide levels today are higher than at any point in at least the past 800,000 years. Levels of CO_2 have increased by more than 40 per cent since the Industrial Revolution began in earnest in 1850. CO_2 levels were c.280 parts per million (ppm) in the 1800s and have increased to 400 ppm in 2020 (Ritchie and Roser, 2017).

Climate.gov notes: 'the last time the atmospheric CO_2 amounts were this high was more than 3 million years ago, when temperature was 2°–3°C (3.6°–5.4°F) higher than during the pre-industrial era, and sea level was 15–25 metres (50–80 feet) higher than today' (Lindsey, 2020).

The 'greenhouse effect'

The so-called 'greenhouse effect' relates to the inbound and outbound radiation that causes the earth's temperature to rise. It is called the greenhouse effect because a common or garden greenhouse functions in precisely the same manner.

FIGURE 4.5 The global carbon cycle

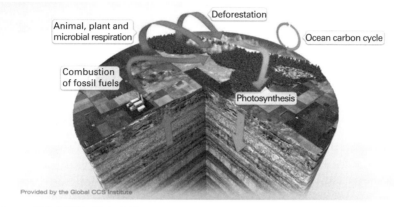

Provided by the Global CCS Institute

SOURCE Global CCS Institute, 2018a

Inbound ultraviolet (UV) radiation from the sun passes through the glass greenhouse windows and is taken on board by the plants and structural material inside. Infrared (IR) rays, which aren't as strong as UV rays, remain trapped inside the greenhouse, causing the temperature to rise. The same effect can be experienced on a cold but sunny day within a parked car, van or truck.

CO_2 cycles through the earth's atmosphere as a natural process. Plants and trees absorb and make use of CO_2 to produce energy; humans and animals exhale CO_2 as we convert air into energy – see Figure 4.5.

However, there is also a human-caused greenhouse effect. Increases in GHGs caused by human activities are trapping the sun's energy and warming our planet's land and seas above the normal temperature experienced up to 1850. 2016 has been recorded as the warmest year since temperature records began. 2017 was the third-hottest year on record, signifying that 17 of the 18 warmest years have been experienced since the year 2000 (Climate Central, 2019).

Burning fossil fuels such as coal in an electricity generation plant releases large amounts of CO_2 into the earth's atmosphere. CO_2 is also released from the ground into the atmosphere during the production of natural gas. Markets such as China, the United States, Australia and Poland have high CO_2 emissions per capita as a direct result of dependencies on coal for power. Huge amounts of CO_2 are also released into the atmosphere as a by-product of oil refining and in the manufacture of construction industry products such as iron, steel and cement.

EU CO_2 emission standards include exhaust emissions from cars, trucks, ships and aeroplanes, and from domestic sources such as heating your home (Global CCS Institute, 2018a).

The impact of large-scale land clearing, especially in South America and Indonesia, is a key factor contributing to the increasing amount of CO_2 in the atmosphere. This is because there are significantly fewer trees and plants to naturally regulate greenhouse gas levels by absorbing excess CO_2.

Planting billions of trees across the world is the most cost-effective and efficient way to reduce CO_2 levels in the atmosphere, according to the scientists who did the research. 'This new quantitative evaluation shows [forest] restoration isn't just one of our climate change solutions, it is overwhelmingly the top one,' said Professor Tom Crowther of the Swiss university ETH Zürich, who led the research (Carrington, 2019).

They have calculated that there are 1.7 billion hectares of land without trees on the planet, upon which 1.2 trillion native tree natural tree saplings could potentially grow; these figures exclude urban and crop areas but include a few trees on grazing land which would benefit sheep and cattle (Carrington, 2019).

Global CO_2 emissions from road freight transport

With its heavy reliance on oil-based products, road freight transport is an important contributor to global energy-related CO_2 emissions. The transportation sector emitted 7.8Gt of CO_2 in 2015. This was around 22 per cent of global CO_2 emissions as a result of energy generation (IEA, 2017).

Over the period 2000–2015, emissions from road freight vehicles rose in line with oil demand: in 2000, CO_2 emissions from road freight vehicles were only 1.7 Gt. CO_2 emissions attributable to road freight vehicles have risen by 2.8 per cent per year since 2000 and contributed to more than 40 per cent of CO_2 emissions growth from transport and around 10 per cent from the entire energy sector over that period. More than 90 per cent of global emissions growth from road freight vehicles was in emerging economies, led by China (around 25 per cent), and this growth was in parallel with their contribution to global economic growth over that period (IEA, 2017).

CO_2 emissions from road freight vehicles have grown in most countries since 2000, but their contribution to total emissions growth varies by region.

In industrialized countries, road freight vehicles were the main contributor to transport-related emissions growth and bucked the wider energy trend of declining CO_2 emissions in many, but not all, of these countries.

FIGURE 4.6   Tailpipe CO_2 emissions from road freight transport by region 2000–2015

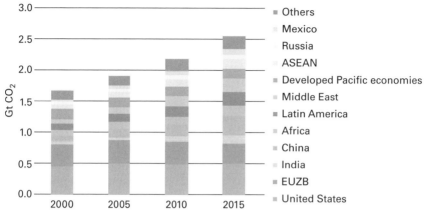

SOURCE IEA, 2017

In the United States (where emissions from road freight grew by more than 50 Mt CO_2), emissions growth from road freight vehicles more than offset the decline in emissions from passenger vehicles.

The rising trend of road freight vehicle emissions in the United States marks a sharp contrast to the efforts to reduce the total CO_2 emissions from fuel combustion, which fell by around 650 Mt over the same period.

In developing and transition economies, emissions generally grew across all parts of the energy sector, given the economies' need to fuel economic growth and lift their populations out of poverty.

Since 2000, road freight transport has contributed to 40 per cent of the growth in CO_2 emissions from road transport in the countries shown in Figure 4.6 and 8 per cent to the overall growth of CO_2 emissions from fuel combustion (IEA, 2017).

A third EU Mobility Package was developed and introduced as part of a new industrial policy strategy in September 2017 and completes the process initiated with the 2016 Low Emission Mobility Strategy (European Commission, 2016) and the Europe on the Move packages from May and November 2017 (European Commission, 2018).

All of these initiatives form a single set of consistent policies addressing the many interlinked facets of our mobility system.

A summary of the EU Commission's plans from the European Commission in 2018 includes:

- New road safety policy framework for 2020–2030. It is accompanied by two legislative initiatives on vehicle and pedestrian safety, and on infrastructure safety management.

- Communication on connected and automated mobility to make Europe a world leader for autonomous and safe mobility systems.
- Legislative initiatives on CO_2 standards for trucks, on their aerodynamics, on tyre labelling and on a common methodology for fuel price comparison.
- A 'strategic action plan for batteries'. Those measures reaffirm the EU's objective of reducing greenhouse gas emissions from transport and meeting the Paris Agreement commitments – see Chapter 6.
- A legislative initiative to streamline permitting procedures for projects on the core trans-European transport network (TEN-T) (European Commission, 2018).

To enable this, the Commission put forward new CO_2 standards for light vehicles in November 2017, followed by the first-ever CO_2 standards for trucks (European Parliament, 2019).

In parallel, the Commission took actions to strengthen the internal road freight market and to better protect drivers. Put together, all these initiatives will offer safe, clean and competitive mobility to Europeans by 2025, delivering on this vision.

Some of the key transport-related activity arising from the 'Europe on the Move' programme can be summarized as follows:

- promoting the 'user pays' and 'polluter pays' principles through road charging and fuel taxes;
- improving the functioning of the road haulage market;
- common European specifications for electronic tolling;
- improved design of cabins – making space for electric powertrains.

A European strategy for low-emission mobility

The transport sector in Europe has been a laggard when compared to other industry sectors in activity designed to reduce emissions. European Energy Agency reports have highlighted the fact that emissions from transport remain higher in 2007 than in 1990 and represent almost a quarter of Europe's greenhouse gas emissions (European Commission, nd).

Road transport is by far the biggest emitter, accounting for more than 70 per cent of all GHG emissions from transport in 2014 (European Commission, nd).

FIGURE 4.7 GHGs from transport by mode in 2014

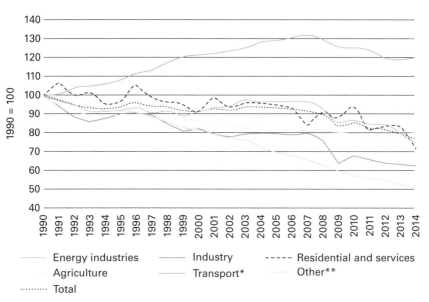

Energy industries ——— Industry ----- Residential and services
Agriculture ——— Transport* ——— Other**
·········· Total

* includes international aviation but excludes international maritime
** includes fugitive emissions from fuels, waste management and indirect CO_2 emissions
SOURCE EEA, 2019

With the global shift towards a low-carbon, circular economy already under way, the Commission's low-emission mobility strategy, adopted in July 2016, aims to ensure Europe stays competitive and able to respond to the increasing mobility needs of people and goods – see Figure 4.7.

The transport 'graph line' shown in Figure 4.7 shows a steady decline in transport CO_2 emissions within the EU, which is encouraging. Zero- and low-emission vehicles (ZLEVs) have to be Europe's full answer to the emission challenge. It is clear that by the time we reach 2050 GHGs from all forms of transport must be 60 per cent lower than those reached in 1990. Ideally the trend should be towards zero emissions to prevent a 2°C temperature rise or more. Transport-related emissions that are harmful to human and animal health need to be significantly reduced as a priority. (European Commission, nd).

Following the 'Dash for Diesel' in the 1990s the industry has recognized the need to address not only CO_2 emissions but also the dangerous levels of pollutants and NO_x emissions. NO_x is produced by the chemical reaction of nitrogen and oxygen gases in the air during the combustion process, and is more prevalent when combustion takes place at higher temperatures. In areas of high motor vehicle density such as large cities, the level of NO_x air pollution emitted into the atmosphere can be very substantial (Icopal Noxite, nd).

FIGURE 4.8 Industry sector emissions monitor

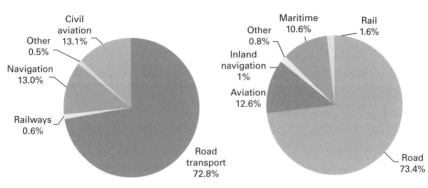

SOURCE EEA, 2019

Many European governments have acted, with the development and implementation of low-emission and zero-emission zones for major cities. This has had the effect of accelerating the adoption of zero-emission and low-emission vehicles.

To get close to the targets and obligations set out in the Paris Agreement by 2050, greenhouse gas emissions from transport will need to be at least 60 per cent lower than in 1990 and be firmly on the path towards zero (European Commission, 2016).

Referring to Figure 4.8, 72.8 per cent of all GHGs are generated from the transportation sector – see left-hand chart. Looking deeper into individual segments of the transportation sector, road transport is the clear major contributor at 73.4 per cent.

At the heart of the EU strategy in support of a low-carbon economy that will create better employment opportunities and investment in complementary green technology businesses will be measures to deliver improvements in urban congestion, reductions in noise levels from freight traffic, and improvements in air quality and public safety through the avoidance of traffic accidents.

This will require attention on not only the development of intelligent traffic management systems and energy innovation hubs that provide alternative energy refuelling infrastructure, but also a determination by national and local government to rethink how urban regeneration plans are developed. In an era where long-haul diesel will be banned from city centres, the integration of fossil-fuelled freight movement with urban electric delivery vehicles will be a primary task to deliver a successful low-carbon transport ecosystem for the future.

Reducing CO$_2$ emissions from heavy-duty vehicles

The first-ever EU-wide CO$_2$ emission standards for heavy-duty vehicles, adopted in 2019, set targets for reducing the average emissions from new lorries for 2025 and 2030:

- Trucks, buses and coaches are responsible for about a quarter of CO$_2$ emissions from road transport in the EU and for some 6 per cent of total EU emissions.
- From 2025 on, manufacturers will have to meet the targets set for the fleet-wide average CO$_2$ emissions of their new trucks registered in a given calendar year. Stricter targets will start applying from 2030 onwards (European Commission, 2019a).

The Regulation (EU) 2019/1242 setting CO$_2$ emission standards for heavy-duty vehicles entered into force on 14 August 2019. The regulation also includes a mechanism to incentivize the uptake of zero- and low-emission vehicles, in a technology-neutral way (European Commission, 2019a).
   The new regulation (EU) 2019/1242 will:

- contribute to the achievement of the EU's commitments under the Paris Agreement;
- reduce fuel consumption costs for transport operators – mostly small and medium enterprises – and consumers;
- help maintain the technological leadership of EU manufacturers and suppliers (European Commission, 2019a).

Expected benefits include:

- around 54 million tonnes of CO$_2$ reduced in the period 2020 to 2030;
- savings at the pump amounting to around €25,000 in the first five years of use for a new truck bought in 2025 and up to about €55,000 in the first five years of use for a new truck bought in 2030;
- oil savings of up to 170 million tonnes of oil over the period 2020 to 2040;
- GDP increases resulting in the creation of new jobs (European Commission, 2019a).

VECTO

VECTO is the new simulation tool that has been developed by the European Commission and will be used for determining CO$_2$ emissions and fuel consumption from heavy-duty vehicles (trucks, buses and coaches) with a gross vehicle weight above 3,500 kg.

From 1 January 2019 the tool will be mandatory for new trucks under certain vehicle categories in application to the certification legislation under type approval.

As of 2019, the CO_2 emissions and fuel consumption data determined with VECTO, together with other related parameters, will be monitored and reported to the Commission and made publicly available for each of those new trucks (European Commission, 2019b).

VECTO is a powerful tool that will assist operators and government agencies to validate the reporting of emission reduction activity necessary to support National Declared Contribution (NDC) reporting required for future Paris Agreement audits of government activity.

CO_2 target levels

In 2025, the average CO_2 emissions of new heavy-duty vehicles will have to be 15 per cent lower than the average emissions in the reference period (1 July 2019–30 June 2020). It is anticipated that this 15 per cent reduction target can be fully achieved using technologies that are already available on the market.

In 2030, the average emissions have to be 30 per cent lower than the average emissions in the reference period. This target will be assessed in 2022 as part of the review of the Regulation (EU) 2019/1242. A review of the Regulation for heavy trucks will be implemented in 2022.

Reducing emissions from heavy trucks, which account for 60 to 70 per cent of all CO_2 emissions from heavy-duty vehicles will be the commission's initial priority and focus (European Commission, 2019a).

After the 2022 Commission review an assessment to extend the scope to other vehicle types such as smaller trucks, buses, coaches and trailers should be considered (European Commission, 2019a).

Funding to support low-emission mobility in the EU

The above strategy could not be achieved without suitable funding. The European Commission stated that in 2016 €70 billion would be available for transport under the European Structural and Investment Fund, including €39 billion for supporting the move towards low-emission mobility, of which €12 billion is for low-carbon and sustainable urban mobility alone (European Commission, 2016).

Under the research programme Horizon 2020, €6.4 billion is available for low-carbon mobility projects as stated by the EU Commission.

Incentive mechanisms for zero- and low-emission vehicles (ZLEVs)

- A zero-emission vehicle (ZEV) is defined as a truck that has no tailpipe CO_2 emissions.
- A low-emission vehicle (LEV) means a truck with a technically permissible maximum laden mass of more than 16t, with CO_2 emissions of less than half of the average CO_2 emissions of all vehicles in its group registered in the 2019 reporting period (European Commission, 2019a).

In order to incentivize the uptake of ZLEVs and reward early action, the commission has introduced a credits system for manufacturers who can demonstrate the adoption of ZEV or LEV during the period from 2020 to 2030. The key information to understand is that for producing vehicles that are not LEV or ZEV or that do not contribute to the CO_2 reduction goals, a fine of €4,250 per gCO_2/tkm will be levied against the manufacturer from 2025. This penalty rises to €6,800 per gCO_2/tkm from 2030.

All major OEMs will be studying the potential financial impact of any failure to accelerate plans to deliver effective product capable of complying with these new environmental regulations (European Commission, 2019a).

UK clean growth strategy

The UK is a world leader in promoting an effective climate change response. Early on in the discussion regarding climate change the UK Government spotted the potential for both security and economic threats. The UK therefore set out five-year limits on GHGs which were named 'Carbon Budgets'. These Carbon Budgets were enshrined in the Climate Change Act of 2008. In this legislation the UK Government set out targets to reduce GHGs by at least 80 per cent by 2050, when compared to 1990 levels. The Carbon Budgets approach has been adopted by the UN and is included in the Paris Agreement.

The UK has been one of the most successful countries in the developed world in growing its economy while reducing CO_2 emissions. Since 1990, UK emissions have reduced by 42 per cent while the economy has grown by 66 per cent. According to the UK Government's 'Clean Growth Strategy',

FIGURE 4.9 UK and G7 economic growth and emission reductions

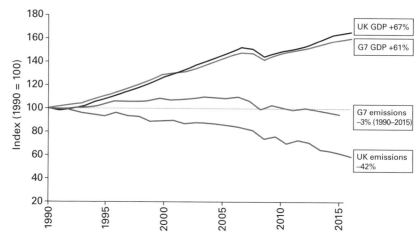

SOURCE Energy and Climate Intelligence Unit, 2020

the UK has taken a leadership position within the G7, reducing emissions faster than other G7 nations, while staying at the top of growth in national income – see Figure 4.9.

This progress demonstrates that the UK outperformed the target emissions reductions of its first carbon budget (2008 to 2012) by 1.5 per cent and is projected to outperform against its second and third budgets, covering the years 2013 to 2022, by almost 5 per cent and 4 per cent respectively. The UK economy is expected to grow by 12 per cent over that time (BEIS, 2018).

In 2016, 47 per cent of the UK's electricity came from low-carbon sources, around double the level in 2010. The UK now has the largest installed offshore wind capacity in the world (BEIS, 2018).

Automotive engine technology has helped drive down emissions per kilometre by up to 16 per cent and driving a new car bought in 2015 will save car owners up to £200 on their annual fuel bill compared to a car bought new in 2011. England also recycles nearly four times more than it did in 2000 (BEIS, 2018).

This progress has been aided by the falling costs of many low-carbon technologies: renewable power sources like solar and wind are comparable in cost to coal and gas in many countries; energy-efficient light bulbs are over 80 per cent cheaper today than in 2010; and the cost of electric vehicle battery packs has tumbled by over 70 per cent in this time (BEIS, 2018).

Because of this technological advancement, new high-worth occupations, ventures and organizations have been created. Furthermore, this is driving a new, technologically innovative, high-growth and high-value 'low carbon' sector of the UK economy.

Leading UK positions on climate change include:

- There are more than 430,000 jobs in low-carbon businesses and their supply chains, employing people in locations right across the country (BEIS, 2018).

- The UK has played a key role in demonstrating international leadership on tackling climate change through its domestic action, climate diplomacy and financial support (BEIS, 2018).

- The UK quickly recognized climate change as an economic and political issue as opposed to solely an environmental one. The UK has used its world-leading economic, science and technical skills to shape the global debate around climate change, for instance making the economic case for climate action in the landmark Stern Report in 2006 (Stern, 2006).

- The UK has also used its influence and resources to help developing countries with their own clean growth – and our actions to date are expected to save almost 500 million tonnes of carbon dioxide over the lifetime of the projects, more than the entire annual emissions of France. While we do not count these results against our domestic targets, we can be proud of the impact of the UK's commitment to global climate action (BEIS, 2018).

- One in every five electric vehicles driven in Europe is made in the UK (BEIS, 2018).

The opportunities and challenges in the UK

The UK played a central role in securing the 2015 Paris Agreement (UNFCCC, 2015) in which, for the first time, 193 countries (representing over 90 per cent of global economic activity) agreed stretching national targets to keep the global temperature rise below 2°C (BEIS, 2018).

The actions and investments that will be needed to meet the Paris commitments will ensure the shift to clean growth will be at the forefront of policy and economic decisions made by governments and businesses in the coming decades (BEIS, 2018).

It is estimated that *c*.$13.5 trillion of public and private investment in the global energy sector alone will be required between 2015 and 2030 if the countries who have signed up to the Paris Agreement are going to meet their national targets (HM Government, 2017a).

The Trump administration formally informed the UN in November 2019 that they would withdraw from the Paris Agreement, setting off a 12-month countdown to departure. The implementation of this decision will be subject to the result of the US presidential election in November 2020. This decision caused a strong response from the other signatories to the accord. Commitment from the other signatories remains high but there are concerns that US budget cuts will affect long-term goals and international cooperation as it is the largest western economy.

The UK is well placed to take advantage of this economic opportunity. Early action on clean growth means that we have nurtured a broad range of low-carbon industries, including some sectors in which we have world-leading positions (HM Government, 2017a).

The UK low-carbon economy could grow by an estimated 11 per cent per year between 2015 and 2030 – four times faster than the rest of the economy – and could deliver between £60 billion and £170 billion of export sales of goods and services by 2030. This means that clean growth can play a central part in the UK's industrial strategy, building on existing strengths to drive economic growth and boost earning power across the country (BEIS, 2018).

There are of course considerable additional benefits to a clean air growth approach, including a cleaner environment with cleaner air, which would in turn improve public health, take the pressure off the NHS, and help drive the economy forward.

The UK has thus far achieved positive improvements in the energy production and waste management sectors. The expansion of the low-carbon economy now needs to happen across the other important sectors responsible for CO_2 and greenhouse gases including transportation, business and industry. Without this roll-out across all sectors it will be difficult for the UK to achieve the carbon budgets it has set.

UK Industrial Strategy Green Paper

Every action taken to cut emissions must be done while ensuring the UK economy remains competitive. As set out in the Industrial Strategy Green Paper, great importance is attached to making sure our energy is affordable (HM Government, 2017b).

In August 2017 the UK Government commissioned an independent review into the cost of energy, led by Professor Dieter Helm CBE. This review recommended ways to deliver the government's carbon targets and ensure security of supply at minimum cost to both industrial and domestic consumers. The report's recommendations into the further development of the 'clean growth strategy' focused on security of supply, and energy policy regulation relevant to a low-carbon market (Helm, 2017).

The Energy Market Reform programme (EMR) that resulted from this research saw the government take much more direct control of how the market worked and develop policy to influence the accelerated adoption of greener alternative energy.

This has seen initiatives like the RE100 programme become catalysts for global corporate enterprises, for example Tesco, to change their energy supply to 100 per cent renewable sources as a key part of managing and reducing their carbon footprint.

Another imminent challenge is to manage any impact of leaving the European Union as the government fulfils its commitment to the British people. Leaving the EU will not affect our statutory commitments under our own domestic Climate Change Act 2008 and indeed our domestic binding emissions reduction targets are more ambitious than those set by EU legislation. The exact nature of the UK's future relationship with the EU and the long-term shape of our involvement in areas like the EU Emissions Trading System are still to be determined (HM Government, 2008).

'Europe on the Move'

In his 'State of the Union' address in September 2017, President Juncker set out a goal for the EU and its industries to become a world leader in innovation, digitization and decarbonization (European Commission, 2018).

Key facts and figures supporting mobility in Europe:

- The mobility sector employs 11 million people accounting for 5 per cent of total EU employment.
- Road transport accounts for 50 per cent of total freight transport activity.
- Transport accounts for 13 per cent of total household expenditure.
- From 2010 to 2050 it is estimated that passenger transport will grow by 42 per cent. Freight transport is expected to grow by 62 per cent.

Building on the previous 'Europe on the Move' of May and November 2017, the Juncker Commission put forward a third and final set of measures to make this a reality in the mobility sector. The objective is to allow all Europeans to benefit from safer traffic, less-polluting vehicles and more advanced technological solutions, while supporting the competitiveness of EU industry (New Mobility, 2020).

Initiatives include an integrated policy for the future of road safety with measures for vehicles and infrastructure safety; the first-ever CO_2 standards for heavy-duty vehicles; a strategic action plan for the development and manufacturing of batteries in Europe; and a forward-looking strategy on connected and automated mobility (European Commission, 2018).

With this third 'Europe on the Move', the Commission is completing its ambitious agenda for the modernization of mobility – an agenda for a socially fair transition towards clean, competitive and connected mobility for all (European Commission, 2018).

The one noticeable absentee from this catalogue of policy initiatives is the scrapping of older, environmentally unfriendly vehicles.

In the UK there exists an active population of over 350,000 commercial vehicles in the 7.5-tonne to 40-tonne range. Unfortunately, over 60 per cent of them, 210,000 units, are below the Euro 3 standards and over 10 per cent are also registered as Statutory Off the Road, ie non-operational (SMMT, nd).

This means two-thirds of the UK Commercial Vehicle parc (running fleet) would be liable for significant penalties should they attempt to gain access to the emerging zero-emission zones. In London this would be £100 per day. Such penalties for being non-compliant would be totally unsustainable for every commercial operator.

In the rest of mainland Europe it is not difficult to imagine that the older vehicle parc, which is not subject to the strict preventative maintenance requirements of the UK O Licence laws, will be as high if not higher than that in the UK. This means there is an opportunity for the metals recycling industry to process and recapture usable components from over a million vehicles and in the process create job opportunities that could be explored as part of the development of the freight-port concept that is outlined in more detail in Chapter 5.

Many of the current EU Commissioners have been quoted in various press reports applauding the 'Europe on The Move' goals but the absence of a scrappage policy for ageing vehicles is a huge gap in the goal to accelerate the move towards a carbon-free transport policy.

When the transition period following Brexit ends on 31st December 2020, the UK government should seriously review the scrapping of vehicles as part of its updating of transport policy.

FIGURE 4.10 'Europe on the Move'

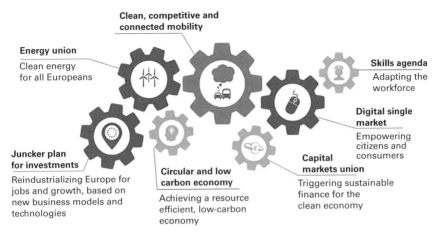

Clean, competitive and connected mobility

Energy union
Clean energy
for all Europeans

Skills agenda
Adapting the
workforce

**Digital single
market**
Empowering
citizens and
consumers

**Capital
markets union**
Triggering sustainable
finance for the
clean economy

**Juncker plan
for investments**
Reindustrializing Europe for
jobs and growth, based on
new business models and
technologies

**Circular and low
carbon economy**
Achieving a resource
efficient, low-carbon
economy

SOURCE UNFCCC, 2015

Summary

- Research by the Global CCS Institute reveals that the level of CO_2 released into the atmosphere has increased significantly since the beginning of the industrial era. Unless we do something to reduce this, the world will continue to experience the effects of climate change (Global CCS Institute, 2018a).

- In 2019 the EU Commission completed its agenda for a low-emission mobility system by putting forward the first-ever CO_2 emissions standards for heavy-duty vehicles. This is the first time trucks have been subject to Regulation (EU) 2019/1242.

- 'Europe on the Move' packages (Figure 4.10) form a single set of consistent policies addressing the many interlinked facets of our mobility system. As a concrete illustration, the Commission proposed in May 2017 to reward the most environmentally friendly vehicles with reduced road charges (European Commission, 2018).

- €70 billion is available for transport under the European Structural and Investment Fund, including €39 billion for supporting the move towards low-emission mobility, of which €12 billion is for low-carbon and sustainable urban mobility alone. Under the research programme Horizon 2020, €6.4 billion is available for low-carbon mobility projects (European Commission, 2018).

- The UK was one of the first countries to recognize and act on the economic and security threats of climate change. The Climate Change Act, passed in 2008, committed the UK to reducing greenhouse gas emissions by at least 80 per cent by 2050 when compared to 1990 levels, through a process of setting five-year caps on greenhouse gas emissions termed 'Carbon Budgets' (HM Government, 2008).

- The UK was among the first to recognize climate change as an economic and political issue as opposed to solely an environmental one and has used its world-leading economic, science and technical skills to shape the global debate around climate change, for instance making the economic case for climate action in the landmark Stern Report in 2006 (Stern, 2006).

- Operators will be required to report CO_2 emissions or face significant fines, using the Vehicle Energy Consumption Calculation Tool (VECTO) (European Commission, 2019b).

- Europe's answer to the emission reduction challenge in the transport sector is an irreversible shift to low-emission mobility. By 2050, greenhouse gas emissions from transport will need to be at least 60 per cent lower than in 1990 and be firmly on the path towards zero.

- The omission of a Government-backed scrappage programme for Euro 3 and below vehicles is a serious error of judgement and needs to be urgently reconsidered.

References

BEIS (2018) Clean Growth Strategy. Retrieved from: https://www.gov.uk/government/publications/clean-growth-strategy/clean-growth-strategy-executive-summary (archived at https://perma.cc/T4RG-F7KN)

Carrington, D (2019) Tree planting 'has mind-blowing potential' to tackle climate crisis, *Guardian*. Retrieved from: https://www.theguardian.com/environment/2019/jul/04/planting-billions-trees-best-tackle-climate-crisis-scientists-canopy-emissions (archived at https://perma.cc/QHL4-TNZD)

Climate Central (2019) The 10 hottest global years on record. Retrieved from: https://www.climatecentral.org/gallery/graphics/the-10-hottest-global-years-on-record (archived at https://perma.cc/N2VV-P4VW)

EEA (2019) Greenhouse gas emissions from transport in Europe. Retrieved from: https://www.eea.europa.eu/data-and-maps/indicators/transport-emissions-of-greenhouse-gases/transport-emissions-of-greenhouse-gases-12 (archived at https://perma.cc/XXP4-6MCR)

Energy and Climate Intelligence Unit (2020) Net zero: economy and jobs.
    Retrieved from: https://eciu.net/analysis/briefings/net-zero/net-zero-economy-
    and-jobs (archived at https://perma.cc/7EQS-CA7J)

EPA (nd) Global Greenhouse Gas Emissions Data. Retrieved from: https://www.
    epa.gov/ghgemissions/global-greenhouse-gas-emissions-data (archived at
    https://perma.cc/KHY5-V3YY)

European Commission (nd) Transport emissions. Retrieved from: https://ec.europa.
    eu/clima/policies/transport_en (archived at https://perma.cc/4ZCS-GV87)

European Commission (2016) Commission publishes strategy for low-emission
    mobility. Retrieved from: https://ec.europa.eu/transport/themes/strategies/
    news/2016-07-20-decarbonisation_en (archived at https://perma.cc/LCP8-
    EH9C)

European Commission (2018) Europe on the Move. Retrieved from: https://ec.
    europa.eu/commission/news/europe-move-2018-may-17_en (archived at
    https://perma.cc/2VT6-E8YW)

European Commission (2019a) Reducing CO_2 emissions from heavy duty vehicles.
    Retrieved from: https://ec.europa.eu/clima/policies/transport/vehicles/heavy_en
    (archived at https://perma.cc/N6RZ-WMUB)

European Commission (2019b) Vehicle energy consumption calculation tool
    - VECTO. Retrieved from: https://ec.europa.eu/clima/policies/transport/vehicles/
    vecto_en (archived at https://perma.cc/4WTV-VXJY)

European Parliament (2019) CO_2 emission standards for heavy-duty vehicles,
    European Parliament, Strasbourg

Global CCS Institute (2018a) Meeting the climate challenge with CCS. Retrieved
    from: https://www.globalccsinstitute.com/why-ccs/meeting-the-climate-
    challenge/ (archived at https://perma.cc/3QMX-4YPP)

Global CCS Institute (2018b) CCS is a climate change technology. Retrieved from:
    https://www.globalccsinstitute.com/why-ccs/what-is-ccs/ (archived at
    https://perma.cc/86QE-YUTQ)

Helm, D (2017) Cost of energy review, Gov.Uk. Retrieved from: https://www.gov.
    uk/government/publications/cost-of-energy-independent-review (archived at
    https://perma.cc/B78W-V9SH)

HM Government (2008) Climate Change Act 2008, HM Government, London

HM Government (2017a) The Clean Growth Strategy, HM Government, London

HM Government (2017b) Industrial strategy: building a Britain for the future.
    Retrieved from: https://www.gov.uk/government/publications/industrial-
    strategy-building-a-britain-fit-for-the-future (archived at https://perma.cc/
    M7MK-VHLE)

Icopal Noxite (nd) Nitrogen oxide (NOx) pollution. Retrieved from: http://www.
    icopal-noxite.co.uk/nox-problem/nox-pollution.aspx (archived at https://
    perma.cc/8DJ9-XPVE)

IEA (2017) *The Future of Trucks*, IEA, Paris. Retrieved from: https://www.iea.org/reports/ the-future-of-trucks (archived at https://perma.cc/7ZWA-ULSJ)

IPCC (2018) Global warming of 1.5°C. Retrieved from: https://www.ipcc.ch/sr15/ (archived at https://perma.cc/J3SH-Y64M)

Lindsey, R (2020) Climate change: atmospheric carbon dioxide, *Climate.gov*. Retrieved from: https://www.climate.gov/news-features/understanding-climate/climate-change-atmospheric-carbon-dioxide (archived at https://perma.cc/MQM6-VD2T)

New Mobility (2018) EU undertakes third and final set of actions to modernise Europe's transport system. Retrieved from: https://www.newmobility.global/future-transportation/eu-undertakes-third-final-set-actions-modernise-europes-transport-system/ (archived at https://perma.cc/6J3M-SEWG)

Ritchie, H and Roser, M (2017) Our World in Data: CO_2 and greenhouse gas emissions, University of Oxford. Retrieved from https: https://ourworldindata.org/co2-and-other-greenhouse-gas-emissions (archived at https://perma.cc/4VWX-A3VL)

SMMT (nd) Heavy goods vehicle registrations. Retrieved from: https://www.smmt.co.uk/vehicle-data/heavy-goods-vehicle-registrations/ (archived at https://perma.cc/5FR3-WNZS)

Stern, N (2006) *The Economics of Climate Change: The Stern Review*

UNFCCC (2015) Report of the Conference of the Parties on its twenty-first session, held in Paris from 30 November to 13 December 2015, UNFCCC, Paris

05

Infrastructure challenge and the role of government

This chapter will familiarize the reader with:

- Clean air zones and ultra-low-emissions zones.
- Pollution levels comparing trucks with cars.
- Costs associated with battery electric commercial vehicles (BEVs) vs internal combustion engines (ICE).
- The challenge of 'last-mile' urban delivery.
- The role of government and the private sector to establish relevant infrastructure activity that supports low-emission zones (LEZs).
- The impact of urban consolidation centres (UCCs).
- Freight quality partnerships (FQPs) and freight-ports.

Europe and UK clean air zones and compliance

The International Council on Clean Transport has reported a benchmark study showing the relative fuel economy performance of vehicles in the world's leading markets. Europe has committed to an ambitious target of being the most fuel-efficient population of vehicles while Japan claims to have already achieved its goal. However, fuel efficiency has been overtaken by air pollution and other environmental concerns in the race to deliver a carbon-neutral transport system. And what we are witnessing today is the design and implementation of clean air, and zero- or low-emissions zones in cities around the world.

The establishment of clean air and zero- or low-emission zones, with significant penalties for non-compliance, is a good example of how carbon taxing is being administered, but also a reason for governments to think seriously about introducing a scrapping policy for older trucks, similar to that introduced for cars some years ago.

In 2018, research into statistics from the Society of Motor Manufacturers & Traders (SMMT) established that over 60 per cent of the UK's Heavy Truck population was Euro 3 or below. The impact of this fact is that over 250,000 registered trucks would be liable for significant daily fines/penalties if they ventured into the low-emission or clean air zones being established (SMMT, nd).

European clean air zones

In 2020, in mainland Europe, we are witnessing the increasing roll-out of stringent bans on vehicles that do not meet environmental standards. Cities in Germany such as Cologne, Stuttgart – the home of Mercedes and Porsche – are imposing citywide bans.

The air quality law suits behind this activity were the work of an organization called Environment Action Germany, known by the acronym DUH. This movement is largely funded by donations from central and regional governments and also Toyota. However, before we celebrate yet another funeral for diesel it's worth considering some facts about what is recognized by many as a good alternative to petrol, as well as being tax beneficial.

In September 2015, Euro 6-engined vehicles became mandatory in Europe. Euro 6-engined trucks are exceptionally clean, almost acting as vacuum cleaners for particulates in many cities due to the screening effect of their diesel particulate filters.

The International Council on Clean Transportation (ICCT) reported in May 2017 that modern diesel cars produce up to 10 times more toxic air pollution than modern heavy trucks. Current Euro 6 trucks emit about 210 mg/km NO_x, less than half that of a Euro 6 standard car, reported as $c.500$ mg/km (ICCT, 2017).

The dramatic reduction in NO_x per litre of fuel is a result of homologation testing that reflects real-world operation. In contrast to Euro 6 cars,

Euro 6 trucks do not emit significantly more NO_x in everyday operation than the level they are certified to. Diesel still has its place in transport and will do so for many years to come.

One of the biggest impacts on the market will be the oil companies and energy utility corporations. According to BP, in 2019 the world consumed nearly 100 million barrels a day of oil – see Figure 5.1 (BP Plc, 2019).

The transport sector, which covers motor vehicles, airlines and shipping, accounts for 60 per cent of this. The balance is consumed by industry (25 per cent), residential homes and commercial property (10 per cent) and electricity (6 per cent) (IEA, 2019).

Over the next five years, from 2000 to 2024, oil will continue to dominate energy usage, along with coal and natural gas. Oil will remain the mainstay of the global energy system. However, it is forecast by the International Energy Agency that global diesel demand from commercial vehicles will drop by 3 million barrels per day by 2030, equivalent to 40 per cent of today's demand (IEA, 2017).

During a 10-year period of transition from 2020 to 2030, various alternative energy sources will be developed and trialled by the transport sector. Natural gas alternatives such as CNG and LNG will make inroads, and similarly biodiesel and bioethanol will remain partial substitutes. But neither of these alternatives will make a significant dent in the dominance of oil (IEA, 2017).

OEM – future vehicle design developments

Vehicle manufacturers will have to develop modifications to current powertrain platforms to use natural gas products, and energy distribution suppliers will have to make significant investments in refuelling infrastructure. Remember it took 50 years for 19th-century factories to convert from steam to electric in the early days of the 20th century.

There is a common international commitment to generate economic growth via a low-carbon future. China is planning a carbon intensity reduction of 65 per cent by 2030 and India intends to produce 40 per cent of its energy from non-fossil fuels in the same timeframe (Climate Action Tracker, nd).

The development of home shopping, e-commerce and home delivery logistics will require 'smart' delivery vans and light trucks, with 'zero tailpipe

FIGURE 5.1 Global oil production and consumption by region

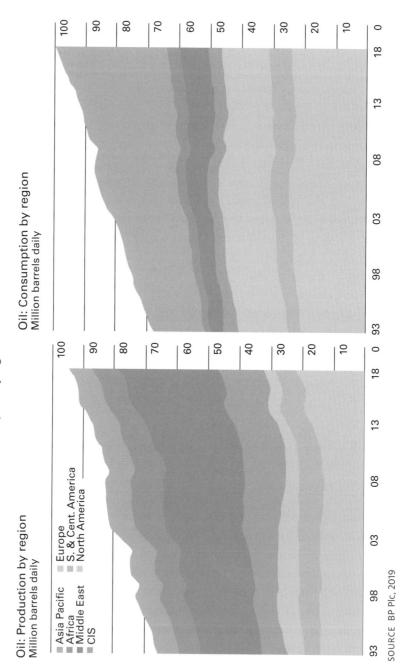

Oil: Production by region
Million barrels daily

Oil: Consumption by region
Million barrels daily

Asia Pacific   Europe
Africa   S. & Cent. America
Middle East   North America
CIS

SOURCE BP Plc, 2019

emissions', reinforcing the demand for 'plug-in' battery electric. The use of BEVs makes a lot of sense in cities, operating over relatively short journeys and returning to base regularly.

The change in vehicle design and requirements for component parts necessary in ICE vehicles will see many components become redundant, such as water pumps, gaskets, rubber hoses, exhausts, filters, gearboxes, engines, pistons, brake and clutch parts and in many cases even exterior wing mirrors. In October 2018 Mercedes-Benz became the first truck manufacturer to replace the traditional exterior door-mounted mirrors with 'MirrorCams' – a system using cameras to present the rearward view on door-mounted LCD screens (Blakemore, 2018).

These reductions in conventional components will have a dramatic impact on traditional Tier 1 and Tier 2 suppliers. This is part of the trade-off calculations operators will be forced into understanding as they weigh the cost of diesel-powered trucks vs BEVs.

The future of trucks

The global sales of commercial vehicles in the major markets of the United States, Europe and Asia/China numbered *c*.2.7 million in 2017. The sales of light commercial vehicles (LCVs) were estimated as double that of medium and heavy trucks. Forecasts suggest that urban light-duty trucks in Europe could reach 35 per cent of total sales by 2030. Globally, eTrucks are forecast to account for 15 per cent of global truck sales (IEA, 2017).

Electric vehicle cost comparisons and adoption rates

It was forecast by McKinsey in 2019 that many countries will reach the point at which BEVs can achieve running cost parity with diesel-powered cars and some trucks by 2025–2030 (McKinsey, 2019).

The most cost-effective segment is in the light-duty truck sector – trucks that are driven less than 200 km per day and avoid high battery costs. Parcel delivery, small retail delivery, self-employed plumbers, electricians, builders and utility company repair and maintenance will see a clear economic benefit for using BEVs as soon as they are available on the market (McKinsey, 2019).

The heavy-duty truck segments will be the last to reach parity with current diesel versions in Europe. Regional characteristics will determine the different timings of when cost parity will be reached in Europe, China and the United States (McKinsey, 2019).

In the United States, cost differences between the prices of diesel and electricity mean that it is later than Europe in adopting electric trucks for heavy-duty applications. China will be last to adopt in heavy duty truck (HDT) sectors due to the availability of cheaper ICE products (McKinsey, 2019).

Overall the switching behaviour towards electric vehicles is expected to be faster for fleet operators than private consumers who are considering electric passenger cars.

There are two main reasons for this:

1 Commercial vehicle operators are more concerned with operating costs than car owners. They will own and operate multiple vehicles and being competitive in their sectors requires attention to detail of fuel consumption, route planning and driver style. All of these are now monitored effectively by in-vehicle telematics. LDV prototype e-vehicle studies in 2019 have demonstrated fuel cost comparisons where diesel fuel cost per 100 km is c.€43 compared to €5 for the equivalent electric vehicle (LDV, 2020).

2 Initial investment in electric trucks is higher, and operators need to be willing and able to pay the higher upfront costs. Current differentials for a 2.5-litre diesel 3.5-tonne van are c.€15,000 vs €60,000 for the electric version. This is offset by major fuel and maintenance cost reductions, eg €80 pm vs €5 pm. In addition, access to the increasing number of city locations that are low-emission or clean air zones will be easier for electric vehicles than non-compliant diesel vehicles (LDV, 2020).

There is no doubt that new technology will take getting used to. Drivers might initially run out of power, as they may not stick to recharging schedules or know how to conserve energy. OEMs will need to train truck operators how best to operate these new drivetrains effectively.

The importance of government and industry collaboration

However, the real challenge in the short term is for industry and government to collaborate on developing and implementing relevant regulations that will not only deliver the low-carbon future necessary, but also build a better infrastructure to enable a profitable and sustainable logistics and distribution supply chain to evolve.

The development of urban consolidation centres (UCCs)

In their book *Green Logistics*, the authors McKinnon, Browne, Piecyk and Whiteing state that the main purpose of UCCs is to avoid the need for goods vehicles to deliver part loads into urban areas. The objective can be achieved by providing facilities in or close to the urban area whereby deliveries (retail, restaurant, office, residential or construction) can be consolidated for subsequent delivery into a target area in an appropriate vehicle with a high level of load utilization. A range of other added-value logistics and retail services can also be provided at the UCC (McKinnon *et al*, 2015).

Much of the historical research undertaken on urban logistics has concentrated on transshipment centres and focused on traditional break-bulk forms of transshipment on a communal shared-user basis; attention has been focused on the use of smaller vehicles for the urban delivery. However, as the automotive, logistics and distribution businesses face challenges that threaten the very future of automotive manufacturing and assembly operations and the impact that will have on tier supply chains, there is an absolute priority to re-examine how our long-haul and urban freight transport system operates.

The scope of UCCs, while notable in the goal of seeking economic and environmental deliverables, is not going to be enough to deliver the kind of radical and innovative transport infrastructure required. In the next 5–10 years, UCCs have the opportunity to evolve as relevant energy innovation hubs (EIHs); there are already live EIH examples such as Tyseley Energy Park in Birmingham. EIHs will not only need to comply with city clean air and environmental objectives but also have the potential to regenerate 'brown field' sites and create the thousands of job opportunities necessary to replace those jobs that will be lost from existing OEMs.

Witness what has happened to Ford and Honda workers in Dagenham, Southampton, Bridgend and Swindon. Liverpool, Sunderland and Solihull are next in line and we need to listen to pundits who are increasingly vocal on the rise and dominance of Asian battery manufacturers.

The Asian battery manufacturers will dominate the future automotive landscape, and where batteries are made cars and trucks will be assembled.

There is a threat to over 250,000 direct jobs in the UK automotive industry unless we face up to this challenge. The role of government is to act as the coordinator of action to bring together the interested parties and deliver the required transport infrastructure necessary (Faraday Insitution, 2019).

Freight quality partnerships

In addition to the attempt at improving urban freight shipment through UCCs, the Freight Transport Association (FTA) launched an initiative in 1996 called the Freight Quality Partnership (FQP). This brought together industry, local government and local environmental interest groups to pursue the following agenda (McKinnon *et al*, 2015):

- identification of problems perceived by each interest group relating to the movement and delivery of goods into the city;
- identification of measures within the group's competence to resolve or alleviate such problems;
- identification of best practice measures and principles for action by local government and industry to promote environmentally sensitive, economic and efficient delivery of goods in towns and cities.

The FQP initiative was tested in four UK urban centres in 1996: Aberdeen, Birmingham, Chester and Southampton. The outcome demonstrated that the role of FQPs would effectively be to become a means whereby local policy makers, businesses, freight operators, environmental groups, the local community and other stakeholders could work together to address specific transport-related problems. The FQP provides a forum to achieve good practice in environmentally sensitive, economic, safe and efficient transport. The partners can exchange information and initiate projects regarding urban freight transport.

More than 120 FQPs have been developed in the UK since 2008, according to FTA reports, and have resulted in a wide range of successful urban freight projects including:

- the production of specialist maps for freight operators and truck drivers;
- improved road signing;
- roadside information boards and online truck information in lay-bys and service stations;
- reviews of parking and roadside loading enforcement regimes.

The FQP initiative is achieving some success in raising the level of communication and dialogue between the various parties, but whether it can deliver the innovative sustained progress required of the transition from a fossil fuel-dominated transport ecosystem to one envisaged for alternative fuels and particular electric vehicles remains to be seen.

Moving towards a modern transport infrastructure

Localis, a leading independent think-tank, established in 2001, identified that common to delivering successful air quality across the country and the world is the central role of infrastructure. By improving efficiencies of existing infrastructure and building much-needed new infrastructure, places can shift people and businesses onto lower-emitting transport or can reduce the need to travel (Localis, 2019).

In a February 2019 document titled 'A modern transport infrastructure strategy', the research identified a plan introduced in Paris that focused on how to better manage the 'last mile' urban delivery challenge. This would require a high degree of collaboration and cooperation between city planners and distribution and logistics operators but nevertheless the potential environmental rewards were significant.

The project in Paris necessitated the building of delivery terminals on urban peripheries. Logistics hotels are being built on the edge of the city on brownfield sites. One, Chapelle International, is being built along the Gare Du Nord rail network and the development includes industrial, office and residential space. Here in the heart of France is a great example of a forward-thinking local authority looking to develop an innovative light freight consolidation terminal by an effective partnership approach and using public land close to road and rail links.

In the UK there are many such examples of Brownfield sites that potentially exist to deliver similar infrastructure project plans.

'Freight-ports' – a radical new idea for transport infrastructure

Imagine an infrastructure policy, driven by the UK Government's clean air policies, that is capable of re-imagining automotive manufacturing plants as 'freight-ports'. Freight-ports would be 'regenerated industrial and distribution hubs', sited on the edge of clean air zones. They would incorporate recharging centres for electric vehicles, recycling centres for older ICE commercial vehicles and vans, battery manufacturing operations, battery storage centres, carbon capture storage plants and would be supported by a solar energy plant.

The Honda manufacturing plant in northeast Swindon is about 370 acres, and Honda announced in May 2019 that it would close in 2021. This site could potentially be reimagined as a solar power plant or a new industrial 'freight-hub'. This would avoid a solar power plant being built on farming land (Chapman, 2019).

The largest solar power plant in the UK – Landmead Solar Farm – is in East Hanney, Oxfordshire, near Abingdon, and is built on 125 acres of low-grade farmland, which was previously used for sheep farming. Landmead produces 46 MW (megawatts) of electricity – enough power to electrify 14,000 homes. Regenerating the Honda site on half its land with a solar-powered infrastructure supporting the development of the logistics, distribution and manufacturing industries described above would be a realistic option going forward (Vaughan, 2014).

The same redundant plant situation as Honda applies to probably 10–12 automotive plants in cities in the Midlands and the north of England. Perhaps they could be alternatives to major investments such as the third runway at Heathrow Airport – cost c.£2.4 billion – or the new high-speed railway 2 (HS2) – cost forecast c.£100 billion (BBC News, 2020):

- HS2 is the largest infrastructure project in Europe. This high-speed railway will connect London to Birmingham and go on to Manchester and Leeds (BBC News, 2020).

- London Heathrow Runway 3 was first discussed by the then Labour government in December 2003. After many protests from environmentalists and lobbyists the project got the go-ahead from the government in 2018. However, the build probably won't start until 2021 and is scheduled for completion in 2028–29 (Saraogi, 2019).

Reimagining redundant automotive plants, as opposed to massive UK infrastructure investment on the above projects, would have an incredibly positive impact on job creation and the environment, and at a fraction of the cost.

At such an imaginative industrial hub one can imagine the complete reduction of air-polluting HGVs entering city centres, a place where workers in newly created 'green technology' jobs go to work on 'free transport' provided by subsidized electric buses. A place where long-haul distribution meets urban delivery powered by zero-emission energy platforms.

Energy innovation hubs

The future of public/private investment plans will emerge from this kind of integrated planning and thinking. A great example of it being developed by progressive city councils is Birmingham City Council's Energy Innovation Hub programme and the example of the Tyseley Energy Park.

CASE STUDY
Birmingham Tyseley Energy Park

Tyseley Energy Park (TEP) is part of an energy innovation hub putting together a collection of green technology-led businesses in support of clean air and low-emission transport.

The following information is from the Tyseley Energy Park Masterplan (Tyseley Energy Park, 2019).

Phase One

On the first phase of Tyseley Energy Park, £47 million was invested into a 10 MW waste wood biomass power plant. This plant supplies Webster and Horsfall's manufacturing operation and tenants across the 16-acre site with renewable electricity.

This provides the foundations for a decentralized controllable distributed energy system in this location. The biomass power plant has created 19 new jobs and diverted 72,000 tonnes of waste wood from going to landfill. The sustainable power generated is equivalent to the amount required to power 17,000 local homes.

Phase Two

Phase two at TEP is the UK's first low- and zero-carbon refuelling station. Strategically located between the city centre and Birmingham airport, this station supplies public and commercial vehicles with a range of sustainable fuels that reduce emissions.

The fuels that will be available include hydrogen from ITM Power, commercial-scale electric chargers, compressed natural gas from CNG fuels, and drop-in bio-diesels with reduced emissions such as Shell GTL fuel from Certas Energy.

FIGURE 5.2   Tyseley Park 10 MW Biomass Power Plant

SOURCE Tysley Energy Park, 2019

FIGURE 5.3   Low- and zero-carbon refuelling station

SOURCE Tysley Energy Park, 2019

Phase Three

As part of a relentless drive to make industry in the city greener, the next generation of waste reprocessing technologies will be developed on phase three, using clean energy linked to city-wide grid infrastructure. Power generated within the site will be from renewable sources including the biomass plant on phase one and the energy from the waste plant planned for phase three.

This clean energy will be used to support the growth of the Webster and Horsfall Group's manufacturing operation, helping to achieve its sustainability goals and reduce the unit price of products manufactured.

Phase Four

Phase four of the TEP site will be home to the University of Birmingham's Innovation Hub. The first phase of the building will have space for research facilities around thermal energy storage, strategic elements and critical materials, hydrogen and fuel cells and thermo-catalytic reforming.

This hub will also have facilities to support teaching and business development. A later phase of development includes a business incubation space, skills academy and community hub. The hub will help companies successfully engage with the revolution that is happening in transport, energy and the circular economy.

FIGURE 5.4   Energy storage unit

SOURCE Tysley Energy Park, 2019

The importance of city planning and the transformation of urban infrastructure

With the acceleration and adoption of clean air zones, congestion zones and zero-emission zones that will prohibit non-compliant vehicles from entering urban environments, there is no doubt that city planners will focus their minds on how best to transform urban mobility through effective infrastructure development. In their report on the future of technology and how it will transform mobility, Boston Consulting Group describe how on-demand mobility will require a new transport ecosystem (BCG, 2018).

It will require traffic management control centres, pick-up and drop-off hubs (freight-ports), dedicated automated driving lanes, purpose-built vehicles and related insurance and finance, and a technology platform that provides the customer interface, routing and trip assignments, and payment processing. Local/regional operations will represent the largest share of costs, potentially making them a critical source of competitive differentiation.

The road to zero emissions will depend enormously on cities to actively shape the future of urban mobility. To be successful they will need to design and implement an integrated mobility strategy that addresses a future transport ecosystem through relevant partnerships, actively manage traffic and consumer demand, and ensure fair and balanced competition. This will include defining the respective roles of public transport agencies and on-demand mobility companies.

Cities will have to ensure the availability of required infrastructure by setting priorities for investments in charging points, dedicated AV lanes, and intermodal hubs. The changes will require cities to find new ways to accurately measure commuter demand and traffic patterns.

Summary

- Clean air zones and ultra-low-emissions zones are appearing in cities outside London and will continue to exercise penalties on offending products until zero emissions is achieved.
- Most BEVs in the light and medium commercial vehicle sectors can achieve cost parity with diesel-powered equivalents within the next 10 years.

- The last-mile urban delivery challenge requires a high degree of collaboration and cooperation between city planners and distribution and logistics operators

- Urban consolidation centres and freight quality partnerships point the way towards innovative transport solutions.

- The concept of 'freight-ports' offers the opportunity to create thousands of new zero-emissions jobs in innovative industry/business parks located on the peripheries of urban city clean air zones, replacing redundant car factories.

- Birmingham City and Paris are exemplars of how future energy innovation hubs can establish a relevant transport infrastructure ecosystem for the future.

References

BBC News (2020) HS2: When will the line open and how much will it cost? Retrieved from: https://www.bbc.co.uk/news/uk-16473296 (archived at https://perma.cc/Y5FV-N3FS)

BCG (2018) By 2035, new mobility tech will drive 40% of auto industry profits. Retrieved from: https://www.bcg.com/d/press/11january2018-automotive-profit-pools-180934 (archived at https://perma.cc/V7FR-LXZJ)

Blakemore, T (2018) New Mercedes Actros pioneers mirrorcams and more, *The Truck Expert*. Retrieved from: https://thetruckexpert.co.uk/new-mercedes-actros-pioneers-mirrorcams-and-more/ (archived at https://perma.cc/C6XM-USJA)

BP Plc (2019) *BP Statistical Review of World Energy*, BP Plc, London

Chapman, B (2019) Honda to close Swindon plant by 2021 with loss of 3,500 jobs, *Independent*. Retrieved from: https://www.independent.co.uk/news/business/honda-swindon-manufacturing-plant-closure-jobs-employees-latest-a8911766.html (archived at https://perma.cc/79UC-5JPT)

Climate Action Tracker (nd) Country Tracker – China. Retrieved from: https://climateactiontracker.org/countries/china/ (archived at https://perma.cc/VVT5-YMHL)

Faraday Institution (2019) *UK Electric Vehicle and Battery Production to 2040*, Faraday Institution, Cambridge

ICCT (2017) [Press release] European Union: Emissions of toxic nitrogen oxides by Euro 6 diesel passenger cars are more than double modern diesel trucks. Retrieved from: https://theicct.org/news/press-release-EU-NOx-emissions-HDV-LDV-comparison (archived at https://perma.cc/ET6X-JPH5)

IEA (2017) The Future of Trucks. Retrieved from: https://www.iea.org/reports/
the-future-of-trucks (archived at https://perma.cc/LG8C-EBH8)

IEA (2019) Global Energy & CO$_2$ Status Report 2019. Retrieved from: https://
www.iea.org/reports/global-energy-co2-status-report-2019 (archived at
https://perma.cc/2LSR-WXTK)

LDV (2020) LDV marketing, Sheffield

Localis (2019) A modern transport infrastructure strategy. Retrieved from: http://
www.localis.org.uk/research/modern-transport-infrastructure-strategy/ (archived
at https://perma.cc/NNT5-32B8)

McKinnon, A *et al* (2015) *Green Logistics: Improving the environmental sustainability of logistics*, Kogan Page, London

McKinsey (2019) Global Energy Perspective 2019: Reference Case. Retrieved from:
https://www.mckinsey.com/industries/oil-and-gas/our-insights/global-energy-
perspective-2019 (archived at https://perma.cc/8QNE-YAK9)

Saraogi, V (2019) The Heathrow Airport expansion timeline: how far have we
come? *Airport Technology*. Retrieved from: https://www.airport-technology.
com/features/the-heathrow-airport-expansion-timeline/ (archived at https://
perma.cc/22QS-WLFN)

SMMT (nd) Heavy goods vehicle registrations. Retrieved from: https://www.smmt.
co.uk/vehicle-data/heavy-goods-vehicle-registrations/ (archived at https://perma.
cc/LD27-UV8L)

Tyseley Energy Park (2019) Tyseley Energy Park Masterplan. Retrieved from:
https://www.tyseleyenergy.co.uk/masterplan/ (archived at https://perma.
cc/69F3-EUSD)

Vaughan, A (2014) UK's biggest solar farm connects to national grid, *Guardian*.
Retrieved from: https://www.theguardian.com/environment/2014/dec/19/
uks-biggest-solar-farm-connects-to-national-grid (archived at https://perma.cc/
F4ZB-9PM7)

06

'Shock waves' in the global battery market

This chapter will familiarize the reader with:

- The value of the battery market by 2030.
- Current locations of existing global 'gigafactories'.
- The importance of battery manufacturing in the UK.
- Automotive industry job threats.
- Rare earth materials.
- Lithium-ion vs solid-state batteries.
- Commoditized vs customized powerpacks.

The strategic importance of battery manufacturing

Global governments seeking CO_2 reduction solutions are more and more committed to replacing fossil-fuelled vehicles with electric vehicles (EVs). Many vehicle manufacturers are also committing to ending the production and sale of internal combustion engines (ICE). The question is no longer whether this transition will occur, but where most EVs will be produced in the future (Faraday Institution, 2019).

BloombergNEF stated in 2019 that more than 2 million battery EVs were sold in 2018 compared to a few thousand in 2010 (figures include plug-in hybrid vehicles). BloombegNEF forecasts that passenger EV sales will increase to 10 million in 2025, 28 million by 2030 and 56 million by 2040.

This would mean by 2040, 57 per cent of global passenger vehicle sales will be electric-powered and 30 per cent of the global vehicle parc (running fleet) will be electric (BloombergNEF, 2019).

With regard to trucks and buses, BloombergNEF states that by 2040 they expect 56 per cent of light commercial vehicles sales and 31 per cent of medium commercial vehicle sales will also be electric. Heavy trucks for long-haul operations present a different challenge because the weight of the required battery power would have a detrimental effect on range, payload and 'turnaround time' due to extended charging time. It is anticipated that natural gas and hydrogen fuel cells will play a major role in heavy transport (HT) (BloombergNEF, 2019).

Due to the surge in EV sales there will be a corresponding annual increase in the demand for lithium-ion batteries (see Figure 6.1), which will also promote a fall in battery prices. China will continue to be at the forefront in terms of battery manufacturing capacity, with Europe being the second-largest manufacturing region.

There are sufficient lithium reserves to meet demand until 2020. Thereafter, with the continuing increased demand for REMs, cobalt and nickel mining capacity will inevitably increase. Solid-state batteries are under development that promise to offer increased power – potentially twice that of lithium-ion – at lower weight or higher 'energy density'. Major OEMs such as Toyota, BMW, Honda and Hyundai are investing in

FIGURE 6.1   Annual lithium-ion battery demand

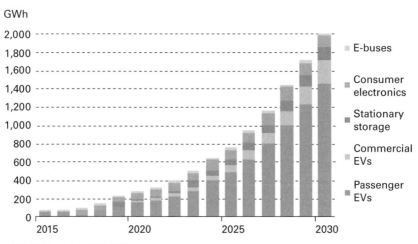

SOURCE BloombergNEF, 2019

technology development by collaborating with R&D institutes, battery material manufacturing companies and battery manufacturers. However, the fully commercialized solid-state battery-based EVs aren't expected to be launched until 2025.

There is currently no battery gigafactory in the UK; Tesla decided to build its first European gigafactory in Berlin, Germany. Speaking to *Auto Express*, Musk said Brexit uncertainty made it 'too risky' to consider constructing a gigafactory in the UK. This came immediately after the Tesla CEO announced he had selected Berlin as the site for the company's first European factory (Asher Hamilton, 2019).

For the UK this poses a significant risk to hundreds of thousands of jobs in vehicle manufacturing and the tier supply chains involved.

It's also clear there are large barriers in the way.

David Bailey, Professor of Business Economics at the University of Birmingham, is quoted in *Autocar* as saying, 'We're in serious danger of missing out for a number of reasons; Brexit is a serious issue and we are lagging in terms of electric vehicle take-up and infrastructure. Why would a company want to invest in a massive battery plant here?' (Autocar, 2020).

Critical to the future of car and commercial vehicle manufacturing in the UK is the location of the manufacturing of batteries. The demise of vehicle manufacturing and the UK becoming an importer of vehicles would have a negative impact on the UK economy and cause a trade deficit.

As the global automotive industry responds to the climate change challenge and the demands from government and regulators, who are introducing zero-emission zones prohibiting the use of non-compliant vehicles in city and urban environments, what will determine the future location of EV manufacture is the geographic location of battery production.

Currently the concentration of EV manufacturing and battery technology know-how and production capacity resides in Asia.

The aim of this chapter is to introduce details of the key players in the world of EV battery manufacturing, what the market is worth today, and what it is likely to be in 2050 and beyond.

Since the 1990s we have seen other industries experience sudden changes in fortune. In October 1998, Nokia was the best-selling mobile phone brand in the world, with annual profits increasing from $1 billion in 1995 to around $4 billion by 1999. However, in 2007 Apple launched the first smartphone – the Apple iPhone. By 2013 Nokia's market value had declined by over 90 per cent and it was eventually acquired by Microsoft. Simply put, Nokia failed to see the emergence and subsequent demand for smartphones (Multiplier, 2018).

In the electrical audio-visual market, there was a 'battle royal' between Betamax and VHS. Sony launched its Betamax video cassette recorder format in 1975 and in 1978 JVC launched its VHS format. VHS won the initial battle due to its lower price and longer recording time despite Sony having better video and audio quality. Sony continued producing Betamax machines until 2002 and by this time VHS was also on its way to being substituted by DVD and digital audio recorders.

The consequences of these technological advances saw the rapid decline of bricks and mortar retail operations like Blockbuster Video and the emergence of Amazon as the market-leading virtual global retailer.

In 2020, lithium-ion is understood to be the leading technology platform for EV batteries and has played a big role in driving uptake of passenger car EVs. Its features have delivered high energy density and charge retention capacity alongside low maintenance requirements However, there are signs that this dominance is reaching its limitations (Future Bridge, nd).

In this chapter we will continue exploring the next generation of battery technology that will respond to the challenge of cost, weight, combustion, and also more sustainable and humane sourcing strategies necessary to purchase the rare earth materials (REMs) required for the massive volume that will be demanded up to 2050 and beyond.

Many people currently engaged in the automotive manufacturing, tier supply chains, logistics, distribution and transport industries who consider themselves knowledgeable about the electric vehicle industry would be hard pressed to name more than a handful of EV battery suppliers.

Battery technology originated in Japan and was then further developed in South Korea, but the centre of the world's battery production for EVs is shifting to China. China's cell production already has a larger share of global production than Japan, and China's global market share is rapidly approaching 70 per cent (Perkowski, 2017).

The success of Tesla in conjunction with Japan's Panasonic in creating the first gigafactory in Nevada, United States, will come to mind. South Korea's Samsung and LG Chem are also players. Increasingly, Chinese company BYD is now universally recognized as the world's largest EV battery manufacturer.

In addition to these major players there are now more than 140 EV battery manufacturers in China. They are engaged in building a market whose value will soar to €240 billion in the next 20 years (Perkowski, 2017).

Understanding BEV vs ICE

In order to understand the transition from ICE to BEVs it is important to have a basic understanding of the technical differences between BEV and ICE products.

This information will not only improve awareness of the changes to the emerging supplier landscape but also inform those responsible for future purchasing decisions on how to make the best choice for the operations that you are responsible for.

Purchasing a conventional ICE truck or car today requires an understanding of the vehicle's residual value, maintenance or total cost of ownership factors, in addition to understanding basic features and specification of options, especially when deciding on a heavy truck's operations. We can explore the factors that need to be considered for BEVs as well.

Purchasing battery electric vehicles

The decision criteria necessary for purchasing electric cars or trucks requires a little more understanding of the component that is 40–50 per cent of the vehicle cost and is central to its operation, ie the battery powertrain.

Key purchasing criteria:

- What range it can deliver?
- What charging time is possible?
- Is the powertrain configuration a commodity component or can it be customized?
- Will the range be compromised in cold weather conditions?
- What additional options will compromise performance, eg seat heating, window defrosting, mirror heating, etc?

These are critical decision factors facing the future buyers of EVs.

Rare earth materials (REMs) – centres of activity

OEMs are facing the challenge of building the best EV powertrain package. This challenge is also one of material sourcing as this is an area very dependent on the supply of REMs.

Three regional centres of activity are approaching the challenge to achieve a presence in a future industry that will see the emergence of battery-producing gigafactories, research laboratories and start-up enterprises set to deliver 'electric shocks' to established OEM corporations.

Successful entrants could position themselves as the Shell or BP of the 21st century in a race to create a trillion-dollar industry. Before looking in detail at the emerging vehicle and alternative fuel developments in the world it is important to understand the current status quo in the key regional markets (IEA, 2017).

The three regional centres of activity for batteries are:

- Asia including China and India;
- Europe;
- United States.

Global market for new heavy-duty trucks

Globally, sales of small trucks (LCVs) are more than twice those of heavy-duty trucks (MFTs and HFTs) combined. Between MFTs (medium-freight trucks) and HFTs (heavy-freight trucks), global sales shares are roughly evenly distributed, but with substantial variation at the national and regional levels.

In 2015, MFTs constituted about one-fifth of heavy-duty trucks sold in the EU market; in the United States, the split was 50:50; and across the ASEAN member states the MFT sales share in MFTs and HFTs was about three-quarters of total sales.

Due to the differences in national and regional classification frameworks as well as the fact that MFTs and HFTs make up the largest share of road freight activity and energy use, this section focuses only on heavy-duty (ie MFT and HFT) truck sales.

Global registrations of heavy-duty trucks, including both new vehicle sales and second-hand imports, have grown by about 60 per cent since the turn of the century, from 2.7 million units sold in 2000 to nearly 4.4 million in 2015.

Global sales dropped by 10 per cent during the financial crisis but rebounded sharply in the subsequent two years. China surpassed the United States and European Union as the largest global sales markets for heavy-duty trucks in 2009, indeed, while global sales decreased.

Asia – China

In China, the truck manufacturing sector is far less consolidated than in the United States and the EU. China's sales grew by 75 per cent between 2008 and 2009. In the subsequent years, China's market share continued to grow rapidly; by 2015 it accounted for 20 per cent of new heavy-duty truck sales globally.

As shown in Figure 6.2, no single manufacturer in China controls more than 12 per cent of the market. The share of medium-weight trucks dropped rapidly over the first 10 years of the 21st century and now has reduced from around 50 per cent to 15 per cent.

India

In India, industry consolidation is more pronounced than in any of the other markets. Four manufacturers account for more than 95 per cent of medium

FIGURE 6.2   Heavy truck sales in China

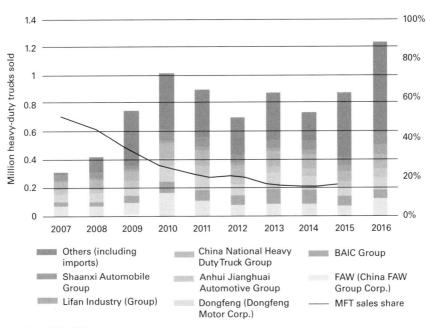

SOURCE   IEA, 2017

FIGURE 6.3 Heavy truck sales in India

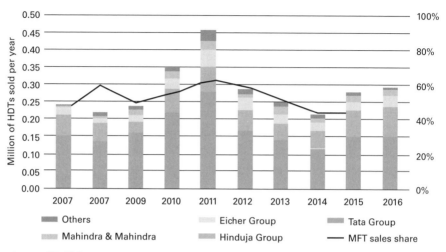

SOURCE IEA, 2017

FIGURE 6.4 Truck sales in the EU

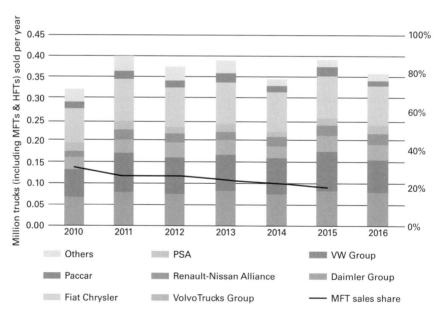

SOURCE IEA, 2017

FIGURE 6.5   Truck sales in the United States

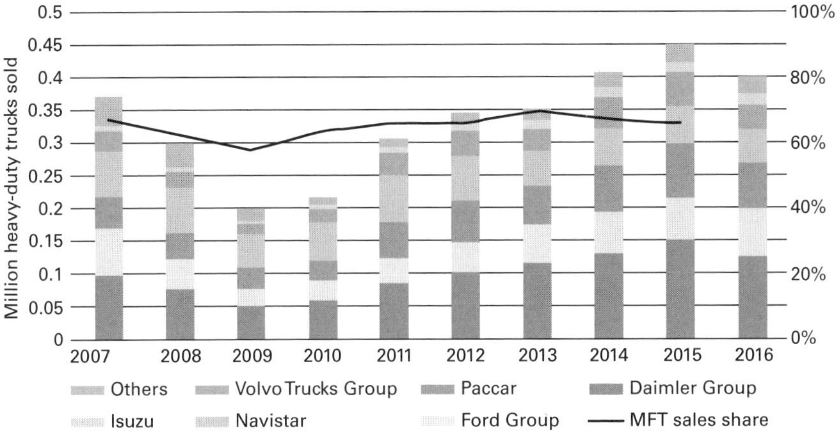

SOURCE IEA, 2017

and heavy truck sales – see Figure 6.3. Tata dominates the truck market in India and Cummins engines account for more than a third of heavy truck sales.

Europe

In the European Union, new truck sales grew moderately through 2008 before plunging more than 40 per cent; as of 2015, they had not returned to their 2000 level. Four manufacturers – Daimler, VW Group, Volvo and Renault-Nissan Alliance – account for more than 60 per cent of new truck sales, as seen in Figure 6.4. Germany is the largest market for new truck sales in the EU.

Since 1995 the trend towards heavier trucks with larger and more power-ful engines is very much like the United States.

United States

The US new truck market is even more consolidated than the EU. Many of the same manufacturers – Daimler, Paccar and Volvo – operate in both the US and in the EU but using different brand names. In the United States, brand names are used such as Freightliner in the case of Daimler, Kenworth and Peterbilt in the case of Paccar, and Mack for Volvo. The market share of these manufac-turers is similar in both the US and the EU – please refer to Figure 6.5.

The global market is dominated by 10 major manufacturers whose futures will be determined by how they manage to balance the following key activity:

- the need to maintain profitability through existing ICE products;
- how they develop new manufacturing methods for electric vehicles and alternative fuels;
- effectively managing the sourcing of rare earth materials;
- developing the tier supply chain relevant to low-emission vehicle manufacture;
- developing new business models for new sales and aftersales.

Trade wars and tariffs threaten to stifle growth and industry collaboration

The global distribution of REMs and the battle to overcome trade barriers and gain a sustainable competitive position in the developing battery market will not be helped by trade wars between major nations. Where there is a trend for investment in key industries by a foreign nation in a domestic market there will be political, social and economic tensions to manage. This will be especially so in the battery market as the demand for BEVs increases rapidly, especially as China is such a major player in the high-growth battery market.

There are similar tensions in the 5G telecoms market as new-generation equipment is sought from global suppliers with market-leading expertise. The 2020 debate over Huawei between China and the EU, UK and the United States is a prime example of the effects of a trade war. The perceived threat of a Chinese telecoms giant to the defence and national security of either the United States or Europe has provoked intense debate not just in the media but also at the United Nations and NATO, which would have been unthinkable prior to 2000.

We are seeing the legislative branches of governments hold serious investigations into how to manage these sensitive commercial events in the context of far-reaching national security or military impacts.

The flip side to the coming 'electric revolution', of course, is that for every battery pack that is put into a vehicle, one less internal combustion engine is needed. While the growth of EVs will give rise to a large global battery industry, it will also make obsolete the substantial investments that have been made in global engine and engine component capacity, and tariff imposition and trade wars in this sector of business will hasten its predicted decline and drive more unwanted social unrest (Perkowski, 2017).

You only have to look at the 2019 United Automotive Workers (UAW) trade union disputes with General Motors in the United States to witness the potential for civil unrest.

By any definition, the global EV industry appears to be at an inflection point. In fact, UBS – a large securities firm – believes that significant change is on the way and predicts that a growing global electric vehicle fleet will be disruptive to petrol demand by 2031 (Perkowski, 2017).

Recently, the International Energy Agency (IEA) stated that the rise of EVs will impact oil production by predicting that overall demand for energy is set to increase by 1 per cent per every year until 2040, but that demand for crude oil will plateau in 2030, 10 years earlier than predicted, due to a rise in the use of EVs (Sharma, 2019).

Cutting down battery costs

Much progress on cost reduction and performance improvement has been made between 2015 and 2020. The cost of a lithium-ion battery is now just one-seventh of what it was and in the world's two largest automobile markets – China and the United States – charging infrastructures are now being put in place (Perkowski, 2017).

A typical cost profile of a lithium-ion battery is detailed in Figure 6.6.

In 2010, the cost of a lithium-ion battery was $750 per kilowatt hour (kWh). Today, General Motors claims that the cost of the battery cells in its Chevrolet Bolt is an industry-leading $145 per kWh. Moreover, GM says that its goal for battery cost is $100 per kWh by 2022 (Perkowski, 2017).

2020 battery prices are a key factor in determining purchase decisions and justifying the switch from an internal combustion engine to a battery electric version. But so too is the range and charging time compared to fossil-fuelled alternatives.

However, from 2020 onwards it is certain that existing lithium-ion battery platforms will be challenged on price, range, charging rate and safety by the development of solid-state battery technology. These batteries will be smaller, lighter, safer, faster to recharge, and have better range capability. All of the major car and truck OEMs are watching these developments; many are making strategic investments in technology start-ups that have been spun out of academic institutions and hold the intellectual property rights to developing the product that will compete with established lithium-ion product available in 2020.

FIGURE 6.6 Lithium-ion cost reduction challenge

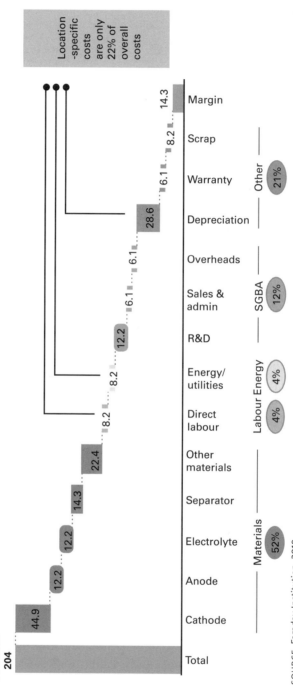

SOURCE Faraday Institution, 2019

United States and EV battery market development

According to BloombergNEF, every time lithium-ion battery sales doubled over the past decade it led to production costs dropping by 18 per cent. The result is that a lithium-ion battery of 20 kWh capacity like those typically found in plug-in hybrids now costs €3,500 compared to €23,000 in 2010 (BloombergNEF, 2019).

The Tesla Corporation has led the way in developing and producing battery packs for EVs and in 2014 opened its first gigafactory in Nevada in a partnership with Panasonic. Tesla will produce a million EVs per year by 2025, and has developed three generations of battery since the first Tesla hit the road in 2008. Tesla has stated that the 'fundamental constraint' on increasing the production of Tesla products is the supply of batteries (O'Kane, 2019).

Customized vs commodity battery packs

Elon Musk and his engineers have focused on a battery powertrain package for the latest Model 3 vehicle with a nickel-cobalt-aluminium battery cell. And with the new generation design of the 2170 cell Tesla aims to deliver a powertrain package with a kWh cost below $100. The 80 kWh 2170 battery pack will contain 4,416 battery cells, packaged in 14 modules and weighing 1050lbs. The Tesla battery platform is designed as a commodity module with the aim of providing a standard pack or an extended range option (Ali, 2018).

This is quite different to those chosen by BMW and GM, who have gone down a more customized cell route, which can be more expensive and also not as economic to repair when any maintenance is required.

GM also chose to outsource its battery manufacturing to LG Chem, while Tesla's gigafactory operation is a vertically integrated enterprise in partnership with Panasonic.

Critical sourcing factors for REMs

Global EV manufacturers are aware of the importance of rare earth materials as the key components to battery manufacture. Cobalt is also a critical element that is found in 0.003 per cent of the earth's crust, while Lithium is only found in 0.0017 per cent – 50 times less than cobalt (Periodictable, nd).

According to the latest US Geological Survey numbers, global supply increased in 2018, up slightly to 140,000 metric tonnes (t) from 120,000 MT the previous year (Barrera, 2020).

Sixty per cent of the world's cobalt is mined in the Democratic Republic of Congo (DRC) – 90,000 MT were mined in 2018. DRC-produced cobalt dominates world supply, and as demand for cobalt is rising, efforts are being taken to deal with possible human rights abuse and child labour (Barrera, 2020).

Russia mines around 5 per cent of cobalt globally, producing 5,800 MT in 2018. Cuba, Australia and the Philippines each produce 3.5 per cent – around 4,700 MT in 2018, and the rest of world accounts for 32 per cent of global reserves (Barrera, 2020). While China is only acknowledged in 2018 by *Investing News* as producing 2.2 per cent of mined cobalt – 3,100 MT – production remained static in 2018. However, according to the US Geological Survey, China was the world's leading producer of refined cobalt and has been a leading supplier of cobalt imports to the United States. Most of the Asian country's production was from partially refined cobalt imported from the DRC. In 2019, China was also the world's leading consumer of cobalt, with more than 80 per cent of its consumption being used by the rechargeable battery industry (Barrera, 2020).

The biggest lithium producers are Australia, Chile, Argentina and China. The largest lithium importers are China, Japan, South Korea and the United States.

The price per pound for battery-grade lithium carbonate in 2018 was $13 while the price for cobalt was $38 per pound (Statista, nd).

The race to develop a battery platform that reduces its dependence on cobalt is one all OEMs are facing. Cobalt, unfortunately, is not a primary metal as it is produced as a by-product of nickel and copper mining. It's a chemical process that is undertaken in conditions where employee welfare is a matter of great concern; almost two-thirds of world cobalt is found in the Democratic Republic of Congo and China has achieved a dominant position through its acquisition of mining operations.

Estimates from mining reports indicate that 140,000 tonnes of cobalt are produced per year, 50 per cent of which is used by irreplaceable industrial product to manufacture aeroplane parts, wind turbine propellers and gas turbines, for example (Barrera, 2020).

China controls 50 per cent of the world's cobalt production, 70,000 tonnes, and 80 per cent of that volume is used in battery production (Barrera, 2020).

The United States now has the major challenge to do two things:

- increase its capacity to mine REMs and to produce cobalt in the United States;
- find an alternative to lithium-ion batteries such as solid-state zinc-air batteries.

Unfortunately, there is only one current rare earth mine operating in the United States, based in California, which has no refining capacity. The Mountain Pass Rare Earth Mine (MPREM) is owned by JHL Capital Group and employs 200 people producing 'rare earth concentrate', which it sells 100 per cent to… China! (Scheyder, 2019).

Ironically, MPREM has relied on China for REM processing, fuelling national security concerns. In 2020 MPREM plans to be the first US company to refine REMs since 2015, to diminish the US reliance on China. Scheyder reports:

> China is the world's largest processor and producer of the 17 specialized minerals used to build weapons, consumer electronics and a range of other goods. There are no known substitutes. In June 2019, China more than doubled tariffs on US REM imports for refining to 25 per cent. On Friday, Beijing said it would add an additional 10 per cent on top of that tariff rate starting next month, the latest tit-for-tat exchange in a protracted dispute between the world's top two economies (Scheyder, 2019).

The interest in exploiting REMs from the Arctic Circle is very topical when considering the interest in the competition to lithium-ion battery technology from solid-state battery developments. The *Financial Times* reported in August 2019 that the United States showed interest in acquiring Greenland from Denmark because of the REMs abundant on the island. It is estimated that 38.5MT of REMs is available in Greenland – a third of the world's reserves, which stand at 120–140MT (Dempsey, 2019).

Solid-state battery science is very different to lithium-ion; it does not require liquid electrolyte and has a reduced need for cobalt. Credited as the inventor of lithium-ion, John Goodenough, a US Nobel Prize-winning professor is championing the development of solid-state batteries and also sees in these developments the opportunity to improve sustainability and ethical sourcing from more stable markets.

Alternative material in the form of zinc and nickel required for the solid-state product is available and sourced from US-controlled mining operations in the Arctic Circle. Red Dog Operations is one of the world's largest zinc mines, located about 170 kilometres north of the Arctic Circle in northwest Alaska. In the event that solid-state battery technology replaces lithium-ion this will certainly change the balance of power between the United States and China in the race to dominate the supply of REMs for the electrification of transport product (Teck, 2020).

European EV market development

In January 2019 it was reported by Reuters UK that Anja Karliczek, the German Minister for Education and Research, said battery technology was an 'existential matter'; she wasn't stoking fears but was highlighting what the German car industry needs to stay relevant in the future (Nienaber, 2019).

Anja Karliczek said her ministry would invest €500 million ($568 million) to support research into both existing and next-generation EV battery cell technology. 'The German car industry shouldn't depend on Asian suppliers,' Karliczek told a business conference in Berlin. 'This is not only a question of independence, but also a question of keeping the German economy competitive' (Nienaber, 2019).

VW, BMW and Mercedes account for one-seventh of the country's jobs, one-fifth of its exports and one-third of its spending on research. But these giants of the internal combustion engine era are facing a new challenge (Rathi, 2019).

As the world looks to clean up its cities and cut carbon emissions to fight climate change it has pivoted to battery-powered electric vehicles. There is an estimated £5 billion market opportunity in the UK and £50 billion across Europe by 2025 (Faraday Institution, 2019).

There is currently only one battery factory in the UK, owned by Nissan, opened in 2010 and with a manufacturing capability of 2 GWh per annum – see Figure 6.7. This is only 1.5 per cent of the forecast capacity development in Europe, leaving the UK behind. Gigafactories in Poland, Sweden and Hungary are forecast to produce 130 GWh per annum by 2025 (Faraday Institution, 2019).

FIGURE 6.7 European lithium-ion battery capacity ramp-up until 2025

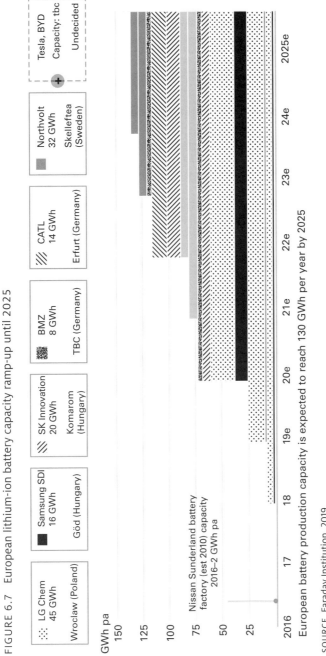

European battery production capacity is expected to reach 130 GWh per year by 2025

SOURCE Faraday Institution, 2019

BMW and CATL join forces

In 2018 Germany produced over 5 million cars (more than every country except China, the United States and Japan), but it does not have a 'battery gigafactory' (Rathi, 2019).

In July 2019 construction began on the country's first gigafactory, which will manufacture batteries to sell to BMW. It's being built by CATL, the world's largest manufacturer of lithium-ion batteries. In the heart of Germany's proud auto industry, this critical new player isn't home grown; the eight-year-old company is valued at $29 billion and is Chinese (Green Car Congress, 2020).

When CATL went public in June 2018, only seven years after it was founded, it minted four new Chinese billionaires. The Ningde-based company investors hoped it would take on LG Chem of South Korea and Panasonic of Japan. But founder Zeng Yuqun stated that his objective did not focus on competing with other battery manufacturers and that his goal was to challenge the internal combustion engine industry itself (Global Casino, 2019).

After early success in the production of US-licensed lithium-polymer batteries for use in smartphones, CATL was approached to supply lithium-ion batteries for a demo fleet of electric buses for the Beijing Olympics. The smog problem in Chinese cities drove a programme to promote electric cars and buses and laid the foundations for the electrification of transport in China.

In 2012, CATL spun off its electric vehicle battery business and has since maximized the use of government subsidies and reached agreements and supplied batteries to more electric car and truck makers than any other battery manufacturer (Global Casino, 2019).

European market development for batteries

Germany announced a €1 billion federal support programme for EV battery production. In Poland and Hungary special economic zones have been set up that offer tax relief for EV battery production. The Faraday Institution stated that the top five battery manufacturers in Europe all announced significant investment plans in 2018 (Faraday Institution, 2018):

- LG Chem: 45 GWh plant in Wroclaw, Poland.
- Samsung: 16 GWh plant in Göd, Hungary.

- CATL: 14 GWh plant in Erfurt, Germany.
- Northvolt, a Swedish company, has selected Skellefteå for the location of its planned 32 GWh battery manufacturing plant. The total amount to be invested through 2023 is estimated at nearly €4 billion (Faraday Institution, 2019).
- By 2025, total battery manufacturing capacity will grow to 130 GWh (Faraday Institution, 2019).

UK automotive industry threats

When analysing the competitive landscape and business environment, the United Kingdom is the fourth-largest vehicle manufacturer in Europe. The UK has a decade of experience of EV battery cell and packaging production, so it should be in a good place to prosper from the future demand for EVs (see Figure 6.8) (Faraday Institution, 2019).

FIGURE 6.8   UK future battery demand

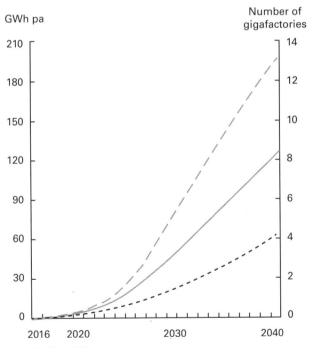

SOURCE Faraday Institution, 2019

FIGURE 6.9 Threat to UK employment

ICE and EV employment 2017 to 2040

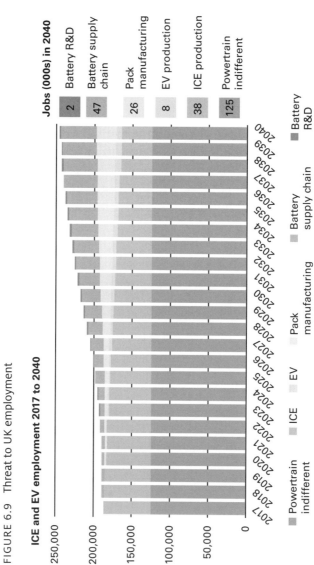

Jobs (000s) in 2040	
2	Battery R&D
47	Battery supply chain
26	Pack manufacturing
8	EV production
38	ICE production
125	Powertrain indifferent

Legend: ■ Powertrain indifferent ■ ICE ■ EV ■ Pack manufacturing ■ Battery supply chain ■ Battery R&D

SOURCE Faraday Insititute, 2019

Based on the three scenarios in Figure 6.8, UK and EU demand for UK-produced batteries could reach 60–200 GWh per annum by 2040; the equivalent of 4–13 gigafactories. While global growth is forecast to be 1.3 per cent per annum, this model predicts a more conservative 1.1 per cent growth in demand for the UK (Faraday Institution, 2019).

Unless the UK takes urgent action to increase the investment first made in 2010 at the AESC plant in Sunderland, there is a clear and evident threat to over 200,000 jobs currently engaged in the UK's automotive manufacturing and supply chains (Faraday Institution, 2019).

In order to realize a successful transition through a ramp-up of UK battery manufacturing capacity by 2040, investment in the range of £5–18 billion is necessary (Figure 6.9) (Faraday Institution, 2019).

Other complicating factors affecting future manufacturing location decisions are going to be influenced by the UK's decision to exit the EU.

With the 'Road to Zero Strategy' launched in 2018, the UK Government has set ambitious targets for UK sales of electric vehicles. The strategy sets out the goal that at least 50–70 per cent of new vehicle sales in 2030 will be ultra-low emission. In addition, EV battery manufacturing is now a strategic priority (Department for Transport, 2018).

This will be very dependent on global battery manufacturers' willingness to invest in the UK. A battery gigafactory generally takes five to seven years to reach full operating capacity so decisions on the siting of these plants need to be made now in order to meet the demands from EV production in the mid-2020s.

A key factor in future decision-making on gigafactory location requires the UK Government to match financial and administrative incentives offered by German and Chinese authorities to attract these investments and secure the future of hundreds of thousands of jobs in the UK automotive manufacturing and supply chain.

Failure to achieve this will create perhaps the biggest shock wave to the UK economy since the financial crisis of 2008 and the oil crisis of the 1970s. The UK and the European Union have developed a series of proposals under the initiative known as 'Europe on the Move' (European Commission, 2018) and this will see highly focused attention on the development of batteries and battery technology and skills for the next generation of automotive product. Details of the proposals are summarized below.

Strategic action plan for batteries (European Commission, 2018)

Policy context

Being able to fully manage the battery value chain is a key requirement to maintain a competitive advantage within the European automotive industry. The EU Commission introduced the 'European Battery Alliance' (EBA) in October 2017 to achieve this goal. Key stakeholders were involved in the development of the EBA, including manufacturers, banks and EU member states.

It will be a huge but worthwhile challenge for the EU to achieve the goal of becoming a key player in the battery industry. Quick decisions, rapid investments and urgent action will be needed. However, success in this enterprise could ensure that the EU would have 10–20 gigafactories by 2025. The European battery market is estimated to be worth around £250 billion by 2025 and would satisfy the need for batteries within Europe. An orderly approach is required.

By implementing this strategy the EU Commission plans to develop a competitive advantage in a critical manufacturing industry. Further benefits of this approach are underpinning jobs and creating a cleaner, more environmentally beneficial environment.

FIGURE 6.10   Battery value chain

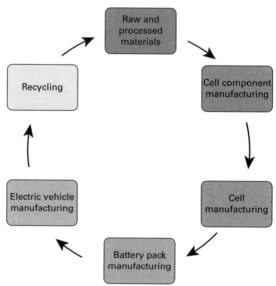

SOURCE European Commission, 2018

This strategy from the EU commission will fully address the complete value chain from sourcing and processing materials, through battery cell and battery pack design, development and manufacturing. It will also cover off the second life of these batteries and include recycling and ultimate disposal.

More specifically the EU Commission aims to:

- Secure access to raw materials from resource-rich countries outside the EU, facilitate access to European sources of raw materials, as well as accessing secondary raw materials through recycling in a circular economy of batteries.

- Support European battery cell manufacturing at scale with a full competitive value chain in Europe; bring key industry players and national and regional authorities together; work in partnership with Member States and the European Investment Bank to support innovative manufacturing projects with important cross-border and sustainability dimensions throughout the battery value chain.

- Strengthen industrial leadership through stepped-up EU research and innovation support to advanced (eg lithium-ion) and disruptive (eg solid state) technologies in the batteries sector. This should target support in all the steps of the value chain (advanced materials, new chemistries, manufacturing processes, battery management systems, recycling, business model innovations), be closely integrated with the industrial ecosystem, and contribute to accelerating the deployment and industrialization of innovations

- Develop and strengthen a highly skilled workforce in all parts of the battery value chain in order to close the skills gap through actions at EU and Member State level, providing adequate training, re-skilling and upskilling, and making Europe an attractive location for world-class experts in batteries development and production.

- Back the long-term viability of the EU battery cell manufacturing industry by utilizing renewable energy in the build process. Apply clear goals to ensure secure and balanced long-term battery production. Should a solid-state battery be successfully developed between 2025–2030, a reduced requirement for cobalt would be achieved and possibly alternative materials could be available from more desirable market locations.

- Ensure consistency with the broader enabling and regulatory framework (clean energy strategy, mobility packages, EU trade policy, etc) in support of batteries and storage deployment (European Commission, 2018).

Strategic action areas

ACTION TO SECURE THE SUSTAINABLE SUPPLY OF RAW MATERIALS

Following the development of the European Innovation Partnership (EIP) in 2012 the EU has made clear its battery strategy (European Commission, 2018):

- sustainable sourcing of raw materials from global markets;
- sustainable domestic raw materials production; and
- resource efficiency and supply of secondary raw materials.

In September 2017, the EU Commission adopted a renewed EU industrial policy strategy, which highlighted the importance of raw materials, particularly critical raw materials, for the competitiveness of all industrial value chains, for the EU economy (European Commission, 2018).

A number of raw materials are required to produce lithium-ion batteries, and few of these materials exist within the EU. They include lithium, cobalt, nickel, manganese, graphite, silicon, copper and aluminium. Cobalt in particular has limited supply sources, with 50 per cent of the world supply coming from the Democratic Republic of the Congo (DRC), which has a troubled human rights record (Statista, nd).

The EU must gain access to raw materials from countries outside the EU with access to these REMs.

FIGURE 6.11 Battery pack pricing

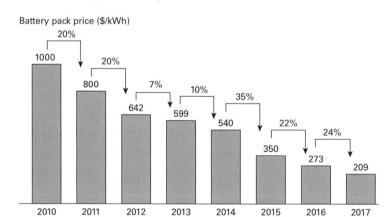

SOURCE BloombergNEF, 2019

SUPPORTING EUROPEAN PROJECTS COVERING DIFFERENT SEGMENTS OF THE
BATTERY VALUE CHAIN (EUROPEAN COMMISSION, 2018)

The 'European Battery Alliance' is moving fast. There have already been concrete developments with the announcements of industrial consortia or partnerships aiming at development of battery cell manufacturing and related ecosystems. To maintain the EU's world-leading position in automotive manufacturing and innovation, action is needed to rapidly increase battery cell manufacturing capability in Europe; action is already taking place (European Commission, 2018).

PUTTING THE UK AT THE FOREFRONT OF THE DESIGN AND MANUFACTURING
OF BATTERY TECHNOLOGIES AND ZERO-EMISSION VEHICLES

In the next 10 years, from 2020 to 2030, the sector will see more change than in the previous 100. Technology is changing what the industry looks like and providing new business opportunities as demand shifts to ultra-low-emission vehicles.

New conditions require new thinking and we want to work in partnership with the sector to provide this. We have set out our ambition in the automotive Sector Deal. This builds on the long-standing partnership between government and industry, brought to life by the Automotive Council, to work together on shifting the industry to zero-emission vehicles.

It will also create a world-leading test environment for connected and autonomous vehicles and raise the competitiveness of UK suppliers to match the best in Europe.

UK ULTRA-LOW-EMISSION TECHNOLOGY DEVELOPMENTS ACROSS THE UK

Figure 6.12 and Table 6.1 detail the UK locations, the activity and the level of investment of those companies actively developing battery technology and support services for zero/low-emission mobility. This information is included in the UK Government's 'Clean Air Industrial White Paper' (Department for Transport, 2018).

SUSTAINABLE AND ETHICAL SOURCING PLANS

Sustainable and ethical sourcing plans have seen start-up enterprises looking for opportunities to ease the pressure on critical minerals.

Breakthrough Energy Ventures, a £1 billion fund led by Bill Gates, recently invested in Kobold, a Silicon Valley start-up looking to deploy artificial intelligence systems to find cobalt reserves where labour and environmental laws are stricter than those found in the Congo (Breakthrough Energy, nd).

FIGURE 6.12   UK locations and investment levels of battery producers

SOURCE Department for Transport, 2018

Deep Green, a Canadian start-up, is looking to mine battery metals from the sea floor. The company argues that at 4,000 metres below sea level the environmental risk associated with land extraction is significantly reduced. Predictions are that this type of exploration will make land-based extraction redundant (Jamasmie, 2019).

Table 6.1   UK EV and battery manufacturing activity

Company	Investment	Location
Alexander Dennis Ltd	Alexander Dennis has developed a range of low- and zero-emission buses for the global market. In addition to their own investment of more than £30 million, Scottish Enterprise awarded the company a £7.3 million R&D grant to design and manufacture low carbon vehicles, creating 100 new jobs.	Larbert, Stirlingshire
Entek International Ltd	Have announced a £10 million investment in a new generation of battery separator for the automotive industry. It is the only manufacturer of its kind in the UK and currently employs 130 staff at its Camperdown Industrial Estate base and another 305 staff worldwide.	Newcastle Upon Tyne, Tyne and Wear
Nissan	Nissan have invested in production of the next generation of the Nissan LEAF at Sunderland, which also makes EV batteries for the LEAF and eNV200 electric van.	Sunderland, Tyne and Wear
Paneltex	Manufacturer of 3.5 tonne–11 tonne trucks, including refrigerated and temperature-controlled vehicles, which offer a zero-emission range of up to 150 miles.	Hull, North Humberside
Magnomatics Limited	Magnetic gear manufacturer, part of a consortium with Romax Technology and Changan UK to produce the next generation in efficient hybrid powertrains, with £38 million of funding from OLEV and Innovate UK.	Sheffield, South Yorkshire
Formula-E	Formula-E has operational headquarters at Donington Park – housing teams, manufacturers and suppliers competing in the ABB FIA Formula E Championship.	Donington Park, Leicestershire
HORIBA MIRA	Located at the MIRA Technology Park, a globally-recognized transport R&D facility – it is Europe's largest transport technology park.	Nuneaton, Warwickshire

(continued)

TABLE 6.1 (Continued)

Company	Investment	Location
London Electric Vehicle Company (LEVC)	LEVC have invested £325 million in a dedicated electric vehicle manufacturing facility in Coventry, which will create 1,000 new jobs. The company's first product, a range-extended electric taxi, is currently on sale and LEVC will be bringing an electric van to market next year that uses the same range-extended EV technology.	Coventry, West Midlands
Equipmake Ltd	Equipmake Ltd supplies electric drive technology to British sports car company Ariel who are producing the Hipercar. They are also developing a low-cost electric bus drivetrain to enable more widespread adoption of electric buses.	Hethel, Norfolk
Mercedes-Benz	Mercedes will enter Formula E in 2019 and will produce an electric drivetrain for new electric motorsport cars at their base in Brixworth near Northampton.	Northampton, Northamptonshire
Cummins	Cummins have committed to launch a leading all-electric powertrain to market by end of 2019 for buses and delivery vehicles incorporating a Cummins-developed battery pack. This is part of an overall £380 million global investment by Cummins to be a leader in electrified power for commercial markets.	Milton Keynes, Buckinghamshire
Tevva	Chelmsford-based company producing range-extender electric 7.5–14 tonne trucks to delivery companies, such as UPS, Kuehne+Nagel and others.	Chelmsford, Essex
Ford	The Ford Dunton Technical Centre is a global centre of excellence for the development of both commercial vehicles and powertrains. Electrified powertrains are playing an increasing role in CO_2 and air quality improvement, as demonstrated by the plug-in hybrid Transit van fleet Ford is trialling in London.	Queen Elizabeth Olympic Park, London

(continued)

TABLE 6.1 (Continued)

Company	Investment	Location
BMW	Electric MINI to be produced in Cowley, near Oxford from 2019, where currently 4,500 staff are employed at this site.	Cowley, Oxfordshire
Yasa	Growing Oxford-based electric motor manufacturer.	Kidlington, Oxfordshire
Arrival	In August 2017, the Royal Mail announced an agreement with Arrival to trial nine electric vehicles in the ranges of 3, 5, 6 and 7 tonnes gross vehicle weight (GVW). The manufacturing facility will be based in Banbury and will represent the first electric-only truck manufacturing facility in the UK.	Kidlington, Oxfordshire
Detroit Electric	To invest £304 million in Leamington Spa facilities to build electric sports cars and SUVs, creating 120 new engineering jobs and 100 new manufacturing jobs.	Royal Leamington Spa, Warwickshire
Jaguar Land Rover (a)	Jaguar Land Rover's £150 million investment established the National Automotive Innovation Centre (NAIC) at the University of Warwick. The centre houses approximately 1,000 scientists, engineers, academics, technicians and support staff working on future automotive technology, including electric vehicles; carbon reduction; and smart and connected vehicles.	Coventry, West Midlands
Jaguar Land Rover (b)	Manufacturing centre in Cannock for research into reducing emissions and weight, employing 1,400 people.	Cannock, Staffordshire
Toyota	In February 2016, Toyota invested £5.8 million in hybrid electric powertrain manufacture in Deeside, helping to secure 400 jobs.	Deeside, Clwyd
INEX	Established in 2002, INEX produces innovative micro/nano technology and semiconductor-based systems.	Newcastle Upon Tyne, Tyne and Wear

(continued)

TABLE 6.1 (Continued)

Company	Investment	Location
McLaren	McLaren Automotive is building a £50 million centre of excellence for innovating and manufacturing lightweight materials, creating around 200 direct jobs focusing on the development of advanced composites technologies.	Sheffield, South Yorkshire
Wrightbus Ltd	Northern Ireland-based company designing and manufacturing battery electric and fuel cell electric buses.	Ballymena, County Antrim

SOURCE Department for Transport, 2018

Next-generation battery technologies and trends

Due to the potential to overheat, lithium-ion cell packs need protection circuitry to ensure they stay within safe operating limits. They also suffer from ageing, storage conditions can have a significant impact on their usability, and they currently cost more to power a medium-sized car than an internal combustion engine would.

Perhaps the most significant breakthrough has been the potential of the solid-state battery. The main difference between lithium-ion batteries and solid-state batteries is that lithium-ion uses liquid electrolyte solution and solid-state uses solid electrolyte. Solid-state batteries claim to be safer, require less cobalt, and can deliver 400 kWh capacity and a range of 500 miles on a single charge. Charging is also measurably faster than with lithium-ion. Ford, Hyundai and BMW have all been working on solid-state battery technology (Faraday Institution, 2019).

Summary and conclusions

- Critical to the future of car and commercial vehicle manufacturing is the location of manufacturing of batteries. Failure to build gigafactory capacity in the UK risks 200,000+ jobs in the UK's automotive industry.

- The concentration of electric vehicle manufacturing and battery technology know-how and production capacity resides in Asia.

- The market for EV batteries is forecast to be worth in excess of $250 billion by 2030.

- Sixty new gigafactories are forecast to be necessary to supply a demand for over 40 million electric vehicles per annum by 2040.

- In July 2019 construction began on Germany's first gigafactory, which will manufacture batteries to sell to BMW. It's being built by Chinese company CATL, the world's largest manufacturer of lithium-ion batteries.

- Sourcing of rare earth materials is going to be a critical core competence for OEMs over the next 10–20 years.

- Solid-state battery technology will compete with current lithium-ion to become the dominant element in battery production.

- China will capture significant electric car and light commercial share of global sales in the 2020–2025 period. It will dominate supply chain for the rare earth materials required for EV battery development.

References

Ali, I (2018) Battery expert: Tesla Model 3 has 'most advanced large scale lithium battery ever produced', *Evannex*. Retrieved from: https://evannex.com/blogs/news/tesla-s-battery-pack-is-both-mysterious-and-alluring-work-in-progress (archived at https://perma.cc/ZZU3-8SFG)

Asher Hamilton, I (2019) Elon Musk says the UK lost out on Tesla's new Gigafactory because of Brexit, *Business Insider*. Retrieved from: https://www.businessinsider.com/elon-musk-blames-brexit-no-tesla-gigafactory-in-uk-2019-11?r=US&IR=T (archived at https://perma.cc/46AM-WAFR)

Autocar (2020) Analysis: Why the UK needs a battery gigafactory – and fast. Retrieved from: https://www.autocar.co.uk/car-news/industry/analysis-why-uk-needs-battery-gigafactory-and-fast (archived at https://perma.cc/JG2N-R3GQ)

Barrera, P (2020) Top cobalt production by country, *Investing News*. Retrieved from: https://investingnews.com/daily/resource-investing/battery-metals-investing/cobalt-investing/top-cobalt-producing-countries-congo-china-canada-russia-australia/ (archived at https://perma.cc/A3BZ-EWA3)

BloombergNEF (2019) Electric Vehicle Outlook 2019. Retrieved from: https://about.bnef.com/electric-vehicle-outlook/ (archived at https://perma.cc/6GXR-QPKH)

Breakthrough Energy (nd) Advancing the landscape of clean energy innovation. Retrieved from: https://www.b-t.energy/research/ (archived at https://perma.cc/2AES-6YAM)

Dempsey, H (2019) US enticed by Greenland's rare earth resources, *Financial Times*. Retrieved from: https://www.ft.com/content/f418bb86-bdb2-11e9-89e2-41e555e96722 (archived at https://perma.cc/ZP5H-3YQQ)

Department for Transport (2018) *Clean Air Industrial White Paper*, Department for Transport, London

European Commission (2018) *Europe on the Move*, European Commission, Brussels

Faraday Institution (2019) *UK Electric Vehicle and Battery Production to 2040*, Faraday Institution, Cambridge

Future Bridge (nd) Solid-State Batteries. Retrieved from: https://www.futurebridge.com/blog/solid-state-batteries/ (archived at https://perma.cc/7Z86-B8QK)

Global Casino (2019) CATL. Retrieved from: https://www.facebook.com/globalcasinoguide/posts/catlthe-entrance-of-catls-headquarters-in-ningde-chinawhen-contemporary-amperex-/2149289192029631/ (archived at https://perma.cc/5N2S-R7RR)

Green Car Congress (2019) CATL starts construction of Li-ion factory in Germany; 14 GWh by 2022. Retrieved from: https://www.greencarcongress.com/2019/10/20191018-catl.html (archived at https://perma.cc/Y2NT-ZNPQ)

IEA (2017) The Future of Trucks. Retrieved from: https://www.iea.org/reports/the-future-of-trucks (archived at https://perma.cc/7ZWA-ULSJ)

Jamasmie, C (2019) DeepGreen closer to ocean mining battery metals after Swiss cash injection, *Mining [DOT] COM*. Retrieved from: https://www.mining.com/deepgreen-closer-mining-battery-metals-sea-150m-injection/ (archived at https://perma.cc/2ZLJ-NYSP)

Multiplier (2018) Why did Nokia fail and what can you learn from it? Retrieved from: https://medium.com/multiplier-magazine/why-did-nokia-fail-81110d981787 (archived at https://perma.cc/8SL4-PPZE)

Nienaber, M (2019) Germany to fund research facility for EV battery technology, *Reuters UK*. Retrieved from: https://uk.reuters.com/article/us-germany-batteries/germany-to-fund-research-facility-for-ev-battery-technology-idUKKCN1PH1NT (archived at https://perma.cc/SD2A-NYTX)

O'Kane, S (2019) Tesla still isn't getting enough batteries from Panasonic, *The Verge*. Retrieved from: https://www.theverge.com/2019/4/11/18305976/tesla-panasonic-gigafactory-batteries-model-3 (archived at https://perma.cc/6VTL-LC2P)

Periodictable (nd) Abundance in Earth's crust of the elements. Retrieved from: https://periodictable.com/Properties/A/CrustAbundance.an.html (archived at https://perma.cc/FWQ8-72VP)

Perkowski, J (2017) EV batteries: a $240 billion industry in the making that China wants to take charge of, *Forbes*. Retrieved from: https://www.forbes.com/sites/jackperkowski/2017/08/03/ev-batteries-a-240-billion-industry-in-the-making/#734bfe503f08 (archived at https://perma.cc/HU64-L4HZ)

Rathi, A (2019) The complete guide to the battery revolution, *Quartz*. Retrieved from: //qz.com/1582811/the-complete-guide-to-the-battery-revolution/ (archived at https://perma.cc/PY4K-43BG)

Scheyder, E (2019) California rare earths miner races to refine amid U.S.-China trade row, *Reuters*. Retrieved from: https://www.reuters.com/article/us-usa-rareearths-mpmaterials/california-rare-earths-miner-races-to-refine-amid-u-s-china-trade-row-idUSKCN1VD2D3 (archived at https://perma.cc/4BGK-QDT5)

Sharma, G (2019) Are electric vehicles really about to plateau oil demand? *Forbes*. Retrieved from: https://www.forbes.com/sites/gauravsharma/2019/11/25/are-electric-vehicles-really-about-to-plateau-oil-demand/#4c762a033b13 (archived at https://perma.cc/64Z3-FELA)

Statista (nd) Average lithium carbonate price from 2010 to 2019 (in U.S. dollars per metric ton). Retrieved from: https://www.statista.com/statistics/606350/battery-grade-lithium-carbonate-price/ (archived at https://perma.cc/VT4H-AYDF)

Teck (nd) Red Dog. Retrieved from: https://www.teck.com/operations/united-states/operations/red-dog/ (archived at https://perma.cc/4YGM-L4A4)

07

Global energy systems and the impact of electric vehicles

This chapter will familiarize the reader with:

- The impact of EV electricity demand on the national grid.
- Global market development and investment plans for charging infrastructure.
- Access to charging infrastructure, costs and investment.
- Costs associated with charging an electric vehicle.
- Cost benefits associated with ownership of electric vehicles.
- Tax benefits of EV ownership.
- Smart charging and availability of charging apps to help locate public charging access.

The impact of EV energy demand on the national grid

There has been an explosion of interest in the production and sale of electric vehicles, in part following the 'Dieselgate' scandal in 2015 and the anxiety levels created by concerns over global warming.

This has raised concerns about what is the likely future demand on national grids and the ability to satisfy demand from current electricity power production capacity. A recent research report by the McKinsey Centre for Future Mobility has detailed key facts and forecasts that are outlined in the figures below (Engel *et al*, 2018).

The demand for the electrification of vehicles has prompted a genuine increase in concern for how electricity generation capacity will be affected.

McKinsey forecasts that by 2030 the worldwide requirements for EVs will increase to 120 million units. Meanwhile, the market share for EVs in the United States and Europe is currently around a modest 2 per cent, but McKinsey expects that by 2030 the US market share will reach 18 per cent and Europe a substantial 30 per cent (Engel *et al*, 2018).

Furthermore, McKinsey research suggests that plug-in hybrid vehicles (PHEVs) will be far more common than BEVs in the United States. In China, sales of EVs are expected to increase dramatically from the existing 4 per cent to leading the market with a 74 per cent share by 2030. China, unlike the US and Europe, is expected to see BEVs take 50 per cent of the market and PHEVs reach 26 per cent (Engel *et al*, 2018).

FIGURE 7.1 Electric vehicle adoption base case

Our base case for adoption suggests approximately 120 million electric vehicles could be on the road by 2030.

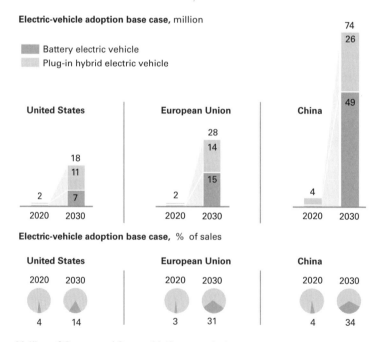

McKinsey&Company | **Source**: McKinsey analysis

SOURCE Engel *et al*, 2018

Energy demand on national grids from electric vehicles

Evidence that any increased power demand will not require significant capacity from the national grid has been produced by a recent research analysis by McKinsey; details are in their 'Insights' report that looked at the potential impact of electric vehicles on the global energy systems (Engel *et al*, 2018).

Due to the rapid increase in sales of EVs, energy demand is forecast to increase from 18 billion kW in 2020 to 280 billion kW by 2030 – a 15-fold rise (see Figure 7.2). Most of the incremental power generation capacity required will come from renewable energy sources including wind, wave,

FIGURE 7.2   Charging-energy demand for electric vehicles in four regions studied

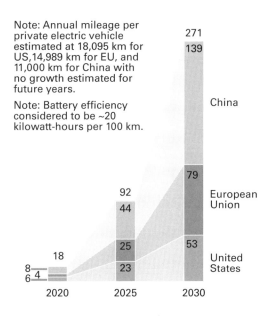

McKinsey&Company | **Source:** Mckinsey analysis

SOURCE Engel *et al*, 2018

solar and some gas-powered generation. While 280 billion kWh of global demand per annum might seem colossal, it only represents about 8 per cent of the full annual electricity demand in the United States (Engel *et al*, 2018).

McKinsey expects that 50 per cent of all electricity demand will come from renewable sources by 2050. With many of the world's largest companies joining the RE100 initiative, renewable energy will play a far more significant role in the future.

How that demand is generated has been analysed as part of the McKinsey Energy Insights research and Figure 7.3 details how demand will be influenced by a number of factors:

- Where the population lives and what type of home they inhabit, ie with or without garages compared to urban high-rise accommodation with no parking.
- What journey patterns drivers choose, eg short, regular to work and back dependent on home charging vs long-distance beyond EV range capacity and requiring public charging.
- The energy capacity differences between the use of hybrid and full BEV product characteristics.
- The cost associated with AC level 1 and 2 and the rate of charge, eg time to recharge compared to access to 'fast direct charging' infrastructure.

Evident from the McKinsey research on energy demand from EV charging infrastructure are the following trends:

- In the United States, EV users will most likely rely on home charging 70–80 per cent of the time. This is primarily due to single family home occupation with a garage for accommodating chargers.
- In Europe the initial chosen option will primarily be home charging but as EV adoption rates increase between 2025 to 2030, access to faster public access charging and the utilization of web-based apps assisting in the notification of public charging capacity and availability will see EV owners move towards public charging from 4 per cent to almost 50 per cent by 2030.
- China is very different to the US and Europe. Already in 2020 it is evident that a population residing in structurally dense inner-city locations relies on access to fast DC public charging 60 per cent of the time and it is predicted that this will be over 80 per cent by 2030 (Engel *et al*, 2018).

FIGURE 7.3   EV charging options by region

There are home- or public-based scenarios for electric-vehicle charging by region.

Energy demand, public-centred scenario, % of kilowatt-hours[1]

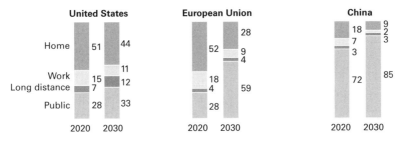

Energy demand, home-centred scenario, % of kilowatt-hours[1]

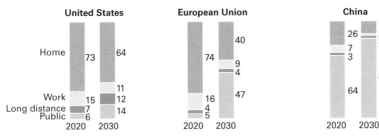

[1]Figures may not sum to 100%, because of rounding.

McKinsey&Company | **Source:** McKinsey analysis

SOURCE Engel *et al*, 2018

EV energy demand by charging technology

EV owners are currently faced with a choice of recharging options. Currently there are three established and recognized charging methods using AC and DC charging infrastructure and in the future the possibility of relevant wireless charging capability (see Figure 7.4).

The differences between the available charging technologies are detailed below:

- **Alternate-current (AC) charging (referred to as level 1 or level 2 charging)**
  Alternating current (AC) is converted by an inverter installed in the vehicle to direct current (DC). The vehicle battery is then charged up as follows:

  – Level 1 (120V) as in the United States.

- Level 2 (240V) as in Europe.
- Level 1 and 2 tend to be home and workplace systems suitable for overnight charging.
- Levels 1 and 2 are expected by McKinsey to provide 60–80 per cent of the charge capability until 2030.

- **Level 3 direct charging (DC) or direct current fast charging (DCFC)**
In level 3 applications the AC from the grid is converted to DC prior to reaching the vehicle – a vehicle-installed inverter is not required.

- DCFC functions at 25–350 kW.
- DCFC chargers are best suited to fast public charging, eg at a service or fuel station or at a public car park.
- DCFC is expected to be very common in China, as due to the take up of EVs demand for public charging will be higher.

FIGURE 7.4   Energy demand by charging technology

Level 1 and Level 2 charging will likely remain the dominant source of charging energy demand.

Energy demand by charging technology, % of kilowatt-hours,[1] home-centered scenario

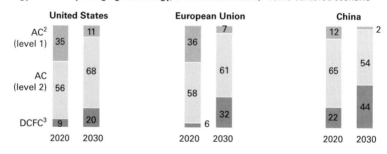

[1]Figures may not sum to 100%, because of rounding.

[2]Alternating current.

[3]Direct current fast charging.

McKinsey&Company | **Source:** McKinsey analysis

SOURCE Engel *et al*, 2018

EV owner charging cost scenarios

The key question is who will provide the necessary capital for public charging while utilization rates remain low, particularly in China, and where the need for public charging is higher?

Charging infrastructure development and likely investment costs

McKinsey forecasts a likely requirement for 40 million chargers across China, Europe and the United States. This infrastructure would require around $50 billion of investment capital from 2020–2030:

- The United States will therefore need to increase charging capacity up to 20 million chargers by 2030, requiring *c.*$10 billion of investment.
- By 2030, 25 million chargers will be required in the EU with a *c.*$15 billion investment.
- China's resource need is 20 million chargers and an investment of *c.*$20 billion

As the demand for EVs rises the cost of batteries is forecast to fall. The number of gigafactories will increase to deliver the batteries required, and new 'green technology' businesses are forecast to emerge as the transition from ICE to EVs takes place.

These emerging 'green challengers' are expected to disturb the status quo within the automotive arena. The 10 major global automotive manufacturers will be forced to balance short-term investments in fossil-fuel vehicles with the increasing demand for EVs and heavy investment in innovative new component technology, distribution methods and changing after-sales requirements.

Automotive competitors will need to abandon the established 'vehicle franchise' sales and service model and build a new direct vertically integrated factory-to-market platform. The disruption to the traditional automotive business model will be discussed further in Chapter 11.

The lack of charging infrastructure is a huge barrier for potential EV purchasers and is currently a major reason preventing the early adoption of EVs. Access to charging relieves what is commonly known as 'range anxiety' – the fear that there isn't sufficient range to get to your destination and back. Tesla has invested heavily in charging stations and in 2019 had 13,000 DCFC 'supercharger stations' globally. Morgan Stanley suggested in February 2019 that Tesla had possibly built a 'competitive

FIGURE 7.5 Investment requirements in charging capability

The industry may need to invest $50 billon in the four regions studied through 2030 to meet the need for chargers.

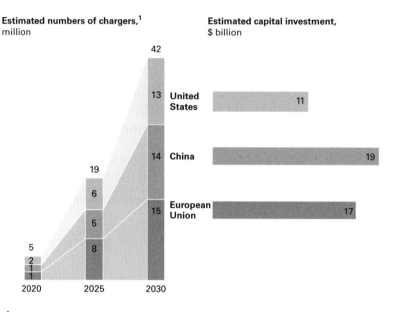

[1]Figures may not sum, because of rounding.

McKinsey&Company | **Source:** McKinsey analysis

SOURCE Engel *et al*, 2018

moat', providing a significant barrier to competitor entry. These 'super-chargers' refuel most Tesla batteries in about an hour (Sheetz, 2019).

Investment in EV charging infrastructure similar to Tesla also provides OEM car and commercial vehicle manufacturers with an opportunity to harness revenue potential. This could also be an offset for the expected downturn in existing aftermarket revenues. McKinsey expects repair and maintenance (R&M) volumes to be 50 per cent lower than current levels generated by ICE vehicles (Engel *et al*, 2018).

McKinsey states that it is key to the survival and future profitability of the existing OEMs to understand the specific local needs for charging services. Rapid adaptation and reinvention will be the key to making effective targeted investments or creating strategic joint ventures, matching demand and supply, and enabling rapid returns on investment (ROI).

The cost of charging an EV at home

A typical electric vehicle (Tesla) with a 60 kWh battery will be able to travel around 200–300 miles on a single charge. Charging at home will cost around £8.40 for a full charge, so the cost per mile at this rate is around 4p. This compares to 15p per mile for the same range from an equivalent ICE vehicle at 2020 diesel pump prices (Pod-Point, 2020).

Charging at work

Workplace charge points offer free access throughout the day and many companies have made these available to staff. Some will opt for a time-based tariff to encourage sharing of charging stations. Other models offer free employee charging for a set period of time; after this a small fee to encourage employees to vacate the station may be applied (Pod-Point, 2020). Governments can influence this charging infrastructure take-up by offering EV tax breaks for vehicle purchase and work charging in order to help reach their reduced national CO_2 targets.

Charging availability at public locations

Many supermarket locations will offer free-to-use charging points for the duration of your stay as part of customer satisfaction and loyalty programmes.

DCFC rapid charging stations

Rapid charging points are more usually found at motorway service stations and will normally charge £6.50 for a 30-minute 100-mile charge.

Details of some of the many charging apps that are available are outlined at the end of this chapter and will direct the EV owner to what is available.

EV financial obligations and tax benefits in the UK

In January 2019, there were 265,000 EV passenger cars running in the UK and 8,700 vans. EVs make up around 3–4 per cent of UK registrations. Meanwhile, there were only around 30,000 charge points, which is approximately 10 vehicles per charge point – totally insufficient (Lilly, 2019).

Registration statistics published by the Society of Motor Manufacturers and Traders (SMMT) reveal that electric car sales in the UK have risen dramatically since 2014. While only around 500 electric cars were registered per month during the first half of 2014, this had increased to an average of more than 70,000 annual registrations by 2019 (SMMT, 2020).

UK sales have been boosted by favourable tax incentives for the initial purchase and downstream savings in maintenance compared to a conventional petrol or diesel car. Since the CO_2 emissions associated with electric and plug-in hybrid vehicles are either zero or well below 100 g/km, all models are categorized in vehicle excise band (VED tax band) rated zero for the standard rate of tax.

Company car tax in the UK

Like all car tax, company car tax is based on its emissions and the benefit in kind (BIK) tax applied will be determined by the company car tax calculator, which currently sets the level for EVs at 7 per cent but will increase by 2 per cent in the next financial year (Pod-Point, 2020).

Electric car capital allowances

In 2020, EVs are eligible for 100 per cent write down in their first year. Compared to the standard tax relief on vehicles of 18 per cent, this represents a cost benefit to company-owned EVs of between £1,000 and £3,000 over four years – equivalent to around 10 per cent of the EV's on-the-road price (NB this benefit does not apply to rental vehicles) (Accounting Web, 2018).

Other EV benefits in the UK

Aside from the electric vehicle benefits outlined above there are further financial benefits associated with electric vehicle ownership (UK Government, 2019a):

- London Congestion Charge – savings of £11.50 per day will be available to EV drivers.
- Maintenance costs – energy costs can be as low as 3p per mile, so over a year it is possible to save around £800 when travelling 10,000 miles pa.

- National Insurance contributions for company cars are based on official CO_2 emissions figures. Employers providing EV company cars will pay lower NIC contributions.
- EV government grants – vans are eligible for £8,000, cars up to £4,500 in government support.

UK government support for EV charging infrastructure

The UK Government has provided home installation grants of £500 to 100,000 homes, and charge points for electric vehicles are being built into future property development. Installed home chargers can cost as little as 4p per mile to power up an EV – a third of the cost of a diesel or petrol equivalent (UK Government, 2019a).

In addition to home charging equipment, most charge points are becoming smart units, which means they are Wi-Fi enabled, manage the charging to enable the cheapest electricity, and provide detailed information about your energy consumption, usually via an app on your mobile phone.

UK EV owners using apps to locate charge points on the move

Apps for life with an electric vehicle are now available and help take charge of your driving. Examples are:

- **ZAP MAP** is a free android and Apple app that has mapped over 6,000 charging points.
- **Electric Highway** is a network of 300 fast chargers located along UK motorways, showing the 10 nearest available charging points with costs ranging from 15–30p/kWh, depending on whether you are an electricity customer.
- **POD Point** has installed 40,000 home chargers and runs 2,000 public charging units, many in supermarket car parks, and provides free charging for short periods.
- **Google Maps** gives you the option of various charging stations while you are on the move. Type 'EV charging stations' into Google and see where ChargePoint, Chargemaster and EVgo charging stations operate
- **Plugsurfing** claims 110,000 charging points across Europe have signed up to its scheme and shows the cost per minute for charging.

FIGURE 7.6 Smart charging

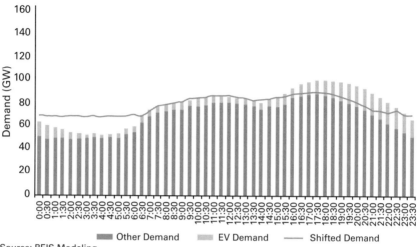

Source: BEIS Modeling

SOURCE UK Government (2019b)

Summary

- McKinsey analysis suggests the projected growth in e-mobility will not drive substantial increases in total electrical grid power demand in the near- to mid-term, thus limiting the need for new electricity generation capacity during that period.

- While the uptake in EV sales is unlikely to cause a significant increase in total power demand, it will likely reshape the electricity load curve. The most pronounced effect will be an increase in evening peak loads, as people plug in their EVs when they return home from work or after completing the day's errands.

- Beyond peak-load increases, the highly volatile and spiky load profiles of public fast-charging stations will also require additional system balancing.

- As the cost of batteries continues to decline rapidly, using energy storage to smooth load profiles will become increasingly attractive.

- Pilot studies have shown a substantial willingness of EV owners to participate in coordinated smart charging.

- Many employers will install workplace charge points and offer free access throughout the day.

- The expected increase in EVs on the road creates a challenge for power companies. While EVs will not lead to a substantial increase in power demand by 2030, they will reshape the load curve, thus placing different strains on the grid.

- In the UK electric vehicles are gaining ground and there were more than 70,000 battery electric and plug-in hybrid vehicles registered in 2019.

- China will be the recognized global leader for electric vehicles and see volumes grow from 4 million to 74 million by 2030.

- Europe will see 2 million EV vehicles in 2020 grow to 28 million by 2030.

- In the United States, 2 million vehicles in 2020 will grow to 18 million by 2030.

- China will see full battery electric vehicles take the lion's share of total volume whereas the US and Europe will have a higher share of electric-hybrid volumes than pure BEV.

References

Accounting Web (2018) Electric car for work – 100% capital allowance? Retrieved from: https://www.accountingweb.co.uk/any-answers/electric-car-for-work-100-capital-allowance (archived at https://perma.cc/SQ6K-UD88)

Engel, H *et al* (2018) Charging ahead: Electric-vehicle infrastructure demand, *McKinsey*. Retrieved from: https://www.mckinsey.com/industries/automotive-and-assembly/our-insights/charging-ahead-electric-vehicle-infrastructure-demand (archived at https://perma.cc/4TPJ-PV4L)

Lilly, C (2019) Electric car market statistics, *Next Greencar*. Retrieved from: https://www.nextgreencar.com/electric-cars/statistics/ (archived at https://perma.cc/U4WD-3PCF)

Pod-Point (2020) Cost of charging an electric car. Retrieved from: https://pod-point.com/guides/driver/cost-of-charging-electric-car (archived at https://perma.cc/8DCU-ZWPL)

Sheetz, M (2019) Tesla's charging stations are a massive 'competitive moat,' Morgan Stanley says, *CNBC*. Retrieved from: https://www.cnbc.com/2019/02/12/morgan-stanley-tesla-charging-station-network-competitive-moat.html (archived at https://perma.cc/UWD8-P5FR)

SMMT (2020) Electric vehicle and alternatively fuelled vehicle registrations. Retrieved from: https://www.smmt.co.uk/vehicle-data/evs-and-afvs-registrations/ (archived at https://perma.cc/YV3P-SRQH)

UK Government (2019a) Electric car chargepoints to be installed in all future homes in world first. Retrieved from: https://www.gov.uk/government/news/electric-car-chargepoints-to-be-installed-in-all-future-homes-in-world-first (archived at https://perma.cc/XHE7-JTPA)

UK Government (2019b) Electric vehicle smart charging. Retrieved from: https://www.gov.uk/government/consultations/electric-vehicle-smart-charging (archived at https://perma.cc/3YME-7N8L)

08

EV development and the world's 'top 10' commercial vehicle manufacturers

This chapter will familiarize the reader with:

- The current scale of the global truck and bus markets.
- The 10 key existing OEM plans for alternative fuel solutions.
- Industry forecasts and trends for medium and heavy-duty trucks and buses in the US, Europe and Asia.
- Threats and opportunities for major OEMs in global markets.

World truck and bus markets

Between 2005 and 2018 around 26 million global commercial vehicle sales were recorded (OICA, nd). In 2018 around 2 million commercial vehicles were produced (ACEA, 2019).

Two million trucks are sold around the world per annum, and the top 10 manufacturers account for 90 per cent of world truck sales. The global top 10 truck manufacturing companies generally own a number of brands as there have been a considerable number of mergers and acquisitions (M&As) since the 1970s. However, the trend is that the acquiring company dissolves the acquired brand over time and absorbs the acquired assets and technology into its own organization.

FIGURE 8.1 World production of medium- and heavy-duty trucks

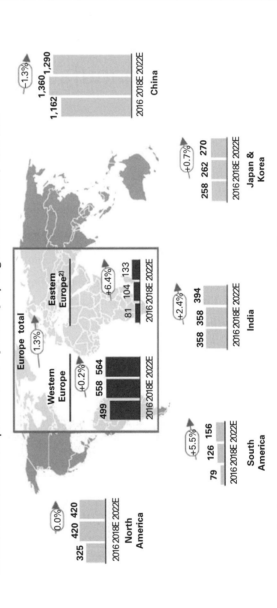

Production of medium/heavy duty trucks and buses is on the rise globally – For Europe, approx 1% annual increase expected

Annual truck and bus production[1] [k units] by region and CAGR, 18E–22E

Demand for commercial vehicles generally tracks economic growth, and the International Monetary Fund (IMF) forecasts global gross domestic product to increase at a rate of around 3.4 per cent in 2020. Meanwhile, the commercial vehicle market worldwide is forecast to continue increasing in size at a compound rate of 4.3 per cent, proving the point (Figure 8.1). This is a very big market set to continue growing, thus increasing the demand for oil. BP states in its 2019 Energy Outlook Report that transport demand continues to be dominated by oil, despite increasing use of natural gas, electricity and biofuels from 2000–2040 (BP Plc, 2019).

The world truck and bus market position 2018

- 2 million new trucks per annum sold (ACEA, 2019).
- 2 million used trucks per annum sold (IEA, 2017).
- Trucks account for 84 per cent of global truck and bus production on average.
- Truck and bus production in China accounts for 42 per cent of global production.
- Europe accounts for 21 per cent, APAC – Japan, Korea and India – account for 20 per cent and North America for 13 per cent of global production on average.

'Top 10' truck manufacturing companies in the world – 2019

There have been around 200 commercial vehicle brands available worldwide over the last century. There were more than 20 commercial vehicle brands in the UK alone and 45 in Europe. Globalization, competition, growing R&D costs and increasingly stringent legislation have caused massive consolidation. Although there are several niche players left in the market there are now only 10 major worldwide truck manufacturing players, each one having additional brands under its direct control (Commercial Motor, 2013).

A major proportion of the world truck industry is in the control of just 10 truck manufacturing companies. Competition is intense. The large market share of these top companies is simply down to industry complexity.

On the face of it the truck industry is simple: design, build and sell a truck that can move a tonne of a given product a kilometre at the lowest price. However, the truck business is not as simple as it seems; the different demands of customers means a plethora of model variants has to be offered and supported. Significant capital investment, resources and infrastructure are required to meet customer needs in a rapidly changing marketplace, heavily influenced by legislation, customer needs, IT and systems developments (Zafar, 2017).

The 10 companies featured in this analysis are developing new powertrain solutions to match the intensifying legislative requirements, reduced emission tolerances and carbon footprint demands.

The analysis provides information about the companies with regard to:

- the number of trucks sold in 2018 and the relative size of the companies;
- alternative fuel source developments other than traditionally fuelled engines.

The top 10 manufacturers of commercial vehicles in the world are, at the time of publication (2020):

1 Daimler Truck AG: including Mercedes-Benz, Freightliner and Mitsubishi-Fuso: 415, 018.
2 Tata Motors: 388,396.
3 Dongfeng Motors: 369,100.
4 Navistar: 313,600.
5 Volvo (including Renault): 300,000.
6 Hino Trucks: 171,800.
7 PACCAR Inc (including DAF): 158,900.
8 Iveco: 134,300.
9 MAN: 83,200.
10 Scania: 81,350.

Figures given are 2018 output.

The challenges facing future manufacturers include what business models will be adopted for alternatively fuelled vehicles, and what is the likely impact of the disruption that will be unleashed on established supply chains and extended enterprises.

Daimler Truck AG (formerly Mercedes-Benz Truck and Bus including Freightliner, Mitsubishi FUSO and Western Star)

Daimler AG established a new corporate structure in November 2019. Daimler Truck AG is now a new global organization and a new branch of the parent company is responsible for e-mobility products. The E-Mobility Group (EMG) will focus across all brands and divisions, define the strategy for electric components and complete electric vehicles, and develop a standardized, global electric architecture similar to Daimler Truck's global platform strategy for conventional engines and drive components. EMG has been set up globally with employees working in various locations throughout the company's worldwide development network (Daimler Trucks, 2018).

MERCEDES-BENZ

Mercedes-Benz (MB) and the 'three-pointed star' have worldwide recognition through their passenger car and van products. Mercedes-Benz offer light, medium and heavy trucks and are widely marketed throughout Europe.

MB's first-announced heavy commercial zero-emission vehicles (ZEVs) utilize battery technology rather than alternative fuels. MB's parent company Daimler Trucks created an e-mobility division in 2018 to focus on electric trucks (Daimler Trucks, 2018).

At the International Automotive Exhibition in 2016 in Hanover, Germany (IAA 2016), Mercedes-Benz became the first OEM in the world to exhibit a heavy-duty electric truck.

An eActros model was launched in 2018, focused on the short-haul distribution market. Typical operations are radial distribution such as food, fuel, brewery, building and industrial products – normally these duties would be performed by diesel-powered vehicles. The range goal for eActros is 200 kilometres (125 miles) with a GVW range of 18–25 tonnes. The chassis frame of the conventional diesel Actros is configured to allow for an electric battery drivetrain (Mercedes-Benz, nd).

FREIGHTLINER AND WESTERN STAR

Freightliner Trucks and Western Star are Daimler Trucks brands for the United States. Freightliner produce trucks in the US weight Class 5 (medium trucks) to Class 8 (tractor trailer articulated units) to meet a broad range of commercial vehicle applications. Western Star of Canada produce heavy trucks for long-haul and specialized applications.

FIGURE 8.2 Mercedes-Benz eActros

SOURCE Daimler Trucks, 2018

Freightliner and Western Star are members of Daimler Trucks North America (DTNA). In 1981, Daimler-Benz AG purchased Freightliner from Consolidated Freightways. In the next decade, vehicle sales more than doubled. With its vast technological resources, Daimler-Benz helped Freightliner reach the top of the North American heavy-duty truck market by 1992. In 2008 Freightliner LLC became Daimler Trucks North America but still markets the Freightliner brand (Daimler Trucks North America, nd).

Martin Daum, a member of the Daimler Board of Management for Trucks & Buses, said in 2018:

> We aim to take the leading role in the field of electric-powered trucks and buses. We started working on electric trucks at an early stage and aspire to set the benchmark in every relevant segment of this industry. By establishing our new global E-Mobility Group we can maximize the effectiveness of our investments in this strategic key technology. This will enable us to provide our customers with the best solutions in battery systems, charging systems or energy management.

Daimler Trucks announced investments of more than €2.5 billion in research and development in 2018 and 2019, more than €500 million of which is set for electrification, connectivity and automation (Daimler Trucks, 2018).

In August 2019 at a US investor and media event named 'Capital Market & Technology Days', Daimler Trucks presented two new, fully

FIGURE 8.3   Freightliner eCascadia and eM2

SOURCE Daimler Trucks, 2018

electric trucks by its US subsidiary Freightliner, built in Portland, Oregon: the eCascadia, a heavy-duty electric truck for long-distance operations (>15 tonne GVW) and a fully-electric variant of the Freightliner eM2 106 to cover the medium segment (9–12 tonne GVW).

The 'drive axle' is a ZF AVE 130 proven in hybrid low-floor buses. Eleven battery packs are distributed around the floor frame and two electric motors are located in the rear axle wheel hubs. Liquid-cooled units develop 125 kW/485 nm torque. Drive performance is designed to deliver on a par with the diesel equivalent, and it has been proven in the EVO Bus.

The 'innovation fleet' of 10 vehicles will be placed with customers in Germany and Switzerland, namely Dascher, Edeka, Hermes, Ludwig Meyer and TBS Rhein Necker.

With the two eFreightliners and the Mercedes-Benz eActros, Daimler Trucks has already established a strong portfolio of fully electric commercial vehicles (Daimler Trucks, 2018).

MITSUBISHI FUSO TRUCK & BUS CORPORATION (MFTBC)
Daimler Trucks also owns Mitsubishi FUSO (MFTBC) based in Japan, which produces light trucks in the 7.5 tonne GVW category.

Daimler Trucks claimed in September 2017 to be the first mainstream manufacturer to make available an electric truck when it launched the FUSO

FIGURE 8.4   FUSO Canter Eco-Hybrid

SOURCE   Daimler Trucks, 2018

eCanter, initially in New York. This was the first opportunity to see the world's first series-produced, all-electric Class 4 truck. The first production models were delivered to customers in the US, Europe and Japan, and MFTBC planned to deliver 500 units of this truck by 2019. Volume production was intended to start in 2019.

The FUSO Eco-Canter aims to provide fleet operators with a zero-emission, low-noise option for inner-city distribution, helping to resolve increasing noise and pollution problems in urban environments. The FUSO eCanter offers a GVW of 7.2 tonnes and has a range of more than 60 miles. The vehicle's electric powertrain contains six 420V Mercedes-Benz lithium-ion battery packs with a total capacity of 82.8 kWh.

Tata Motors

Tata Motors and Indian Oil Corporation are currently carrying out testing on a Tata hydrogen fuel cell bus. A hydrogen fuel cell engine only produces water and heat as a by-product (Singh, 2018).

Trials were announced of this, India's first-ever hydrogen fuel cell-powered bus in March 2018 to understand the efficiency and durability of the new and clean mobility solution in the long run in a better way. The bus

FIGURE 8.5 Tata hydrogen-powered bus

SOURCE Tata Motors

was fuelled at India's first hydrogen dispensing facility at Indian Oils' R&D Centre (Singh, 2018).

Hydrogen fuel cell (HFCV) technology is about three times more efficient than a traditional combustion engine. A fuel cell operates quite like a battery but without having to be charged. The fuel cell generates electricity and the exhaust is water (Singh, 2018).

Tata Motors haven't publicly declared any development plans for electric commercial vehicles; their focus at present appears to be on the development of electric passenger cars.

Dongfeng Motor Corporation (DFM)

Founded in 1969 and based in Wuhan, Hubei Province, China, the Dongfeng Motor Corporation (DFM) is one of China's largest auto groups, with total assets of RMB 240.2 billion (£246 billion) and 176,000 employees. DFM notes:

> DFM's main business covers the full range of commercial vehicles, passenger vehicles, new-energy vehicles, engines, auto parts and components, and other auto-related business, with the business scale exceeding 3.8 million units – including c.370,000 commercial vehicles per annum (Dongfeng Motor Corporation, nd).

FIGURE 8.6 Donfeng electric truck

SOURCE DFM image bank

China is the world's largest truck market, and is leading the charge towards electric mobility in electric passenger cars.

DFM currently offer three pure electric cargo trucks in China from GVW 2280 kg to 7100 kg (Dongfeng Motor Corporation, nd).

Navistar

Navistar is a leading manufacturer of commercial trucks, buses, defence vehicles and engines based in Lisle, Illinois, USA. It mainly operates in the United States, marketed under the International brand.

Navistar unveiled a prototype battery-electric version of its medium-duty International MV truck at the 2019 North American Commercial Vehicle Show. A regular production eMV model is slated to come on the market in 2021.

The eMV prototype features its all-electric drive system and a 'highly swooped-down' aerodynamic front end facilitated by the removal of the traditional MV Cummins diesel engine (Kane, 2019).

Inside EVs notes the following about the specifications, range and origins of the eMV (Kane, 2019):

FIGURE 8.7 Navistar eMV prototype BEVHDT Trucking

SOURCE HDT Trucking Info (David Cullen)

The eMV is based on the current production version of the MV Series. The eMV is powered by an electric motor with a peak power of over 474 kW (645 HP). The prototype's continuous power is 300 kW, or more than 400 HP, which is available at all times.

The vehicle was designed to accommodate multiple battery capacity options that range from 107 to 321 kWh. Navistar stated that 'customers operating a truck with a 321 kWh battery in typical pickup and delivery cycles should expect to be able to travel up to 250 miles on a single charge'.

The eMV was developed in part by tapping technology developed by Navistar's strategic partner, Germany-based Traton Group, the parent of Volkswagen Trucks, MAN Trucks, and Scania Trucks.

Volvo Trucks

Volvo Trucks, based in Gothenburg, Sweden, is one of the largest heavy-duty truck brands in the world. More than 95 per cent of the trucks produced are over 16 tonnes. Volvo makes vehicles that are sold and serviced in more than 130 countries all over the world. Volvo Group also owns Volvo Trucks and Renault Trucks.

FIGURE 8.8 Volvo EV

SOURCE Volvo Trucks

Volvo has invested in the electric vehicle concept. In spring 2018 Volvo Trucks introduced two all-electric truck models – the Volvo FL Electric and Volvo FE Electric. Both trucks are primarily intended for transport operations in urban conditions, such as distribution and refuse collection.

The Volvo FL Electric is designed for operating weights up to 16 tonnes GVW. The Volvo FE Electric is designed for heavier operations, with gross weights of up to 27 tonnes. The Volvo FL Electric is equipped with an electric motor with a maximum power rating of 130 kW. The Volvo FE Electric has dual electric motors and has a maximum power rating of 370 kW and continuous power output of 260 kW.

RENAULT TRUCKS

Renault Trucks is a French commercial truck and military vehicle manufacturer with corporate headquarters at Saint-Priest near Lyon. Originally part of Renault, it has been owned by the Volvo Group, a Swedish multinational manufacturing company, since 2001.

Renault have invested in both hybrid and electric versions of commercial vehicles. Recently a narrow cab Range D 16 tonne and a 26 tonne 6x2

FIGURE 8.9 Renault BEV

SOURCE Renault image bank

version with a wide cab have made an appearance. Electric motors range from 57–300 kW.

The range Renault has focused on is up to 200 km; their research has indicated almost 80 per cent of travel is between 100 km and 150 km round trip in and out of dedicated depots, where recharging infrastructure is available.

Like Scania, MAN and Mercedes, Renault has invested in 'real-world' trials with retail distribution operations including luxury goods vendor Guerlain, delivering overnight to various city centre stores and Delanchy, a seafood wholesaler operating in Lyon, France.

Results from recent trials are to prove cost comparison with diesel equivalents.

RENAULT KANGOO VAN JOINT VENTURE WITH NISSAN AND SEPARATE FROM THE RENAULT TRUCK DIVISION

- Key features: full electric powertrain, zero emissions,106-mile range.
- The Kangoo ZE is quite simply the brand's established small van with its internal combustion drivetrain taken out and replaced by an electric

motor of 44 kW – equating to 60 bhp. In terms of space, the buyer choosing a Kangoo ZE loses nothing over the diesel version – it offers exactly the same 3–3.5 cubic metre carrying capacity and 650 kg payload, with the motor's battery pack not eating into any of the load space.

- The ZE will also be available in two Maxi crew van versions, one a five-seater, and the other a basic van.

- The Kangoo ZE is officially capable of 81 mph, which of course is enough for UK roads, and has a 0–62 mph time of 20.3 seconds, six or more seconds slower than its traditionally engined siblings.

- One display on the dash commands attention throughout the drive – the range. Renault quotes an official range of 106 miles for the Kangoo, regarded as sufficient for a day's work for many companies using such vehicles.

- This will be one of two vital factors for firms deciding whether to join the electric revolution. Recharging the ZE from empty will take six to eight hours, and for the next year at least there won't be a fast-charge option.

- Plugging into a three-pin socket is not advised either (quite apart from the 11 hours or more it will take this way) – you'll need a specific socket, with British Gas being Renault's preferred installation partner.

FIGURE 8.10 Full electric version of Renault's established van

SOURCE Renault image bank

Hino Motors Limited

Hino Motors, commonly known as simply Hino, is a Japanese manufacturer of commercial vehicles and diesel engines, headquartered in Hino-shi, Tokyo, Japan. Hino represents the Toyota Group in the market for medium and heavy-duty diesel trucks in Asia.

Unlike many of the other truck manufacturers, Hino has invested in plug-in hybrid (PHEV) technology.

Hino and Volkswagen have agreed to deepen collaboration on electric trucks, trying to catch up with rivals like Daimler in technology, gaining traction among logistics companies for urban transportation (Nikkei Asia Review, 2018).

The arrangement between truck maker Hino and the Volkswagen truck and bus unit Traton Group represents the first initiative under a broader partnership agreed between the units (Nikkei Asia Review, 2018).

Hino has observed clearly that electric vehicles are important to logistics operators who wish to reduce their carbon footprint, and Hino also plans to release electric trucks in 2020. It would appear at this stage that these products are specifically aimed at the Asian markets including Australia and Singapore. Hino has improved the designs of its 'Diesel Electric', clutches, accelerator pedals and more to improve sustainability (Hino, nd).

FIGURE 8.11 Hino 300 Hybrid truck

SOURCE Hino global website

In addition to this, all Hino hybrid 300 series trucks use a nickel-metal hydride (NiMH) battery for their hybrid driveline systems. The majority of hybrid vehicles in the world today use NiMH batteries, and worldwide the same Toyota Group battery technology has been used in over 3 million hybrid vehicles.

Hino's nickel-metal hydride battery has the advantages of:

- proven reliability, safety and durability, even in high-current applications;
- resilience to overcharging;
- low cost;
- long life and maintenance-free operation.

PACCAR Inc (including Kenworth Truck Co, Peterbilt Motors Co and DAF Truck)

PACCAR is a global transportation technology company manufacturing light, medium and heavy-duty trucks and has its head office located in Bellevue, Washington, USA. Kenworth, Peterbilt and DAF brands are owned and marketed by PACCAR. PACCAR also designs and manufactures advanced diesel engines, provides financial services, information technology, and distributes truck parts related to its principal business (PACCAR, nd).

PACCAR has invested in battery electric vehicle (BEV) and hydrogen fuel cell vehicle (HFCV) technologies. It exhibited three zero-emission vehicles at the CES 2019 show in Las Vegas, Nevada – a battery-electric Peterbilt Model 579EV, a battery-electric Peterbilt Model 220EV, and a hydrogen fuel cell electric Kenworth T680 developed in collaboration with Toyota. PACCAR notes, 'These trucks were designed for a range of customer applications, including over-the-road goods transportation, port operations and urban distribution' (PACCAR, nd).

Presenting at the American Truck Dealers show in January 2019, PACCAR Inc CEO Ron Armstrong said the trucking industry is moving towards ever-cleaner and more energy-efficient vehicles and will adopt increasingly advanced automated driving technology to assist drivers (Clevinger, 2019).

'The future of the industry is very dynamic, with technology accelerating the pace of change,' Armstrong told an audience of truck dealers from across the country. 'Now more than ever, we need to innovate to stay relevant' (Clevinger, 2019).

DAF TRUCKS

DAF Trucks NV is a transportation technology company and one of the main commercial vehicle manufacturers in Europe. DAF is a wholly owned subsidiary of PACCAR Inc. PACCAR also designs and manufactures advanced diesel engines, provides financial services and information technology and distributes truck parts for its product aftermarket needs.

DAF's initial offerings in the zero-emission vehicle (ZEV) market are an LF & CF hybrid and a battery electric vehicle (BEV). In 2020 DAF is testing products in Belgium, Germany and the Netherlands, and in 2019, in partnership with Dutch supermarket Jumbo, it introduced a full BEV CF 4x2. The vehicle has a 170 kW/h battery pack and 210 kW electric motor giving a range of 100 km at 40 tonnes, and a 90-minute recharge capability.

CNH Industrial (formerly Case New Holland)

CNH Industrial is a global leader in the capital goods sector that, through its various businesses, designs, produces and sells agricultural and construction equipment, trucks, commercial vehicles, buses and speciality vehicles, in addition to a broad portfolio of powertrain applications. Present in all major markets worldwide, CNH Industrial is focused on expanding its

FIGURE 8.12 DAF CF Electric

SOURCE DAF image bank

presence in high-growth markets, including through joint ventures. It employs more than 64,000 people in 66 manufacturing plants and 54 research and development centres in 180 countries.

CNH International has 12 principal brands including Iveco and Magirus, from commercial vehicles to agricultural tractors and combines to trucks and buses, as well as powertrain solutions for on-road and off-road and marine vehicles.

IVECO

Industrial Vehicles Corporation (IVECO) is an Italian transportation manufacturer based in Turin, Italy. IVECO designs and builds light, medium and heavy commercial vehicles, with a global manufacturing output of around 150,000 commercial vehicles per year.

Iveco has concentrated its efforts, up to 2020, primarily on its van range; the IVECO Daily in electric form has been available for a few years. Iveco has for many years offered several power sources for its vans and trucks and has recently updated both its Daily Electric and Natural Power CNG vans. Daily Electric can be provided for both a 3.5-tonne or a 5.0-tonne chassis.

FIGURE 8.13 IVECO Daily

SOURCE Iveco image bank

The following information is taken from *Van Fleet World* (Gilkes, 2017):

- Unlike most competitors Iveco continues to use a sodium nickel chloride battery, which it claims is less affected by temperature and weather conditions, is 100 per cent recyclable and offers a high 110Wh/kg energy density.
- Depending on operating weight and chassis length, the vans can be equipped with one, two or three battery packs, capable of delivering 44 miles, 95 miles or 125 miles of range respectively.
- The big problem for the Daily Electric is that of cost. A single battery van costs *c*.£60,000, a two battery variant is *c*.£80,000 and the three-battery version is *c*.£100,000.

In 2020 the UK Government was offering a plug-in grant of up to 20 per cent, to a maximum of £8,000, on a 3.5-tonne vehicle. The grant increases to a maximum of £20,000 for vehicles above 3.5 tonnes GVW (UK Government, 2020).

The UK Government is also looking at the option of raising the GVW of an alternatively fuelled van from 3.5 to 4.25 tonnes for a car licence holder, which would make the van more viable as that would add 350–400kg of payload.

In 2017 a predicted £4,000 a year saving on diesel could be achieved with a further £3,000 saving potential through not having to pay the London Congestion Charge. Payback for the IVECO is estimated to be six years and after that the vehicle would be cost neutral (Gilkes, 2017).

Volkswagen Group AG and Traton SE

The VW Group comprises 12 brands from seven European countries: Volkswagen Passenger Cars, Audi, SEAT, ŠKODA, Bentley, Bugatti, Lamborghini, Porsche, Ducati, Volkswagen Commercial Vehicles, Scania and MAN. Scania and MAN are brands of Traton SE.

Traton SE is a subsidiary of Volkswagen AG and a leading commercial vehicle manufacturer worldwide with its brands MAN, Scania and Volkswagen Caminhões e Ônibus, and RIO. In 2018, Traton group's brands sold around 233,000 vehicles in total.

MAN Truck and Bus

MAN Truck and Bus is one of Europe's leading commercial vehicle manufacturers and transport solution providers, with an annual revenue of some €13.4 billion (in 2019). The company's product portfolio includes vans, trucks, buses/coaches and diesel and gas engines along with services related to passenger and cargo transport.

At the September 2018 Hanover IAA show the Cite Refuge Collection Vehicle was shown – a battery electric vehicle (BEV) featuring a low-entry cab. In addition, MAN is involved with various joint venture trials in Austria with a logistics consortium (Council for Sustainable Logistics) involving a number of major haulage and logistics providers and the University for Natural Sciences in Vienna.

Vehicle details are as follows (Porsche Newsroom, 2018):

- The 'pilot vehicle' is built for evaluation and has a 6x2 chassis with a refrigerated container and is in operation with several supermarket clients.

- A TGS 4x2 18 tonne semi-trailer 'demonstrator unit', fitted with 250 kW electric motor providing drive to the rear axle is also being piloted. A dashboard display keeps the driver abreast of battery charging levels. Truck batteries are arranged under the driver's cab and above the front axle where a diesel engine would normally be located.

- In 2018, MAN also trialled a 32-tonne eTGM with Porsche manufacturing. The truck operates between the Freiberg am Neckar depot of logistics partner LGI and the Porsche manufacturing centre in Stuttgart-Zuffenhausen.

- The rationale supports the movement of components bound for the production of Porsche's electric SUV the Taycan. The aim is to cut CO_2 emissions by 30 tonnes per annum on the 19 km trip between the two locations, undertaken five times a day.

- The MAN eTGM is a 32-tonne 18.360 4x2 that has the same payload and kerb weight as the diesel version. The unit is powered by a lithium-ion battery pack with a storage capacity of 149 kWh enabling a range of 130 km. A 45-minute break between deliveries allows for recharging.

- The plan for 2019 is to operate a fleet of 50 eTGMs in the UK and mainland Europe from Q3 2019 and build a database of critical operational information that will guide the forward development of electric truck component configuration and the design of powertrain packs for a variety of journey types.

FIGURE 8.14 MAN Cite

SOURCE MAN image library

Scania

Scania can trace its roots back to 1891 and has been headquartered in Södertälje in southern Sweden near Stockholm since 1912. The company produces around 80,000 trucks and buses per annum. (Scania, nd).

At the 2018 IAA show, Scania also introduced a Euro 6 hybrid truck (PHEV), a P 320 that can be driven electric-only or powered by renewable sources – fatty acid methyl ester (FAME) or hydrotreated vegetable oil (HVO) biofuels (Scania, 2018)

The new hybrid trucks (HEV) are powered by Scania's DC09, an inline five-cylinder engine that can run on HVO or diesel, working in parallel with an electric machine generating 130 kW (177hp) of power and 1,050 nm. 'The lithium-ion rechargeable battery's energy window is set to 7.4 kWh to secure a long battery life. The trucks can be driven in fully electric mode without any support from the combustion engine, thanks to electric auxiliaries for steering and brake air supply' (Scania, 2018).

Scania's HEV was available from November 2018, and the PHEV followed in 2019 (Scania, 2018).

In September 2018, Jesper Brauer, Product Manager, Urban, Scania Trucks said:

> The lithium-ion technology is still the best proven solution available. Just like in our former HEV truck, the HEV/PHEV trucks are primarily utilizing regenerative braking for their charging by capturing kinetic energy. The intention is to drive the truck in auto zero tailpipe emission (ZTE) mode, which means that the electric machine is always used to start moving and at lower speeds, provided that energy is available in the battery. Using the Auto ZTE mode will result in the lowest possible fuel consumption since it will cut the internal combustion engine (ICE) every time that is favourable (Scania, 2018).

FIGURE 8.15 Scania Hybrid

SOURCE Scania image bank

Commercial vehicle industry forecasts

Most of the industry forecasts for the next decade say that most growth in electric commercial vehicles will be from the light commercial vehicle (LCV) sector. This augurs well for Iveco and Renault, who have positioned themselves as early entrants into this space.

However, Ford, VW, MAN and Mercedes are all making significant investments in light sector product and all expect to be into series production by 2020.

The medium and heavy sector, in addition to the bus and coach market, will see developments come later into the second decade of the 21st century.

Current estimates from various well-informed research studies in Europe, the United States and Asia are predicting that by 2030, up to 40 per cent of global commercial vehicle sales will be from the van and LCV sectors.

The medium and heavy sector will probably remain dependent on diesel due to the inability to deliver total cost of ownership (TCO) parity with fossil-fuelled variants and the absence of charging and refuelling infrastructure when looking at hydrogen or other alternative energy sources.

The truck market in the future

The concern about climate change, coupled with environmental regulation, has led to a new level of commitment to increase fuel efficiency and reduce emissions. New engines are being developed to comply with limits on nitrogen oxides (NO_x) and particulates that were set by the US Environmental Protection Agency in 2012. The greatest challenge remains regulatory differences: some regions have tougher limits than others. The use of alternative powertrain technologies – natural gas, hybrid drives or fuel cells – is becoming more prevalent. Persistent air pollution, particularly in major cities, could ultimately lead to a driving ban on heavy trucks. PWC notes, 'One possible solution is to build lighter vehicles; another is to increase interoperability among different-sized trucks: for instance, using mini-containers that can be swapped from heavy to light vehicles' (PWC Strategy&, 2014).

Characteristics of infrastructure, of vehicle ownership, and even of truck drivers are changing, and these trends point to the development of new kinds of trucks to match. PWC suggests:

The long-haul truck is becoming more of a living space for drivers and their families, and so needs to be suitably equipped. As digital technologies take hold, including for medium and heavy-duty trucks, there is a shortage of skilled drivers, with an associated need to provide driver support' (PWC Strategy&, 2014).

The major global trends that shape the business environment are social, technological, economic, environmental and political (STEEP). In turn, STEEP factors have a profound effect on commerce. Although these trends are quite similar across the world, they affect different world regions much more than in others; the road to zero emissions for large commercial vehicles looks different from one country to another. In that context, each industry player will have its own potential road to success. To help craft an effective strategy for your own starting point and chosen destination, five major factors must be considered (PWC Strategy&, 2014):

1 The evolving business environment (global trends).

2 The potential demand for trucks in every country (sales and markets).

3 The needs and preferences of truck owners and operators (customers and products).

4 The operational opportunities (production and manufacturing).

5 Environmental concerns, safety features and internet connection (innovation).

Summary

- There are approximately 2 million trucks sold around the world per annum. The top 10 manufacturers account for 90 per cent of world truck sales. As you saw from the list, most truck manufacturers own a number of brands.

- Most of the industry forecasts for the next decade predict that most growth in electric commercial vehicles will be from the LCV sector.

- However, Ford, VW, MAN and Mercedes are all making significant investments in light sector products and all expect to be into series production by 2020.

- The medium and heavy sector, in addition to the bus and coach market, will see developments come later into the second decade of the 21st century.

- Current estimates are predicting that by 2030 up to 40 per cent of global commercial vehicle sales will be from the van and LCV sectors.

- The medium and heavy sectors will probably remain dependent on diesel due to the inability to deliver TCO parity and the absence of charging and refuelling infrastructure when looking at hydrogen or other alternative energy sources.

References

ACEA (2019) World commercial vehicle production. Retrieved from: https://www.acea.be/statistics/article/world-commercial-vehicle-production (archived at https://perma.cc/58TJ-7BNA)

BP Plc (2019) *BP Statistical Review of World Energy*, BP Plc, London

Clevinger, S (2019) Paccar CEO outlines path toward zero-emission trucks, automated driving, *Transport Topics*. Retrieved from: https://www.ttnews.com/articles/paccar-ceo-outlines-path-toward-zero-emission-trucks-automated-driving (archived at https://perma.cc/3FE3-7QWG)

Commercial Motor (2013) Decade of change in the 1970s European truck manufacturers. Retrieved from: http://archive.commercialmotor.com/article/7th-march-2013/29/el-ecade-of-change-in-the-1970s-european-truck-man (archived at https://perma.cc/74BU-ANX5)

Daimler Trucks (2018) Daimler Trucks sets up global E-Mobility Group and presents two new electric trucks for the U.S. market. Retrieved from: https://media.daimler.com/marsMediaSite/en/instance/ko/Daimler-Trucks-sets-up-global-E-Mobility-Group-and-presents-two-new-electric-trucks-for-the-US-market.xhtml?oid=40507299 (archived at https://perma.cc/ZG33-MRKS)

Daimler Trucks North America (nd) Defined by Innovation. Retrieved from: https://daimler-trucksnorthamerica.com/company/history/ (archived at https://perma.cc/KX7N-H94E)

Dongfeng Motor Corporation (nd) About Us. Retrieved from: http://www.dongfeng-global.com/index.php/aboutus/overview.html (archived at https://perma.cc/7J3Q-YM5R)

Gilkes, D (2017) Road Test: Iveco Daily Electric, *Van Fleet World*. Retrieved from: https://vanfleetworld.co.uk/road-test-iveco-daily-electric/ (archived at https://perma.cc/LCP4-SL2U)

Hino (nd) The Hino Hybrid System. Retrieved from: https://www.hino.com.au/300/hybrid/features/ (archived at https://perma.cc/T2T6-9C5Y)

IEA (2017) *The Future of Trucks*, IEA, Paris

Kane, M (2019) Navistar launches new business for electrification, *Inside EVs*. Retrieved from: https://insideevs.com/news/379726/navistar-launches-new-business-electrification/ (archived at https://perma.cc/L6EA-WMBF)

Mercedes-Benz (nd) Innovation fleet in practical trial. Retrieved from: https://www.mercedes-benz.com/en/vehicles/trucks/eactros-heavy-duty-electric-truck/ (archived at https://perma.cc/C3LK-WL5H)

Nikkei Asia Review (2018) Hino-VW alliance seeks to gain ground on electric trucks. Retrieved from: https://asia.nikkei.com/Business/Business-deals/Hino-VW-alliance-seeks-to-gain-ground-on-electric-trucks (archived at https://perma.cc/GB97-W5DL)

OICA (nd) OICA sales statistics. Retrieved from: http://www.oica.net/category/sales-statistics/ (archived at https://perma.cc/RUY4-5TW5)

PACCAR (nd) Get to know Paccar. Retrieved from: https://www.paccar.com/about-us/get-to-know-paccar/ (archived at https://perma.cc/DW9S-AZCW)

Porsche Newsroom (2018) Porsche uses electric truck. Retrieved from: https://newsroom.porsche.com/en/sustainability/porsche-etruck-man-etgm-fully-electric-zuffenhausen-16611.html (archived at https://perma.cc/P5YT-KRU3)

PWC Strategy& (2014) The truck industry in 2020: How to move in moving markets. Retrieved from: https://www.strategyand.pwc.com/gx/en/insights/2011-2014/truck-industry-2020.html (archived at https://perma.cc/F7BJ-3EBG)

Roland Berger (2018) Trends in the truck & trailer market, Roland Berger, Aachen

Scania (nd) Scania Annual Reports. Retrieved from: https://www.scania.com/group/en/section/investor-relations/financial-reports/annual-reports/ (archived at https://perma.cc/9GSY-7SJE)

Scania (2018) Versatile hybrid trucks for urban applications. Retrieved from: https://www.scania.com/uk/en/home/experience-scania/news-and-events/news/2018/09/hybrid-truck-for-urban.html (archived at https://perma.cc/CB26-7YDU)

Singh, A (2018) India's first-ever hydrogen fuel cell powered bus by Tata Motors is here! Made in India bus emits only water, *Financial Express*. Retrieved from: https://www.financialexpress.com/auto/car-news/tata-motors-indianoil-corporation-flag-off-countrys-first-hydrogen-fuel-cell-powered-bus/1096895/ (archived at https://perma.cc/39JC-22VV)

UK Government (2020) Low-emission vehicles eligible for a plug-in grant. Retrieved from: https://www.gov.uk/plug-in-car-van-grants (archived at https://perma. cc/63QY-PHNG)

Zafar, S (2017)Top 10 truck manufacturing companies in the world, *all4truck.com*. Retrieved from: https://all4truck.com/blog/2017/12/06/top-10-truck-manufacturing-companies/ (archived at https://perma.cc/4PVH-YGWU)

09

'New kids on the block' – new entrants into the EV market space

This chapter will familiarize the reader with:

- The threat of new entrants into the BEV market.
- The future epicentre of the automotive industry.
- BEVs and total cost of ownership (TCO) planning.
- The alternative power sources being used for different commercial vehicle applications.
- Future range efficiency for alternative fuels.
- New supply chain relationships with OEMs.
- Collaborative R&D on future chassis development.

The race to develop alternative power sources to the diesel engine

The electric lightbulb was not created due to improvements in the candle.

OREN HARARI

All the current major truck manufacturers have deep-rooted investments in the 'energy equivalent of the candle' while all wanting desperately to develop an electric lightbulb to allow them to be able to operate in the world's major cities and avoid increasing financial penalties.

In addition to wanting to pursue ethical environment strategies to deal with the challenge of climate change, we are witnessing a greater demand for cleaner vehicles and operators are increasingly aware of the penalties for non-compliance with city regulations rolling out clean air zones.

However, distribution and logistics operators will need to study carefully what current OEMs have to offer.

The main barriers to the early adoption of electric trucks are:

- initial price – electric trucks can cost tens of thousands of dollars more than diesel-engined equivalents;

- scepticism about the reliability of electric truck technology, and uncertainty about the cost and availability of charging systems.

The main issue when selecting future fleet requirements is that of the energy density of batteries and understanding capacity vs size and weight. Recharging time, range and payload issues will feature in decision making going forward.

When fuel savings and maintenance savings over the life of a truck are factored in, even when you disregard the government incentives that most electric truck purchasers get, there is still a good business case to be made.

For many urban distribution operations involving short distances, regular return to depot and access to refuelling/recharging infrastructure, electric vehicles will dominate the future logistics landscape. For long-haul this requires a different set of calculations.

Across the UK, US, Europe and China we are witnessing the emergence of a number of innovative suppliers of low-emission commercial vehicles that are offering more than conventional conversion kits or special vehicle attributes. The main part of this chapter details the 'new kids on the block' and what they have to offer.

UK

Electra commercial vehicles

The Electra business has the support and common ownership of one of the largest fleet management companies in the UK, NRG Fleet Services, headed up by chairman Sid Sadique. NRG support provides answers to customers who want the security of a 24/7 company that totally understands what it takes to keep vehicles in service for contract periods of seven years or more. This is the backbone of the Electra support offering, which includes full maintenance and spare vehicle support, contract hire and leasing, work-shops and mobile engineer support throughout the UK. Furthermore, the customers of NRG are the very same customers who want Electra prod-ucts – city centre operators.

The role of Electra is that of collaborator, and they have successfully arranged with the leading truck manufacturers the supply of 'glider kit' chas-sis units. These chassis platforms are purpose made for Electra by the likes of Daimler, Iveco and others to allow Electra to utilize their bespoke EV technology and deliver vehicles to customers in advance of other companies.

The rapid technology delivery has been a successful collaboration between manufacturers who are busy developing products for the wider market; Electra is a specialist collaborator who, using OEM platforms, has been able to deliver solutions to customers who are wanting to adopt the new technology quickly.

NRG is Electra's specialist fleet management partner, and through NRG Electra has a national network to support its products (Electra Commercial Vehicles, 2020)

It also positions Electra as one of the few potential third-party partners with a 360-degree view of the commercial vehicle operational space.

The rationale for Electra becoming a leading provider of EV services can be summarized as follows:

- The road transport industry is currently being served by small start-ups, grant-hungry, experimental and technology showcase companies.
- Lack of real logistics and distribution industry experience to support 24/7 transportation sector.
- Truck manufacturers not providing access to systems and factory engineering.
- Truck manufacturers are looking for technology partners and suppliers to provide EV support.
- EV technology would traditionally upscale from vans and cars over a prolonged period.
- Demand is outstripping supply now!
- Electra can deliver to the industry now.

Electra has successfully undertaken the conversion of a Mercedes-Benz Econic refuse truck. This is a three-axle 26-tonne product with a compactor body configuration and bin lift.

FIGURE 9.1 Electra refuse vehicle

SOURCE Electra Commercial Vehicles, 2020

KEY FEATURES OF THE ELECTRA RCV – REFUSE CITY VEHICLE

- Battery size 200 kWh.
- Drive motor max power 350 hp peak.
- Drive motor torque 3400 Nm peak.
- Electricity regeneration system – 12–16 per cent expected on mixed city cycle.
- 'Geesink' 22 m body with electric power take-off (PTO).
- 'Terberg Omnidel' split bin lift.
- Expected use is 100–150 km per shift over nine hours.
- 400 kg payload loss compared to a diesel-powered truck operated at 26 tonne GVW.
- 1,000 kg weight dispensation available on two- and three-axle-trucks.

ELECTRA HAS PRODUCED A TOTAL COST OF OWNERSHIP (TCO) MODEL

- The heavier the fuel use and the longer daily use, the more the EV case stacks up.
- Fossil fuels are going to remain trending upwards in price.

- Carbon reduction pressure will remain through punitive legislation and taxation.
- Clean air requirements will be placed into major towns and cities across the world.
- Alternative power sources such as gas and hydrogen have limited supply infrastructure.
- Electric power is readily available and accessible at reasonable cost.

ELECTRA – OPERATIONAL 'COST PER DAY' STUDY

In six locations Electra analysed the operation of the Electra RCV under a variety of conditions, mileage and bin lift movements. The average cost per day of power/energy required ranged from £13 to £18, which compared favourably to the diesel equivalent cost per day of around £100 (Figure 9.2).

The initial project undertaken was to provide an in-depth study of the critical operational requirement to determine the exact energy needs of an electrified version. This would necessitate detailed analysis of route planning, journey times, climatic and road conditions, and driver behaviour and equipment usage in order that a direct comparison with its diesel equivalent could be assessed.

The Electra team have undertaken a detailed total cost of ownership (TCO) study to illustrate the cost-per-mile comparison and the energy

FIGURE 9.2 Electra RCV operating costs in various locations

	Averages per day					
	Leeds	Teesside	Manchester	Sheffield	Glasgow (trade)	London
Hours on shift	6.75	9	7.17	7	6.31	7.31
Tonnage collected	19.65	18	15.99	21	6.53	8.16
Containers lifted	907	1158	1100	1055	392	1138
Mileage	80	76	66	55	58	35
Battery utilization kW	181	181	140	161	136	134
Battery capacity used	91%	91%	70%	81%	68%	67%
Power cost	£ 18.10	£ 18.13	£ 14.00	£ 16.10	£ 13.60	£ 13.44

SOURCE Electra Commercial Vehicles, 2020

requirement necessary for determining battery size and therefore the weight and payload implications for the EV refuse truck.

They estimate that for a 'refuse city truck' it will see 0.9 miles per kWh as the basis for calculating battery specification to support the range requirement for this type of operation. They have established a very competitive cost per day for the operator of refuse trucks. They comply with all future 'clean air or low- to zero-emission zone' requirements, will be quiet, and most of all will offer tremendous cost reduction in terms of fuel management and maintenance costs over the term of engagement.

Electra are at this point in time probably the UK's best-positioned new entrant into the electric medium and heavy truck product development space. They possess not only the engineering credentials to develop effective OEM partnerships but also the operational and commercial expertise to manage fleets in operation and provide a full-service support programme including energy charging, payment and TCO planning and management.

They are definitely 'one to watch' in the race to become a leading EV producer or Tier 1 supplier to major OEMS.

Arrival

Arrival is a Russian-backed electric vehicle manufacturer with capacity to make a truck in four hours and build 50,000 units per year from a new plant in Banbury, Oxfordshire.

Arrival controls 80 per cent of component requirements through patents on motors, inverters, battery packs and body assemblies, and will sell initial

FIGURE 9.3 Arrival EV

SOURCE Arrival image bank

product for same cost as their diesel equivalent. It will also aim to become a major Tier 1 supplier to other manufacturers.

The company currently employs around 300 staff, with 150 focused on software development. Fifty per cent of the software engineering expertise resides in Russia and hails from the telephony industry, which has deep-rooted expertise in networks and the increasing use of AI software to link products and services to distributed communities providing a whole range of digital added-value services to both Arrival and their extended enterprise relationships. Arrival will be a 'one to watch' future Tier 1 supplier to existing truck OEMs.

In January 2020 Hyundai and Kia Motors announced a £75 million investment into Arrival. *Business & Innovation Magazine* writes:

> This investment marks the start of a partnership to jointly accelerate the adoption of commercial electric vehicles globally. Hyundai and Kia will leverage key Arrival technologies to help achieve their recently announced goal to develop mobility services and electrify their vehicle fleets (Business & Innovation Magazine, 2020).

Paneltex

In 2007, Paneltex, based in Hull, Yorkshire, began a project to design bodywork and integration systems to develop an electric truck in preparation for the eventual shift to alternatively fuelled vehicles.

At the time, however, there was no viable technology available to meet the requirements of the 5–11-tonne GVW truck range. So, Paneltex built their own pilot vehicle and a successful product emerged from a direct cooperation with Isuzu.

They have since spent years refining and improving the concept and the design. Over this time, there have been pilot and demonstration vehicles operating in customer fleets in numerous locations nationwide.

The latest range of Paneltex electric vehicles is based on an Isuzu chassis cab and currently offers a 7.5 tonne GVW, with future development projects planned at higher and lower weight ranges (Paneltex, nd).

Highlights include a range of up to 240 km, zero tailpipe emissions and low pence-per-mile running costs. These vehicles offer a real alternative to similar traditional diesel engine-powered vehicles (Paneltex, nd).

FIGURE 9.4 Paneltex Isuzu EV

SOURCE Paneltex, 2020

Tevva

Tevva is a battery truck specialist. Based in Chelmsford, Essex, their technology capabilities extend to battery system development, telematics, power electronics, software, range extension and platform integration (Tevva, nd).

Tevva has a broad offer including:

- Being both an EV manufacturer and industrial manufacturer of battery packs – this joint expertise has enabled them to develop a bespoke EV battery and battery management solution designed with end of life in mind.

- The ability to offer a 'customer-centric' battery solution. The battery is one of the most expensive inputs to the EV, so the amount of energy stored needs to be right-size and the optimization of that power is key.

- Battery systems that are designed, engineered and manufactured in-house. Tevva batteries have been conceived and developed from the outset for commercial vehicles (Tevva, nd).

In 2020, Tevva can quote a seven-year lease including repair and maintenance for a 10-tonne rigid at £1,900 per month, which compares favourably to £1,450 per month for a diesel equivalent and saves not only a congestion charge in ULEZ clean air zones but also £600 per month in fuel costs.

FIGURE 9.5 Tevva

SOURCE Tevva, 2020

In 2018, Tevva secured a £10 million investment from India via Bharat Forge – an automotive ancillary manufacturer – and will focus its future development on long-term safety, long-term durability and, critically, cost (Hindu Business Line, 2018).

Tevva's electrical and mechanical engineering teams have combined to deliver class-leading battery packs (Tevva, nd).

The four core technologies of Tevva are:

1 Tevva Power™

2 Tevva Drive™

3 Tevva Link™

4 Tevva ReX™ (optional) (Tevva, nd)

Europe

EMOSS, Netherlands

EMOSS is a Dutch specialist converter and manufacturer of vans and trucks, and a future Tier 1 supplier of all battery pack, motor and chassis

FIGURE 9.6 EMOSS EV based on DAF chassis

SOURCE EMOSS web image bank

development. EMOSS is focused on becoming an 'Electric Mobility One Stop Shop'.

They started in 1998 in the agricultural equipment sector but moved into small-scale development of electric municipal vehicles. Their experience in this field led them to become engaged in technology developments used in the original Tesla sports car.

EMOSS is currently focused on the development of electric drivetrain kits and power packs for trucks and passenger vehicles from 7–7.5 tonnes. Astra Vehicle Technologies in Ellesmere Port in the North-West of England is its installation partner.

EMOSS's most significant sector in the short term to be developed is the refuse truck market, as most business opportunities are reliant on meeting strict environmental and in many cases zero-emission targets to be considered as a purchasing option for councils and airport operations.

Also, EMOSS is collaborating with Calor Gas on bottle distribution and has calculated TCO comparison figures for diesel vs BEV by quoting cost per 100 km as around €44 for diesel and €5 for electric (EMOSS, 2020).

EMOSS is very clear in its business statements regarding:

- The cost of its products. In many cases the additional cost for an electric drivetrain can be anywhere from £60,000 to £275,000 over the cost of the base product.

- Cooperation with DAF and MAN on 18-tonne rigid units.

The initial purchase cost of an EMOSS EV needs to be understood. An equivalent ICE-powered truck is around €70,000 whereas the EMOSS truck is around €150,000. Payback will be achieved through the reduced TCO (EMOSS, 2020).

Like Arrival in UK, EMOSS is definitely a one-to-watch Tier 1 supplier of the future.

United States

Tesla Motor Corporation: truck division and Yandell Truckaway

Since 1945 Yandell Truckaway has been serving the Northern California wine industry. Yandell prided themselves by staying at the forefront of technology, making operations more efficient and environmentally friendly. The inclusion of a Tesla Semi truck into the fleet illustrates their commitment to being a leader not a follower in the race to succeed in supporting the transition to zero-emission transport. Tesla has designed its truck to be equipped with four Tesla Model 3-derived electric motors, which allow the heavy-duty unit to accelerate from 0–60 mph in five seconds flat while not carrying a trailer. The Tesla Semi was initially announced for production in 2019, though this date has been adjusted for 2020. One of the reasons for the delay was hinted as the development of the battery electric powertrain capacity being able to deliver a 600-mile range (Teslarati, 2019).

Yandell's future experience with zero-emission transport will depend very much on the successful implementation and access to charging infrastructure. Yandell plan to invest in a dedicated building equipped with solar panels to provide the power necessary for the charging infrastructure. The charging infrastructure will be accessed by its electric material handling equipment too.

Nikola Trucks

Based in Phoenix, Arizona, Nikola trucks is a US manufacturer of vans and Class 8 trucks based on zero-emission hydrogen cell powertrain, an innovative fuel supply strategy with a Norwegian energy company, and a nationwide maintenance agreement with Ryder Trucks USA.

Nikola will sell direct to all end users and offer free fuel for 1,000,000 miles. In conjunction with an energy partner they will own and operate 350 hydrogen fuel stations nationwide (Lambert, 2016).

FIGURE 9.7 Tesla Semi – artist's impression of Class 8 18-wheeler

SOURCE Tesla image bank

FIGURE 9.8 Tesla Semi fleet operated by Yandell Truckaway 2019

SOURCE Teslarati, 2019

- Hydrogen fuel cell technology is in its infancy for long-distance heavy truck operations, primarily due to not only the absence of refuelling infrastructure but also the price of hydrogen, which is currently around $15 per kilogram and needs to be below $3 per kilogram to be competitive with existing diesel-based TCO levels.

- Hydrogen fuel cell will be the superior zero-carbon energy source, but cost and availability will be a critical barrier to it becoming a mainstream alternative energy source in the short term.

Rivian and Amazon

Rivian is an American automaker and automotive technology company. Founded in 2009, the company develops vehicles, products and services related to sustainable transportation.

The company has facilities in Plymouth, Michigan; San Jose, California; Irvine, California; Normal, Illinois; and the United Kingdom. In 2017, Rivian announced it was building an electric sport utility vehicle and pickup truck on a platform that executives claim can be modified for future vehicles or adapted by other companies.

In February 2019, Rivian announced that it will be receiving a $700 million investment from Amazon, just as the start-up finished launching its all-electric R1T pickup truck and R1S SUV. Amazon plans to buy 100,000 vehicles from Rivian over the next decade.

In April 2019 the company announced that Ford will also be investing $500 million in a partnership that would develop an all-new battery pack,

FIGURE 9.9   Nikola Class 8 tractor unit

SOURCE Nikola Motor Company, 2020

FIGURE 9.10 Rivian R1T pickup truck

SOURCE Rivian image bank

which in turn would power Ford's future electric car or cars, for that matter.

Amazon also hopes that by placing such a hefty order, it will stimulate other companies as well as similarly minded start-ups such as Rivian to contribute to the carbon emission-cutting endeavour.

At this point, though, little is known about Rivian's all-electric delivery trucks. What we do know, however, is that for its utilitarian R1T pickup truck, Rivian offers three battery packs: 105 kWh, 135 kWh, and 180 kWh. We reckon the 135 kWh one, as well as the largest, 180 kWh battery, are more suited to the needs of an all-electric delivery truck.

The maximum range on a single full charge ranges from 230 miles to 300 miles and to 400 miles. Although that's less relevant for a delivery truck, Rivian's R1T can reach a top speed of 125 mph and can hit 60 mph from a standstill in anything between three seconds and 4.9 seconds – again, that depends on the specified battery pack.

Asia

Panasonic, South Korea

Battery research has seen a big shift in recent years. At one time, nearly half of the presentations at the Battery Symposium in Japan were about fuel cells and li-ion battery cathode materials. But since 2012, these topics have been supplanted by presentations about three alternative platforms to lithium-ion:

- lithium-air;
- solid-state;
- non-lithium batteries.

While Panasonic has been considered one of the world's leading suppliers of lithium-ion batteries it has not ignored the issues of range and safety that remain critical factors to the success of EV adoption rates.

According to Panasonic's President Kazuhiro Tsuga there remains a trade-off between energy density and safety. While it is possible to improve current energy density levels by 20–30 per cent, solid-state technology has

FIGURE 9.11 Panasonic Lithium-ion battery factory, Dalian, China

SOURCE Panasonic press release

the potential to achieve the improvements that will see better range, safer product (ie less prone to combustion), and lighter, cheaper batteries. It may be another five years until it is available but Toyota, the world's biggest car manufacturer, is now focusing its attention on solid-state developments.

Achieving a product capable of generating 800 to 1,000 watt-hours per litre is the goal to support delivery of a range of 500 km on a single charge. Currently many battery engineering experts believe that lithium-ion is now close to the limits of the energy density capacity and will not see much improvement beyond 2020. So, in the next 5–10 years (2020–2030) the potential of solid-state technology as a competitor to lithium-ion is a very real possibility.

What is of interest in these discussions about the limits of current lithium-ion battery technology and the potential of solid-state alternatives is that the man credited with the invention of lithium-ion batteries, John Goodenough, a renowned professor at Austin Texas University who was awarded the Nobel Prize for chemistry in 2019, is also the current champion of solid-state battery developments.

The current reliance on lithium-ion batteries has some downsides in that the liquid electrolyte is considered a potential fire hazard and prone to combustion. This is due to the existence of a factor known as a dendrite, which essentially is small thread-like particles of lithium that grow inside the battery cell over time in a way that they can short-circuit the battery by piercing the cathode. Both Tesla cars and Samsung phones have made the front pages of newspapers recording such incidents.

Currently a number of emerging battery manufacturers have been working on this problem and developing new solid-state battery options that solve this issue by incorporating metals such as zinc and nickel, which are less volatile and plentifully available in US, China, Australia and Peru.

The development of solid-state battery technology will be a key factor in the future development of low-carbon and zero-carbon transportation. Developments of this nature are being pursued primarily to reduce the world's dependence on cobalt, which is currently essential in lithium-ion battery manufacture but is sourced from many of the most unstable and corrupt regions of the world and in conditions that do not contribute to an ethical and sustainable supply chain (Faraday Institution, nd).

VW, BMW, Toyota, Honda, Nissan and Hyundai are all currently exploring partnerships with various battery technology specialists with the aim of introducing solid-state battery platforms by mid-2025.

BYD Motors, China

Founded in 1995 as a pioneer in battery technology, BYD's stated mission is to change the world by creating a complete, clean energy ecosystem that reduces the world's reliance on petroleum. BYD's innovative products are leaders in multiple sectors, including battery-electric cars, buses, medium and heavy-duty trucks and forklifts, the SkyRail monorail system, solar power generation and energy storage systems, and consumer electronics (BYD USA, nd).

BYD North America's headquarters is located in downtown Los Angeles, with a 556,000-square-foot bus manufacturing facility in Lancaster, California. BYD employs over 800 workers in the United States (BYD USA, nd).

- BYD has ranked first in global EV sales for four consecutive years (2015–2018), and its new energy vehicle footprint can be found in more than 300 cities across over 50 countries and regions around the world. In 2018, BYD sold more than 247,800 new energy vehicles worldwide and currently has more than 50,000 pure electric buses and coaches in service around the world. BYD employs over 31,000 engineers globally, constantly innovating in order to make the world a better place.

- At the heart of BYD's technology is its batteries. One of the largest rechargeable battery manufacturers in the world, BYD develops batteries for a broad range of applications from cell phones and laptops to large-scale, grid-connected energy storage systems. BYD's non-toxic iron-phosphate battery chemistry makes it the safest choice available on the market today.

- BYD is listed on the Hong Kong and Shenzhen Stock Exchanges. Warren Buffett's Berkshire Hathaway is the largest single shareholder at 8.25 per cent.

FIGURE 9.12 BYD 'Pure Electric Vehicle'

SOURCE BYD Images

The development of collaborative partnerships with established OEMs

Electra

The Electra team effectively wrote the book on essential requirements to work with an established OEM. At the start of their project with Mercedes-Benz they made a significant breakthrough with the negotiation for a donor 'glider kit' unit to enable a much faster and commercially viable prototype unit to be developed.

They agreed, in a confidential NDA, how they would have access to vehicle build data and connectivity via the Mercedes-Benz CANBUS platform and ultimately developed a relationship that would enable a factory-coded product to be ordered and the delivery of a complete converted unit in five days.

Electra have also become the approved outsourcing partner for critical components as part of the battery powertrain package:

- drive motor;
- inverters;
- enclosed battery package;
- 'Battery Passport programme' to support recyclability.

The battery cell unit is encased in a robust steel box that is safely secured to the main chassis by a bracket system that is incorporated into the chassis production at the OEM production plant. This again demonstrates the effort put into developing the relationship with the OEM, and has delivered valuable time and commercial advantage to both Electra and its customers.

Electra have successfully engaged with several major OEMs including Mercedes-Benz, Iveco, DAF and Dennis to develop low-entry refuse product, road gritters and other municipal product, and in the process have not only focused on managing the key relationships with OEM engineering and design officers but also made significant progress on the ethical sourcing of key electric powertrain components.

Electra will also be an effective disruptor in this market due to its recycling credentials. A unique feature of the Electra product is the availability of the Battery Passport concept, which has been developed to capture the unique DNA of every individual battery cell and will be a valuable tool for not only predicting future vehicle value but also the usability of batteries at the end of term for the initial vehicle operation. Electra are already looking forward to the future of battery recycling and potential static storage usage. They are associated with an innovative new energy management business Energi Mine Ltd, a leading technology company, which uses blockchain and AI to transform how consumers manage their power consumption. (Electra Commercial Vehicles, 2020).

The system uses crypto currencies in their strategy to allow consumers and companies to pay for their power using a digital coin. Electric vehicles and their power use and management are a challenge for the future, and Energi Mine are at the forefront of this technology, using their vast experience of power management to provide charging infrastructure and payment systems.

VW and BMW enter into collaborative arrangements with battery technology partners

Volkswagen Group is paving the way for the next level of battery power for long-range e-mobility and in 2018 became the largest automotive shareholder in Stanford spin-off QuantumScape Corporation (Volkswagen, 2018).

Furthermore, Volkswagen AG and Northvolt AB created a 50/50 joint venture to build a factory for lithium-ion batteries in 2019. VW will work together within this newly formed joint venture with the aim to enable an industrial level of production of solid-state batteries. One of the long-term targets is to establish a production line for solid-state batteries by 2025 (VW Group, 2019).

In December 2017, BMW partnered with Solid Power to jointly develop its solid-state batteries for use in BMW's future electric vehicle models. The company was established in 2012 as a spinout from the University of Colorado, Boulder, based on research in solid-state battery technology. The company plans to commercialize its technology for not only battery-powered electric vehicles but also portable electronics, aircraft and satellites (McDonald, 2017).

Summary

- New kids on the block are threatening established OEM market position in the UK, US, Europe and Asia.
- Small, agile, innovative start-up businesses will dominate development of light and medium truck prototype development and could become attractive to OEMs looking at acquisition targets.

- The main barriers to the early adoption of electric trucks are the initial price – electric trucks can cost tens of thousands of pounds more than diesel-engined equivalents, scepticism about the reliability of electric truck technology, and uncertainty about the cost and availability of charging systems.

- When fuel savings and maintenance savings over the life of a truck are factored in, even when you disregard the government incentives that most electric truck purchasers get, there is still a good business case to be made.

- For many urban distribution operations involving short distances, regular return to depot and access to refuelling/recharging infrastructure, electric vehicles will dominate the future logistics landscape. For long haul this requires a different set of calculations.

- The road transport industry is currently being served by small start-ups, grant-hungry, experimental and technology showcase companies.

- Truck manufacturers are looking for technology partners and suppliers to provide EV support. VW, BMW, Toyota and Honda have formed effective joint venture arrangements with innovative battery technology partners spun out from established academic institutions.

- John Goodenough, Nobel Prize-winner and inventor of the lithium-ion battery is now championing the development of a solid-state battery that will compete with lithium-ion in the future and change the dynamics of sustainable and ethical sourcing of rare earth materials.

References

Business & Innovation Magazine (2020) Banbury electric vehicle unicorn arrival receives £75 million investment from Hyundai and Kia. Retrieved from: https://www.businessinnovationmag.co.uk/banbury-electric-vehicle-unicorn-arrival-receives-75-million-investment-from-hyundai-and-kia/ (archived at https://perma.cc/UES3-KTUA)

BYD USA (nd) The official sponsor of mother nature. Retrieved from https://en.byd.com/about/ (archived at https://perma.cc/P9P9-2AWD)

Electra Commercial Vehicles (2020) Electra Commercial Vehicles. Retrieved from https://www.electracommercialvehicles.com/ (archived at https://perma.cc/2ZLZ-S2V4)

EMOSS (2020) Electric vehicles for every purpose. Retrieved from: http://www.emoss.nl/en (archived at https://perma.cc/9VRF-88ND)

Faraday Institution (nd) Solid State Batteries. Retrieved from: https://faraday.ac.uk/research/beyond-lithium-ion/solid-state-batteries/ (archived at https://perma.cc/WC6A-2NAC)

Hindu Business Line (2018) Bharat Forge invests £10 m in UK-based Tevva Motors. Retrieved from: https://www.thehindubusinessline.com/news/bharat-forge-invests-10-m-in-uk-based-tevva-motors/article24146154.ece (archived at https://perma.cc/CD5P-XX77)

Lambert, F (2016) Nikola Motor unveils electric truck concept with up to 1,200 miles of range, *Electrek*. Retrieved from: https://electrek.co/2016/05/12/nikola-motor-electric-truck-concept/ (archived at https://perma.cc/V8FX-UXTZ)

McDonald, L (2017) BMW & Solid Power to jointly develop solid-state batteries for electric vehicles, *Clean Technica*. Retrieved from: https://cleantechnica.com/2017/12/18/bmw-solid-power-jointly-develop-solid-state-batteries-electric-vehicles/ (archived at https://perma.cc/DUV5-X7YF)

Nikola Motor Company (2020) Nikola Motor Company Images. https://nikolamotor.com/ (archived at https://perma.cc/24DV-F5Q2)

Paneltex (nd) Paneltex electric trucks and zero-emission vehicles. Retrieved from: https://www.paneltex.co.uk/service/electric-vehicles/ (archived at https://perma.cc/Y99F-2LLH)

Teslarati (2019) Tesla Semi to kick off Yandell Truckaway's transition to an all-electric fleet, *Teslarati*. Retrieved from: https://www.teslarati.com/tesla-semi-yandell-truckaway-all-electric-transition/ (archived at https://perma.cc/Z2NE-BL2C)

Tevva (nd) Retrieved from: https://tevva.com/tevva-technologies/ (archived at https://perma.cc/295P-YXAK)

Volkswagen (2018) Volkswagen partners with QuantumScape to secure access to solid-state battery technology. Retrieved from: https://www.volkswagenag.com/en/news/2018/06/volkswagen-partners-with-quantumscape-.html (archived at https://perma.cc/X985-HG8N)

VW Group (2019)Volkswagen and Northvolt form joint venture for battery production. Retrieved from: https://www.volkswagen-newsroom.com/en/press- releases/volkswagen-and-northvolt-form-joint-venture-for-battery-production-5316 (archived at https://perma.cc/4PYQ-ZUZF)

10

Alternative fuels to diesel and electricity for trucks and transportation

This chapter will familiarize the reader with:

- The impact of climate change and legislation on new product development.
- Major tier suppliers experimenting with the design of alternative powertrain portfolios.
- Current global energy sources for road transport.
- Barriers to adoption of alternative fuels, specifically hydrogen fuel cells.
- The cost parity challenge for alternative fuels to gain market acceptance.
- Is hydrogen the fuel of the future for heavy trucks?

Climate change drives product change

Truck manufacturers are walking an economic tightrope on climate change, but trucking operators won't invest in the technology unless it pays for itself within 18 months. It's a strict measure that highlights the balance between economic and environmental concerns in a sector central to climate concerns.

Road freight accounts for 7 per cent of total emissions, and trucking's share will expand as freight volumes grow. All diesel engine manufacturers are committed to reducing greenhouse gas emissions from heavy-duty trucks, but many are leaving some innovations on the table because trucking customers won't pay for them.

Nearly all market reports on the viability of battery electric for long-haul road transport where heavy batteries would reduce payload and limit range conclude that there will be limited growth for electric heavy-duty trucks. A carbon tax or tougher emissions standards could get operators to spend more on lower-emission technology, though such changes seem less likely in the United States than in Europe as we see the Trump administration aggressively roll back environmental regulations on the auto industry.

Climate change is a major concern globally for the public, political leadership and corporations alike. Action to address this concern will require products that are capable of operating on a zero-emission basis and alternative fuels have been identified as the pathway to succeeding in delivering lower emissions.

However, there is a cost factor that currently prices electric vehicles at a significant premium over internal combustion engine options and a key factor in accelerating the adoption of zero- and low-emission product will be governments considering subsidizing the transition.

China has demonstrated conclusively that subsidies can have a major impact and have been a catalyst for massive increases in the production and sales of electric vehicles.

Europe and the United States are lagging behind China in the provision of and support for state subsidies for both the electrification of transport and solar energy.

In the absence of government subsidies, renewable energy sources and product dependent on that form of energy will be slow to achieve any sizeable market presence.

Energy use and emissions from road freight vehicles

Globally, road freight transport energy consumption has grown by more than 50 per cent over the past decade and a half, from around 23 exajoules (EJ) in 2000 to 36 EJ in 2015. Today, road freight transport makes up 32 per cent of total transport-related energy demand, which accounts for more than 97 per cent of sectoral final energy.

This makes road freight transport an important contributor to global oil demand growth; since 2000, oil use from road freight vehicles has grown by nearly 6 million barrels per day (mb/d) to close to 17 mb/d in 2015, accounting for more than 35 per cent of the net increase in global oil demand over that period (IEA, 2017).

Road freight transport is the primary user of diesel among all energy sectors: 84 per cent (or 14 mb/d) of all oil products used in the sector are diesel fuels, which means that about half of global diesel demand is from road freight transport. Road freight transport alone accounted for 80 per cent of the global net increase in diesel demand since 2000.

Petroleum utilization in road transportation? (IEA, 2017)

The use of petrol plays a much smaller role in road freight transport and is largely confined to light commercial vehicles (LCVs); about two-thirds of petrol use in road freight vehicles is linked to this segment. At 2.6 mb/d, petrol demand from road freight vehicles constitutes 13 per cent of global automotive petrol demand (Figure 10.1).

The share of petrol use in road freight oil demand gets smaller as the size of the trucks increases. For HFTs, nearly all oil use is diesel-based due to the higher energy density of the fuel and the efficiency of diesel engines in heavy-duty applications. The United States is by some distance the largest market for road freight oil use, consuming around 3.3 mb/d of oil-based fuels for road freight transport, about one-fifth of the global total. Around 73 per cent of US road freight oil use is diesel.

FIGURE 10.1   Global oil consumption 2017

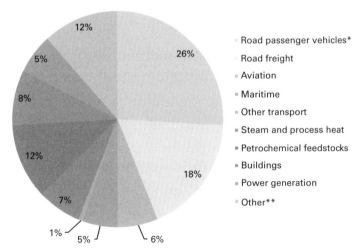

* Passenger vehicles include buses and two- and three-wheelers.
** Includes agriculture, transformation and other non-energy use (mainly bitumen and lubricants).

NOTE The percentages show the shares of oil consumption in 2015.
SOURCE IEA, 2017

The share of petrol in Canada, Mexico and the United States, which is higher than one-quarter in each of these countries, is disproportionally high compared with that of most other industrialized European and Asian countries (where the shares range from less than 1 per cent to 23 per cent in Japan), reflecting these countries' large LCV fleets. The European Union uses about 2.1 mb/d (13 per cent of the global total), practically all of which is diesel.

At 2.1 mb/d, China's oil demand is nearly equal to the European Union's, though about 10 per cent of this comes in the form of petrol. India's oil demand for road freight transport has seen the largest growth among all countries since 2000, growing by a more than a factor of three. Road transport oil use in India and the Middle East has tripled since 2000. Latin America and the Middle East each consumed about 1.4 mb/d in 2015, around 90 per cent and 85 per cent of which was diesel in each region, respectively (Hindu Business Line, 2018).

In Africa, the ASEAN countries and Brazil, road freight oil use has more doubled since 2000. Brazil's consumption now totals about 0.7 mb/d (about 95 per cent diesel), while it is 0.8 mb/d in India (and nearly all diesel) (Hindu Business Line, 2018).

Alternative fuels so far play a minor role in supplying energy to road freight vehicles.

Reducing the future growth of oil demand (IEA, 2017)

Reducing future growth of oil demand from road freight vehicles is a challenging, but possible task; opportunities arise from three main areas.

Systemic improvements in road freight operations and logistics

These changes can reduce growth in road freight trucking activity and improve the on-road efficiency of truck operations:

- Modern Telematic software embedded in the truck's engine management systems using GPS technology to optimize truck routing will deliver better service to time-sensitive deliveries.
- Driver behaviour can be improved through driver training and the use of on-board, real-time feedback devices that monitor many on-road performance characteristics such as use of cruise control, harsh braking, excessive

idle time that tracks fuel economy of trucks, and a wide range of measures to improve the utilization of vehicles and reduce maintenance costs.

- The development of 'open source' internet-based systems can enable better integration of supply chain data and improve areas such as return logistics to enable a reduction in the number of empty trailers returning to base – and could transform road freight operations entirely.

- In 2020, there has been an explosion in the development of logistics systems and services designed to service this area and Chapter 12 details examples of start-up companies who have entered this space.

Vehicle efficiency technologies

Many vehicle efficiency technologies pay back their higher capital costs through fuel savings within only a few years:

- For the existing stock of trucks, aerodynamic retrofits can reduce the drag coefficient and lead to reductions in road load; and low-rolling resistance tyres can translate into immediate improvements in fuel economy.

- For new trucks, additional technologies exist for reducing idling and for improving vehicle efficiency, such as the use of lightweight materials and improvements to truck engines, transmissions and drivetrains.

- Some of these opportunities have longer payback times than operators tend to consider when purchasing new trucks.

Alternative fuels

The use of alternative fuels and alternative fuel trucks could help achieve key energy and environmental policy goals, such as:

- Diversifying the fuel supply of road freight and reducing CO_2 and air pollutant emissions.

- Natural gas, biofuels, electricity and hydrogen are the main alternatives to oil, but they differ in the extent to which they can contribute to policy objectives.

BIOFUELS AS AN ALTERNATIVE FUEL SOURCE

Biofuels are not a new phenomenon. Over 100 years ago, Rudolf Diesel originally developed his engine to run on biofuels as an alternative to diesel fuels

Today, biofuels contribute 2.2 per cent of final energy to road freight transport in shares that roughly mirror those of the petroleum-based fuels they substitute: biodiesel, 1.6 per cent; ethanol, 0.6 per cent; and biomethane, less than 0.01 per cent.

The United States and Brazil are the world's largest producers of fuel ethanol, and the two countries account for more than 80 per cent of global fuel ethanol consumption in road freight vehicles.

Biodiesel is used as a road freight transport fuel in more countries than ethanol and is most commonly used in ASEAN countries, Brazil, China, the European Union, India and the United States. Natural gas supplies the remaining 1.2 per cent of energy to trucking. This primarily goes to dual-fuel trucks but also includes a small but growing share of trucks with engines designed to run on compressed natural gas (CNG) and liquefied natural gas (LNG). Figure 10.2 shows the energy consumption of petrol and diesel in key global regions. However, concerns remain about the fact that LNG is also a significant polluter emitting in many cases five times the NO_x emissions of diesel, and this has elevated the debate about subsidies available for these alternative fuels.

THE CASE FOR HYDROGEN AS A FUEL FOR THE FUTURE

The case supporting hydrogen as a zero-emission fuel option in the future is based on two key factors:

- the time to refuel is very close to that experienced by current diesel;
- the range it can deliver – Nikola Trucks is claiming range goals of 1,200 miles on a tank of hydrogen.

In the absence of significant refuelling stations for commercial vehicles, range anxiety is a big issue until investment in refuelling infrastructure is sorted out.

Hydrogen is stored in rapidly refillable on-board tanks, similar to the process for conventional diesel trucks. Motive power is provided through the electrochemical conversion of energy and produces zero direct emissions of harmful pollutants (including CO_2).

The high cost of hydrogen at €12–€15 per kilogram and the cost for on-board storage systems remain the biggest barriers to accelerating adoption of hydrogen as an alternative to diesel, which translates to about $12 to $18 per diesel gallon equivalent. To be competitive with diesel the cost per kilogram needs to fall below $3.

Hydrogen fuel presents the most promising and most challenging aspects of moving heavy-duty FCVs towards actual commercialization and broad use to displace diesel HDVs.

FIGURE 10.2   Energy consumption of road freight vehicles 2015

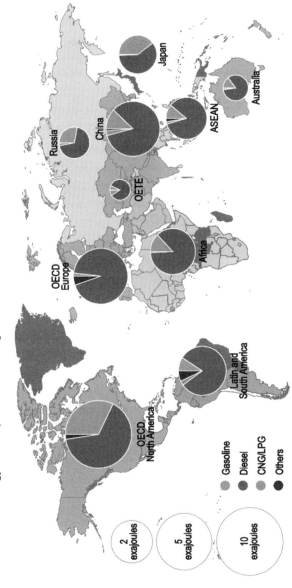

This map is without prejudice to the status of or sovereignty over any territory, to the delimitation of international frontiers and boundaries, and to the name of any territory, city or area.

SOURCE   IEA, 2017

Currently, none of the major truck manufacturers are offering an integrated hydrogen fuel cell platform. That said, the future of fuel cells for commercial trucking looks bright. This is evidenced by recent announcements from OEMs that are launching major research and development efforts, coupled with demonstration projects.

Since mid-2017 Toyota has been testing a prototype Class 8 tractor powered by hydrogen fuel cell technology. Notably, Toyota's apparent ultimate plan is to sell this heavy-duty proton exchange membrane fuel cell (PEMFC) drive system to Class 8 truck OEMs (rather than to become a Class 8 OEM itself).

ZANZEFF: ZERO-EMISSION AND NEAR-ZERO-EMISSION FREIGHT FACILITIES PROGRAMME

Under a collaboration between Kenworth and Toyota, these fuel cell drayage trucks will be built specifically to move cargo from Port of Los Angeles terminals to local distribution centres and inland destinations. The 10 fuel cell tractors will be operated by Toyota Logistics Services, United Parcel Services, Total Transportation Services Inc and Southern Counties Express. In a second phase of the project, two new 'large-capacity heavy-duty hydrogen stations' will be developed by Shell to serve these fuel cell trucks (one in Wilmington, one in Ontario) (Leonard, 2018).

Heavy-duty vehicle solutions

What will make a bigger difference to global warming: sleek electric sedans like those made by Tesla Inc, or heavy-duty trucks, powered by the sort of engines that Cummins Inc is testing at its research centre south of Indianapolis? (Ip, 2018.)

The answer is the latter, for a simple reason: most of the world thinks like a Cummins customer, not a Tesla customer (Ip, 2018).

A Tesla buyer isn't trying to save money: It is 'an emotional buy,' says Wayne Eckerle, Cummins' head of research. Cummins customers are commercial truck operators: 'They don't buy on emotion. At all.' Committed as Cummins is to combatting climate change, any innovation it offers must meet one simple rule: pay for itself within 18 months (Ip, 2018).

Trucking exemplifies both the challenges and the stakes facing the commercial vehicle business. Though less numerous than passenger vehicles, trucks collectively emit almost as much carbon dioxide because they travel further and weigh more. According to the International Energy Agency, road freight accounts for 35 per cent of transport-related greenhouse gas emissions and 7 per cent of total emissions (Ip, 2018).

- **The bad news:** trucks' shares will expand as freight volumes grow and fuel efficiency advances more rapidly for cars than trucks.
- **The good news:** incremental changes actually deliver bigger carbon dividends than with cars.

In 2009 the US Federal Government joined with manufacturers in a project dubbed 'SuperTruck' to raise truck mileage to about 10 miles a gallon, up from six. That would equal a staggering 40 per cent reduction in fuel consumption. For Cummins, that meant raising the efficiency of an engine from about 42 per cent (the share of energy burned that becomes motion, as opposed to wasted heat) to 50 per cent.

Cummins is now incorporating some of the resulting innovations, such as combining the transmission and engine for optimum shifting and increasing cylinder pressure to maximize fuel efficiency. Its flagship heavy-duty engine, rolled out in 2017, gets 3–8 per cent more mileage than its predecessor.

Cummins has yet to implement some innovations because they don't meet customers' financial criteria. For example, it figured out how to boost efficiency by 4 per cent by recycling waste heat back into the engine compartment, but that won't pay for itself in 18 months.

In 2016 a second 'SuperTruck' programme kicked off, aiming to boost mileage to 14 miles a gallon and engine efficiency to 55 per cent. Cummins predicts achieving the new goal will be far harder than the last because the easiest, most cost-effective changes have been made. Indeed, conventional engines may never exceed 60 per cent efficiency.

Cummins would prefer to make battery electric vehicles more attractive by governments applying some form of a carbon tax on vehicle purchase. By forcing customers to internalize the cost of climate change, it would naturally incentivize them to pay up for lower-emission technology, no matter the fuel type (Ip, 2018).

'If we want rules that are more effective, decide the end result we want and let technology compete for the best solution,' says Cummins Chief Executive Tom Linebarger. 'Carbon taxes are much better than all the other choices' (Pressman, 2018).

Yet hopes of such a tax are fading. Voters in the capital of regulation, Washington state, have twice rejected such a tax and France has just been forced to suspend a fuel tax increase because of widespread protests. All of which means businesses must live without the thing they need most to deliver a low-carbon economy: a price signal that aligns their customers' interests with that mission.

Cummins, aligned with other diesel engine manufacturers, is spreading its bets, developing a mix of electric, hybrid and natural gas-powered motors for small and medium-size trucks. But long-haul heavy trucks will, for the foreseeable future, run on diesel. Besides costing a fortune, an electric truck's batteries would reduce payloads and recharging time would lengthen trips.

The upshot is that HDFCVs – heavy-duty fuel cell vehicles – hybridized with battery-electric architectures that improve performance and enable regenerative braking, can provide fleets with greater utility and applicability compared to 'pure' battery-development efforts, coupled with demonstration projects (Leonard, 2018).

Barriers to commercializing hydrogen fuel cell trucks

The current cost of hydrogen fuel is a significant barrier to commercialization of heavy-duty fuel cell vehicles.

For heavy-duty fleets, fuel costs are second only to labour costs in determining total operational costs. The current cost of hydrogen fuel, which is currently much more expensive than diesel, is a significant barrier to commercialization of heavy-duty fuel cell vehicles (Leonard, 2018).

Hydrogen costs approximately $10 to $15 per kilogram. To achieve parity with current global diesel costs the cost per kilogram for hydrogen needs to be closer to $3 per kilogram (Leonard, 2018).

Current diesel costs are around $2.75 per gallon in the United States. The cost per gallon for diesel in the UK is £6, equivalent to €8 in Europe and $8 in the US; therefore, the cost of diesel fuel in Europe is currently three times that of the US. Here is clearly an opportunity for the UK and Europe to be early adopters of hydrogen as a fuel for the future in medium and heavy trucks (Ricardo Energy & Environment, 2019).

On the positive side, the higher cost and relatively small volumes of on-board hydrogen are partially compensated for by the relative higher efficiency of a 'fuel cell electric-drive system' compared to a 'conventional-drive diesel truck' (Leonard, 2018).

Fuel cell makers such as Ballard Power Systems are working hard to further reduce total cost of ownership by improving stack life, reducing capital costs, improving power density, and other advancements (Ballard, 2018).

Ballard indicates that its PEMFC stacks for heavy-duty vehicle applications will be commercially available in 2019 (Leonard, 2018).

Bosch are also a major Tier 1 supplier to the industry of fuel cell stacks. A description of exactly what this component does as part of the hydrogen fuel system is detailed below:

> The fuel-cell stack contains up to several hundred fuel cells; it forms the core of the fuel-cell system. In each one of these fuel cells, arranged in series, a 'cold combustion' process takes place. This 'cold combustion' converts the energy from the chemical reaction between the continuously fed hydrogen and airborne oxygen into electricity. This process takes place when the hydrogen is catalytically split down into electrons and protons (Bosch, nd).

While the protons diffuse through a polymer membrane in the direction of the cathode, the electrons flow from the anode to the cathode via an electrical circuit. In the process, they supply a consumer with electric current. At the cathode, the protons, electrons, and oxygen from the air ultimately react to form the end product: water. No pollutants such as particulate matter or nitrogen oxides are created as by-products of this process (Bosch, nd).

Like compressed natural gas (CNG) vehicles, emerging heavy-duty fuel cell vehicles are designed to use compressed hydrogen, which is stored on board in heavy, expensive high-pressure tanks (Leonard, 2018).

While on-board CH_2 – methylene – storage is robust and proven (using similar technology to CNG tanks), it presents significant trade-offs on cost, range and other factors that are very important to the bottom line in heavy-duty trucking. Further optimization and advancements for hydrogen fuel systems may be required before heavy-duty FCVs can meaningfully penetrate into on-road HDV applications, especially in HDV trucking (Leonard, 2018).

Today there is almost no hydrogen fuelling infrastructure designed to serve medium and heavy-duty FCVs. The limited existing or planned hydrogen fuelling stations designed to serve passenger vehicles are not equipped to fuel heavy-duty FCVs. Except for a few demonstration programmes, the only hydrogen stations that can accommodate heavy-duty FCVs are located on transit properties and designed to refill fuel cell buses. (Leonard, 2018).

It's likely that the initial approach to build out a hydrogen fuelling network for heavy-duty trucks will focus on a 'corridor' concept; this will take many years to orchestrate, and each station will cost roughly $3 million. To build out a national network of heavy-duty FCV fuelling stations, it will likely take decades and cost billions of dollars. Careful coordination will be needed with the pace of rolling out the heavy-duty FCVs that will utilize such stations (Leonard, 2018).

CASE STUDY
European prototype testing of hydrogen fuel heavy-duty trucks

Scania and ASKO test hydrogen gas propulsion

ASKO, Norway's largest convenience goods wholesaler, is continuing its investment in sustainable transport services. In conjunction with Scania, a prototype testing programme was set up in 2016 to test trucks with an electric powertrain. Electrical energy is converted from hydrogen gas in fuel cells on board the vehicles. The hydrogen gas will be sourced from locally generated solar energy. The trucks operate in a distribution service with distances of almost 500 km. The conversion of hydrogen gas to electrical energy on board trucks that are operated for longer distances provides valuable experience for Scania's continued development of electrified powertrains (Scania, 2016).

ASKO has the ambition to achieve a climate-neutral business, where distribution of goods will take place using trucks that run on renewable fuels and in the longer term completely on electricity.

Experience from pilot testing of vehicles and the plant, which was built for local hydrogen gas production, will form the basis for ASKO's decision on a continued investment in hydrogen gas propulsion. The research project was partly financed by the Norwegian government.

Scania provided three-axle distribution trucks with a gross weight of 27 tonnes, where the internal combustion engine in the powertrain will be replaced by an electric engine powered by electricity from fuel cells and hydrogen gas on board the vehicle. The rest of the powertrain is composed of the same standard components used in the hybrid trucks and buses that Scania already delivers.

So far the tests have been positive, and in a 2020 update Scania provided the latest report:

> Hydrogen gas is an interesting option for long haulage electrified transport and early tests show that the technology also works well in colder climates. We will continue to monitor the performance of these trucks closely. I also want to commend ASKO for taking early and bold steps to ensure a supply of hydrogen sourced from renewable sources and infrastructure for fuelling. The company is a player who really takes action to catalyse a shift toward sustainable transport (Thomson, 2020).

As always, Scania's work is based on a modular approach. Scania notes: 'In the four trucks deployed in ASKO's operations, the internal combustion engine in the powertrain is replaced by an electric machine, powered by electricity from fuel cells fed with hydrogen and from rechargeable batteries.' The rest of the powertrain is composed of the same standard components used in the hybrid trucks and buses that Scania already delivers (Scania, 2020).

Funding opportunities available and abundant

Fortunately, more and more grant funding opportunities are becoming available to help fund deployments of heavy-duty fuel cell vehicles, as well as the hydrogen stations that will serve them (Leonard, 2018).

Funding to offset the higher capital costs of heavy-duty FCVs will be critical for fleet managers to purchase the vehicles and take on the risks associated with new fuel technology platforms. California's Zero and Near Zero Emissions Freight Facilities (ZANZEFF) grants provide a recent example of forward momentum (Leonard, 2018).

Each state is just beginning to award its collective $2.925 billion in funds from the VW post- 'Dieselgate' settlement, directed by the EPA to support state activity. Regional agencies like the South Coast Air Quality Management District are dedicating significant portions of their incentive and R&D funds towards heavy-duty FCVs and hydrogen stations (Leonard, 2018). There is solid movement towards hydrogen fuel cell systems meeting their potential to become commercially available.

The greatest reason is the expanded interest and involvement seen from mainstream, fully proven truck OEMs as they iteratively move beyond diesel ICE platforms to zero-emission, battery-electric and fuel cell platforms. Albeit gradual, there is solid movement towards hydrogen fuel cell systems meeting their potential to become commercially available as zero-emission alternatives to conventional diesel HDVs (Leonard, 2018).

Hydrogen fuel cell development

United States

NIKOLA MOTORS
Nikola Motors, based in Scottsdale, Arizona, is the leading manufacturer of hydrogen-electric trucks.

We want to transform everything about the transportation industry. With Nikola's vision, the world will be cleaner, safer and healthier (FutureCar, 2019).

Nikola is building its high-tech hydrogen-powered trucks for autonomous highway driving. All of the Nikola products have been built for the future with autonomous driving hardware in place (Future Car, 2019).

As FutureCar states: 'One of Nikola's biggest clients, Anheuser-Busch, the beverage company, placed orders for 800 Class 8 zero-emission trucks from Nikola as part of its sustainability strategy, which is to reduce CO_2 emissions by 25 per cent across its value chain' (Future Car, 2019).

Nikola's zero-emission trucks already have customers lining up for them. There are currently more than 13,000 Nikola trucks on order. The trucks have lower operating costs than diesel-powered trucks, so there is much interest from the freight industry as a way to cut costs (FutureCar, 2019).

Under the Nikola leasing programme, owners pay a fixed monthly cost for the truck, hydrogen fuel and warranty and maintenance. Owners will have the option to trade in for a new Nikola vehicle every million miles or 84 months, whichever comes first (FutureCar, 2019).

FutureCar lists how 'Nikola's trucks have an advanced surround view system using a 15-inch touchscreen display, which shows the driver a virtual aerial view of the area around the truck and trailer in real time, eliminating all blind spots.' The trucks use several high-definition cameras combined with radar, sonar and computing software and hardware to provide 360-degree views. Nikola also announced a battery-electric vehicle option for the urban, short-haul trucking market (FutureCar, 2019).

For the European market, Nikola President Mark Russell and CEO Trevor Milton unveiled the never-before-seen Nikola Tre, an advanced truck with a clean, contemporary design (FutureCar, 2019).

'With a range between 500 and 750 miles depending upon load, this gorgeous vehicle will have fast hydrogen fuelling in under 15 minutes, even in Europe,' said Russell. 'Think about Europe with no more diesel trucks,' said Milton, 'The roads will be clean, quiet and beautiful' (Nikola Motor Co, 2019a).

Nikola's Executive Vice President of Hydrogen Jesse Schneider discussed the company's hydrogen fuel cell vision. The vision consists of the world's first purpose-built fuel cell Class 8 truck, enabling more hydrogen storage, optimized placement of the powertrain, and a robust 70 MPa hydrogen fuelling network (FutureCar, 2019).

FIGURE 10.3   The interior of the Nikola Two

SOURCE Nikola Motor Co, 2018

Nikola Trucks opened their first hydrogen station at their Phoenix head-quarters in 2019 and are leading the way working with industry and other OEMs to develop hydrogen standards to enable fuelling in less than 15 minutes. The goal is safety and interoperability, so that anyone can fuel at a Nikola station (FutureCar, 2019).

Like Tesla, Nikola Motors have developed a direct sales model and are partnering with key customers for future service and maintenance needs. Nikola has partnered with Ryder System, Inc and Thompson Machinery to offer world-class sales, service and warranty through their over 800 locations across North America (Nikola Motor Co, 2019a).

Nikola Motor Co unveiled a prototype design in 2018, the Nikola Tre, a hydrogen-electric truck aimed at the European market. The Nikola Tre, which means 'three' in Norwegian, was created in response to widespread interest from European customers, said Trevor Milton, founder and CEO of the Phoenix-based company.

The appearance of the Nikola Tre in Europe will be a European first for a zero-emission product in the heavy truck class. The current plan is for the product to be available from 2022–2023.

FIGURE 10.4 The Nikola Two hydrogen-powered truck

SOURCE Nikola Motor Co, 2018

The Nikola Tre was first displayed in Phoenix in 2018. This event was the first time the public had a chance to see the vehicles, including the Nikola Two semi-truck pulling loaded trailers and the Nikola NZT off-road vehicle.

The Nikola Tre is being designed with 500–1,000 horsepower and a range of 500– 1,200 kilometres, depending on options.

The Tre will fit within the current size and length restrictions for Europe, according to Nikola.

Nikola's European testing is projected to begin in Norway around 2020. The company is also in the preliminary planning stages to find a location for its European manufacturing facility, according to a Nikola announcement.

Nikola is working with Oslo-based Nel Hydrogen for its hydrogen stations in the US and it is planning to use Nel's network and resources to develop the market representation strategy for Europe.

NIKOLA MOVES INTO THE EUROPEAN MARKET

As of September 2019 Nikola Motors announced that CNH Industrial, which owns the European Truck maker Iveco and is part of the Fiat Corporation, will be investing £203 million ($250 million) in the Nikola Motor Company. This illustrates the predictions being made that at some stage traditional OEMs will invest in or acquire start-up assets to accelerate their entry into alternative energy market opportunities (Nikola Motor Co, 2019b).

FIGURE 10.5   The Nikola Tre is Nikola Motor Co's European version of its
hydrogen-electric semi-truck

SOURCE Nikola Motor Co, 2018

FIGURE 10.6   Nikola's Tre European semi-truck

SOURCE Nikola Motor Co, 2018

The immediate priority for Nikola and CNH will be to incorporate technology from models such as the Iveco S-Way and the European Nikola
derivative the 'Tre'. This partnership will witness the sharing of manufacturing know-how, purchasing power, validated truck parts, plant engineering
and much more.

In addition to this partnership agreement with CNH, Nikola announced that vehicle component system provider Bosch and Hanwha, which makes solar panels, had invested £186 million ($230 million).

While other OEMS believe zero-emission solutions cannot happen in the timeframe regulators have demanded, Nikola, CNH, CNH Industrial and IVECO are going to prove that the timelines for a zero-emission hydrogen fuel cell heavy truck is not unreasonable.

China hydrogen market development

Wan Gang, China's former minister of science and technology, thinks hydrogen is the future. He announced, during a press conference in Hong Kong in May 2018, a vision to make China an electric-vehicle powerhouse (BloombergNEF, 2019).

He revolutionized the global car industry, cementing a move away from the internal combustion engine. China is now poised to develop hydrogen and, in the process, change the basis of competition for heavy trucks manufacturers

The world's biggest car market is set to embrace hydrogen fuel-cell vehicles the way it did EVs, claimed Wan, who's been called the father of China's electric car movement. His strategy – using government subsidies to bring carmakers and drivers on board – made China home to one of every two EVs sold globally today.

'We should look into establishing a hydrogen society', said Wan, who is now a vice-chairman of China's national advisory body for policymaking, a role that ranks higher than a minister and gives him a voice in the nation's future planning. 'We need to move further toward fuel cells.' That means the government will commit resources to developing such vehicles, he said (BloombergNEF, 2019).

While China plans to phase out the long-time subsidy programme for the maturing EV industry next year, government funding for fuel-cell vehicles may stay in place to some extent, Wan said (BloombergNEF, 2019).

There are key benefits that hydrogen fuel cell-powered vehicles have over electric, the main one being refuelling time, which is close to that of diesel. The main problem is the cost of hydrogen fuel vs diesel – it is currently four to five times more expensive than its fossil-fuel competitor.

Toyota has started to experiment with fuel cell vehicles but there is still a reluctance to see hydrogen as a true competitor until hydrogen cost is reduced and refuelling infrastructure is established nationally. To put the current situation into some perspective, only 1,500 hydrogen vehicles are in use today in China, compared with more than 2 million purely electric vehicles (BloombergNEF, 2019).

For Wan – a mechanical engineer trained in Germany – the shift towards hydrogen is a natural step in realizing a vision of having electric cars dominate inner-city traffic, while buses and trucks filled with hydrogen tanks roam the nation's motorways for long-distance travel.

Then there's the matter of hydrogen's flammability, as evidenced by a recent fire at a refuelling station in Norway. But Wan is confident the many issues facing the adoption of hydrogen will be resolved.

Long-range commercial vehicles are not currently well suited to run on batteries alone because of weight and range constraints, according to a 2019 BNEF report. Fuel cells would be a good bet should the government ease restrictions on hydrogen-refuelling infrastructure (Business Times, 2019).

Beyond hydrogen, Wan voiced scepticism about the notion that computers will completely replace the need for humans in the driver's seat: 'I believe that people still want to drive or have a sense of control,' Wan said. He also said he does not envision China issuing a national ban on the sale of petrol cars as provincial authorities will be left to make their own decisions (Business Times, 2019).

Japan

BloombergNEF has looked at the hydrogen cell future. Efforts are under way in Japan, which plans to increase the number of fuel-cell vehicles on its roads to 40,000 by 2020 – though BloombergNEF estimates that sales so far are not close to that target (BloombergNEF, 2019).

Daimler leads European hydrogen developments

In Europe, Daimler's Mercedes-Benz unit rolled out a fuel-cell version of its popular GLC SUV. In the United States, the California Fuel Cell Partnership is trying to promote the technology, with limited success.

Alternative fuel growth potential conclusions

Creating a market for sustainable fuels is difficult. Many technological breakthroughs are strongly dependent on the car and bus manufacturing industries and the biofuel industry, with truck and van manufacturers having less influence.

Purchasing decision makers in the logistics and major fleet operators will have an influence but not as much as the regulatory authorities and oil companies who will influence the development of refuelling infrastructure and subsidies for consumption of alternative fuels.

Fuels such as natural gas (CNG and LPG), hydrogen and biofuels all face direct market barriers that hinder the future development, which need to be overcome by public policies and private investment strategies.

In countries such as Brazil, the market share of biofuels in the freight sector is likely to increase substantially by 2030, possibly with the use of flexi-fuel vans (Schmitt *et al*, 2011), if land use questions can be resolved. The recent massive destruction of the rainforests in Brazil would appear to be a barrier to this gaining traction.

Attention is turning to second generation biofuels. These are fuels that can be produced by waste material such as residual oil or municipal waste, and cellulosic crops (dedicated energy crops). According to the EU, use of cellulosic biomass feedstock allows new methods of biofuel production from products, by-products, and waste from agriculture, forestry, and wood pulp and paper with more sophisticated chemical processes. The Royal Society (2008) argued that biofuels may form a part of the solution for the future but will contribute just a small part.

Alternative fuels have made inroads but the evidence is that electric-powered trucks remain the dominant product. As of 2019, DHL had a worldwide fleet of around 98,500 vehicles, and about 8,000 were powered by alternative drive technologies.

The trend towards electric fleets in the logistics industry is starting from a very low base, and most current product has a very high price compared to its diesel equivalent. The cost differentials will need to be reduced, the refuelling infrastructure challenges need to be addressed and government financial incentives and environmental accreditation is required to accelerate the adoption of alternative fuels (McKinnon *et al*, 2015).

This chapter has attempted to highlight the areas where progress is being made. We have also examined the players that are active as we enter the third decade of the 21st century. The road to zero emissions looks like a race between:

- Tesla and Nikola among the new entrants;
- the legacy OEMs and tier suppliers such as:
  - Traton Group (VW);
  - Mercedes-Benz;
  - Paccar;
- diesel engine and component manufacturers such as Cummins, Navistar, Bosch and ZF.

Summary

- Road freight transport is the primary user of diesel among all energy sectors: 84 per cent (or 14 mb/d) of all oil products used in the sector are diesel fuels, which means that about half of global diesel demand is from road freight transport. Road freight transport alone has accounted for 80 per cent of the global net increase in diesel demand since 2000.

- Nearly all market reports on the viability of battery electric for long-haul road transport, where heavy batteries would reduce payload and limit range, conclude that there will be limited growth for electric heavy-duty trucks.

- A carbon tax or tougher emissions standards could get operators to spend more on lower-emission technology, though such changes seem less likely in the United States than in Europe.

- Cummins, aligned with other diesel engine manufacturers, is spreading its bets, developing a mix of electric, hybrid and natural gas-powered motors for small and medium-sized trucks. But long-haul heavy trucks will, for the foreseeable future, run on diesel.

- Fuel cell technology is becoming increasingly mature and optimized for HDV applications. Today, it is the hydrogen fuel rather than fuel cell hardware that mostly entails the major remaining challenges for heavy-duty fuel cell vehicles.

- To compete with diesel cost, hydrogen needs to fall from $15 per kilogram to below $3 per kilogram. At current process hydrogen is equivalent to a gallon of diesel being $12–$18.

References

Ballard (2018) Ballard unveils next generation zero-emission fuel cell stack for heavy duty motive market. Retrieved from: https://www.ballard.com/about-ballard/newsroom/news-releases/2018/09/19/ballard-unveils-next-generation-zero-emission-fuel-cell-stack-for-heavy-duty-motive-market (archived at https://perma.cc/55MM-RM39)

BloombergNEF (2019) China's father of electric cars says hydrogen is the future. Retrieved from: https://www.bloomberg.com/news/articles/2019-06-12/china-s-father-of-electric-cars-thinks-hydrogen-is-the-future (archived at https://perma.cc/4SUN-63LD)

BloombergNEF (2019) Electric transport revolution set to spread rapidly into light and medium commercial vehicle market. Retrieved from: https://about.bnef.com/blog/electric-transport-revolution-set-spread-rapidly-light-medium-commercial-vehicle-market/ (archived at https://perma.cc/JVR7-9YX5)

Bosch (nd) Fuel-cell stack: the heart of the fuel cell system. Retrieved from: https://www.bosch-mobility-solutions.com/en/products-and-services/passenger-cars-and-light-commercial-vehicles/powertrain-systems/fuel-cell-electric-vehicle/fuel-cell-stack/ (archived at https://perma.cc/2VUG-V6SJ)

Business Times (2019) China's father of electric cars declares hydrogen as the future. Retrieved from: https://www.businesstimes.com.sg/transport/chinas-father-of-electric-cars-declares-hydrogen-as-the-future (archived at https://perma.cc/33L4-F37G)

FutureCar (2019) Nikola Motors reveals its latest hydrogen-electric vehicles at 'Nikola World 2019'. Retrieved from: https://www.futurecar.com/3142/Nikola-Motors-Reveals-its-Latest-Hydrogen-Electric-Vehicles-at-Nikola-World-2019 (archived at https://perma.cc/U4GA-YJAP)

Hindu Business Line (2018) India, China to drive road freight fuel consumption: IEA *Hindu Business Line*. Retrieved from: https://www.thehindubusinessline.com/news/world/india-china-to-drive-road-freight-fuel-consumption-iea/article9747188.ece (archived at https://perma.cc/G8MA-K2F3)

IEA (2017) *The Future of Trucks*, IEA, Paris

Ip, G (2018) Business's climate challenge: getting customers to pay, *Wall Street Journal*. Retrieved from: https://www.wsj.com/articles/businesss-climate-challenge-getting-customers-to-pay-1544011201 (archived at https://perma.cc/ZWP3-DPFF)

Leonard, J (2018) Hydrogen fuel cell future is promising for heavy-duty trucks, *ACT News*. Retrieved from: https://www.act-news.com/news/hydrogen-fuel-cell-vehicles/ (archived at https://perma.cc/K7UQ-YYF3)

McKinnon, A, Browne, M, Piecyk, M and Whiteing, A (eds) (2015) *Green Logistics: Improving the environmental sustainability of logistics*, Kogan Page, London

Nikola Motor Co (2018) Nikola Launches stunning truck for European market. Retrieved from: https://nikolamotor.com/press_releases/nikola-launches-stunning-truck-for-european-market-53 (archived at https://perma.cc/92RF-RFDF)

Nikola Motor Co (2019a) Nikola showcases five zero-emission products at Nikola World. Retrieved from: https://nikolamotor.com/press_releases/nikola-showcases-five-zero-emission-products-at-nikola-world-61 (archived at https://perma.cc/7G79-Q633)

Nikola Motor Co (2019b) CNH Industrial to lead Nikola's Series D round with $250MM USD investment. Retrieved from: https://nikolamotor.com/press_releases/cnh-industrial-to-lead-nikolas-series-d-round-with-250mm-usd-investment-64 (archived at https://perma.cc/5RJ3-9765)

Pressman, M (2018) Cummins talks Tesla, electric trucks, and the need for a carbon tax, *Evvanex*. Retrieved from: https://evannex.com/blogs/news/cummins-talks-tesla-electric-trucks-and-hopes-for-a-carbon-tax (archived at https://perma.cc/FWK9-U5GW)

Ricardo Energy & Environment (2019) *Zero Emission HGV Infrastructure Requirements,* Ricardo Energy & Environment, Didcot

Royal Society (2008) Sustainable bio-fuels: prospects and challenges. Retrieved from: www.royalsociety.org/policy/publications/2008/sustainable-biofuels (archived at https://perma.cc/9H2Z-GK82)

Scania (2016) Scania and Asko test hydrogen gas propulsion. Retired from: https://www.scania.com/group/en/home/newsroom/press-releases/press-release-detail-page.html/2277739-scania-and-asko-test-hydrogen-gas-propulsion (archived at https://perma.cc/W5DX-YWEV)

Scania (2020) Norwegian wholesaler ASKO puts hydrogen powered fuel cell electric Scania trucks on the road. Retrieved from: https://www.scania.com/group/en/home/newsroom/news/2020/norwegian-wholesaler-asko-puts-hydrogen-powered-fuel-cell-electric-scania-trucks-on-the-road.html (Scania, 2020) (archived at https://perma.cc/2LAF-4CY4)

Schmitt,W F, Schaffer, R and Szklo, A (2011) Policies for improving the efficiency of the Brazilian light-duty vehicle fleet and their implications for fuel use, greenhouse gas emissions and land use, *Energy Policy*, **39** (6), pp 3163–76

Thomson, J (2020). Scania puts hydrogen tests trucks into action in Norway, *Truck & Bus News*. Retrieved from: https://www.truckandbus.net.au/scania-puts-hydrogen-tests-trucks-into-action-in-norway/ (archived at https://perma.cc/E2NW-GP3R)

11

Business innovation in the automotive sector

This chapter will familiarize the reader with:

- Business model innovation in the automotive sector.
- The decline of the UK truck manufacturing industry.
- Case study: MAN Truck & Bus UK Ltd.
- Customer relationship management.
- Adapting to an uncertain future.
- Impact of non-traditional investors.
- Case study: Tesla Motors

Business model innovation

The road to zero emissions will not only challenge the status quo of the traditional automotive manufacturers but will also force them to radically change their current business models and deliver innovation on a gigantic scale.

Business model innovation in the 21st century needs to be more than new product development. The type of industrial revolution envisaged is going to be powered by forces that were unheard of by the likes of Rudolf Diesel, Michael Faraday, James Watt or Nikola Tesla.

Business models that have been in place for a century or more are going to be challenged by technology and innovation that will see established giants of industry today disappear in less than a decade.

Think of Kodak and the Polaroid camera and today's digital image landscape. The original manufacturers of cameras have been replaced by smartphone manufacturers such as Apple and Samsung.

Business model innovation is not restricted to manufacturing. The retail sector has also experienced massive disruption. Retail giants of yesterday, such as Toys'R'Us and Blockbuster Video have been replaced today by Amazon and Netflix.

The traditional retail high street has replaced department stores with pound stores and charity shops, which reflects to a large extent the shape of the disposable incomes of a large part of society.

The industry we have spent our life in is now under massive pressure in terms of profitability, productivity and utilization of plants. Unless radical business model innovation is conceived and acted on, many of today's industrial behemoths will not retire gracefully but, like Rover, ERF, Enron, Pan Am (TWA), Standard Oil and Arthur Andersen, will suddenly announce cessation of business and plunge thousands of people into redundancy or early retirement.

For many existing employers, specifically in the automotive sector, to protect their current business and transition to a new reality there appear to be six key drivers of change and innovation that need to be addressed and which will dominate market development over the next 50 years.

Commoditization

There is constant pressure to drive prices and margins lower. Over the last 50 years in the UK, over 30 British commercial vehicle manufacturers have gone out of business. In fact, the UK market is served by just five non-British truck manufacturers producing seven brands. There is a capacity to build over 400,000 units a year in Europe but currently a demand of around 300,000. As a result of legislation in combination with supply over capacity, commoditization of product has created intense competition and driven prices and margins to ever-lower levels.

Future business models need to provide clear product or service differentiation in order to avoid this race to the bottom.

Digital revolution

Business model innovation (BMI) will be greatly influenced by new technologies that will level the playing field by giving small companies the same computational powers that only big corporations used to have. Big traditional players may have to look at collaboration or cooperation agreements with new digital partners in order to maintain their presence in the marketplace.

Michelin Solutions, for example, works with a team of partners to provide a range of services to the tyre manufacturing company. Services such as TyreCheck, which inspects the tyre while in service, and Effifuel, which checks the fuel efficiency of the vehicle through a telematic capability, are just two examples of digital transformation of old business models. Having access to expertise in exploiting added-value information service platforms will reinforce the notion that it is no longer what you make but what you know that is the key to survival in the next century.

Social media

Social media platforms make it possible for people anywhere in the world to instantly connect, share information and create communities. They have been particularly important in quantifying customer satisfaction through a process of customer reviews.

New online marketing communication channels have been created that have disturbed the traditional means of communication with customers and have led to the development of new methods of both selling and payment.

Globalization

Competitors can now come from anywhere in the world, no matter the product, market or industry. Uber is a great example of how an online software capability has not only threatened traditional taxi services worldwide but is also now entering the world of food delivery.

Increasingly turbulent world

We live in an unsettled world of economic upheavals, territorial and religious disputes, shifting demographics, and a very rapid rate of change. The financial crisis of 2008 started in the United States with delinquent subprime mortgages that resulted in a commercial contagion that affected almost every worldwide banking system.

The current trade and tariff disputes between the US and China are further evidence of how an unsettled world can have profound effects within the world trading community. This dispute is not confined to the US and China, as the big German automotive companies such as Daimler, BMW and VW have seen their fortunes in China nosedive.

Speed of change

The speed of change within many business sectors requires organizations to adopt a fleet of foot and even more agile company culture. For many, however, this has not been possible as existing business models are maintained. Current OEMs are having to balance the need to simultaneously maintain production of fossil-fuelled powertrains with massive capital investment in new design and production capacity for electric vehicles.

Both actions will significantly dilute profitability and shareholder returns in the short term. These pressures will also foster unheard of collaborative activity to share not only cost but experience in the development of future energy platforms necessary to comply with environmental legislative demands. Darwin's theory of evolution comes to mind, where he stated that it is not the strongest or the most intelligent that will survive but those most able to adapt to the new environment.

With these six key drivers in mind it is worthwhile also highlighting the thoughts of Professor Malcolm McDonald of Cranfield University. He has enjoyed a stellar career monitoring and writing about corporate success and failure:

> Today, all products and services are excellent – in the sense that they all work perfectly well, so having a good product will no longer deliver you to the riches that you desire. No, today the only way to get rich is to differentiate yourself in a way that appeals to your customers. A big part of this appeal to customers is *money*. If a customer knows that dealing with you will make them richer, they will deal with you. It really is that simple. The problem is, they need to know how they will be richer, and it is your job to demonstrate this to them (McDonald, 2018).

A good example of how the profitability of a whole industry, from manufacturers through to channels of distribution and through to the end user, can be significantly improved via business model innovation and financially quantified value propositions is the case study of MAN Truck & Bus in the UK. It illustrates that the process is not easy, but also that the rewards to all stakeholders, including society, are significant.

Des Evans, one of the authors of this book, was CEO of MAN Truck & Bus in the UK and received his OBE for services to the transport industry. This case history is but one small part of his massive contribution to an industry that was traditionally working on low margins because of massive waste and inefficiency.

The authors are delighted to have this contribution from Des and its potential influence on persuading readers to take seriously the topic of business model innovation and financially quantified value propositions.

Product launches

When launching new products many companies focus on the product features and benefits, the technical specifications, and end up as another 'me too vanilla product' that all too often becomes commoditized and ends up in a price war with its competitors.

The two important questions to be asked therefore when developing a new business model innovation through a value proposition are:

1 Who are your target markets?

2 What is your differential advantage?

These are very simple questions but invariably very difficult for many organizations to answer.

CASE STUDY
The UK commercial vehicle market 1970 to 2020

This case study looks at the UK commercial vehicle market over a 50-year period from the 1970s to 2020 and highlights how MAN Trucks, a relative newcomer to the UK market, launched a new product range into a declining market with remarkable results. The company achieved its goals of reaching 12 per cent market share and selling 6,000 units per year by carefully selecting its target market and demonstrating a sustainable degree of differentiation from its competitors. Details of how these two key questions were answered will be dealt with later in this case study but first it is important to understand the background to how the market had evolved over the 40-year period.

It is interesting to note that the market leadership changed every 10 years; the cause of this was that the primary strategy was production-led and failed to notice what customers really needed and wanted.

The following timeline indicates the changes in both annual sales and market leadership from 1970–2010:

- 1970 UK Market > 6 tonnes c.70,000 units – market leader Bedford.

- 1980 UK Market > 6 tonnes c.60,000 units – market leader Ford.

- 1990 UK Market > 6 tonnes c.50,000 units – market leader Leyland DAF.

- 2010 UK Market > 6 tonnes c.<30,000 units - market leader DAF.

The UK Commercial vehicle market has experienced tremendous change over the last 40 years (Figure 11.1). Legislation, emission standards, new technology, foreign competition and the banking crisis have combined to such an extent that by 2010 the annual sales volume had shrunk from a high of 70,000 units in the 1970s to less than 30,000 units. More worryingly, as far as UK manufacturers are concerned, over 30 UK commercial vehicle manufacturers had gone out of business during this period to be replaced by just seven European brands owned by five organizations.

Bedford, Ford and Leyland trucks dominated the market for over 30 years but during the late '70s and early '80s the Swedish brands of Volvo and Scania together with Mercedes-Benz from Germany and DAF from Holland entered the UK market.

These four European brands brought with them not only new hardware but also very attractive value propositions that were not available from the 'home' manufacturers. Volvo and Scania provided more stylish vehicles that were very well equipped with sleeper cabs and night heaters. This appealed very much to the drivers, especially as transcontinental transport from the UK to the Middle East was emerging. Mercedes-Benz and DAF supplied similarly equipped vehicles, but they

FIGURE 11.1 Changes in truck annual sales and market leadership

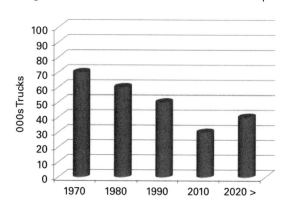

SOURCE Authors

added value through the availability of European-wide service stations that supported transcontinental traffic.

Consequently, the British makes of Bedford, Ford and Leyland very quickly disappeared and today, in a market almost half of the volume of the '70s, the UK market is the 'home market' for DAF, Volvo and Scania. In fact, nearly 60 per cent of the UK market is made up of these three leading brands.

Against this competitive background, UK manufacturers failed to adapt to the new customer needs and focused on product-led 'business as usual'. In addition, the transport business model was also changing with the growth of 'White Van Man' and the significant increases in the van population, with annual sales increasing from 150,000 units to over 300,000 units.

The development of the internet and home delivery business models would further add to the truck manufacturer's misery; however, it also opened up the opportunity for a whole new value proposition to be presented to the UK transport marketplace.

Answering Question 1: Who are the target markets?

Against this background of market volume decline, an example of a new customer value proposition in the UK truck market was developed by MAN Truck & Bus UK Ltd, a wholly owned subsidiary of the German MAN Group of companies.

MAN is a famous German engineering company who celebrated their 250th anniversary in 2008 with the statement: 'MAN – Engineering the future since 1758'. Among their most notable achievements is the invention of the diesel engine, which was developed by the engineer Rudolf Diesel, who was contracted to the MAN company from 1893–1897.

The MAN diesel engine has for many years been the means of differentiation from other brands due to its reputation for reliability, ease of maintenance and good fuel consumption but, as with many engineering-led companies over the last 20–30 years, good basic engineered products are no longer enough.

The customers demand more than good engineering and, more importantly, even good engineering can be copied and sold on price alone. Look what happened to Bedford Trucks, Ford Motor Company and Leyland Trucks!

The Trucknology Generation

On 24 March 2000, the MAN Truck company launched its latest generation of heavy commercial vehicles: the TGA, or the Trucknology Generation, to give it its full marketing description - see Figure 11.2.

FIGURE 11.2 The 'TGA – Trucknology Generation'

SOURCE MAN Truck & Bus UK Limited, 2019

'Trucknology' by MAN Trucks – 'It's not about the Truck!' was the start of introducing a new value proposition that was based on a service strategy that helped transport operators better control their costs with the introduction of telematics. Its target market was operators within a 30-mile radius of the 70 UK workshops as research had highlighted that truck operators were not prepared to travel further than 30 miles to the nearest dealer.

Answering Question 2: What is your differential advantage?

The TGA range represented a new type of product insofar as the vehicle now incorporated electronic, digital components compared to the traditional analogue, mechanical vehicles that dominated the marketplace.

The new product also introduced the concept of 'Trucknology'. Essentially this brought together knowledge of both the trucks and transport industries. The production of this new range had taken place over seven years and at a cost of over €1 billion.

However, the electronic, digital nature of the product enabled a whole new value proposition to be created and delivered to the customer. In the UK several 'key account customers' were consulted, and their views of what truck manufacturers should be supplying were discussed and taken seriously. The main points raised were that the overriding concerns of the operator were not really about the product. Many of the comments were 'All trucks are the same', or 'It's only about the price'.

FIGURE 11.3 MAN, fleet management website

SOURCE MAN Truck & Bus UK Limited, 2019

The real concerns of the operators, however, were the cost of fuel, the performance of their drivers and the service and maintenance schedules in order to keep the vehicles on the road with the minimum downtime. Fuel and uptime were therefore highlighted as critical success factors as far as the launch of this new model was concerned.

Truck profitability

It was further noted that the transport operators' profitability was also a major concern, with average return on sales of 3–4 per cent. For a 44-tonne articulated unit travelling 150,000 km per annum this meant that bottom line profitability would be between £5,000 and £6,000 per vehicle per annum. This represented a relatively very low return for a high-risk operation.

In addition, in terms of uptime, with vehicle availability for 300 days per annum, a 3 per cent return on sales meant that for 291 days the truck operated for nothing. Profitability was only secured in the last nine days of the year and that was on the assumption that no other unscheduled downtime was incurred!

Understanding the total value chain

Figure 11.4 highlights the total operating cost and income of a typical 44-tonne articulated vehicle travelling 150,000 km per annum.

FIGURE 11.4 Total cost of ownership – profit and loss account of a typical haulier

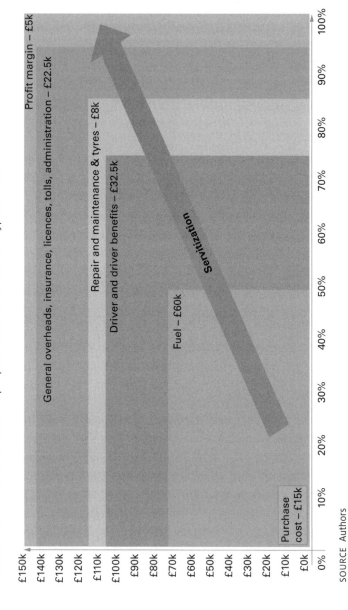

SOURCE Authors

What is interesting to note is that the actual 'product cost' is only 10 per cent of total annual cost. Fuel and driver costs represent over 70 per cent and it is the management of these costs that are important to the customer.

Developing a customer value proposition

A customer value proposition was developed that would focus on helping the customer better control the operating cost by providing real-time management reports that managed fuel consumption and driver performance.

Delivering and communicating value

In its marketing communication (see Figure 11.5) the 'product' was referred to as 'the tip of the iceberg' and the real danger was the 90 per cent of invisible costs that were 'below the waterline'. It was with these costs that the TG range, as a result of incorporating telematics into the service contract offer, was able to support the operator in a way that provided a unique market offer that the competition was unable to match until later.

This value proposition was further validated by the results of monitoring 1,000 drivers who travelled over 3 million km during a prelaunch research study. The telematics data showed very clearly the need for driver training when 90 per cent of the drivers examined in the research were shown to be not operating at benchmark (B) performance levels (see Figure 11.6).

FIGURE 11.5 MAN's customer focus – focusing on operator's whole life costs

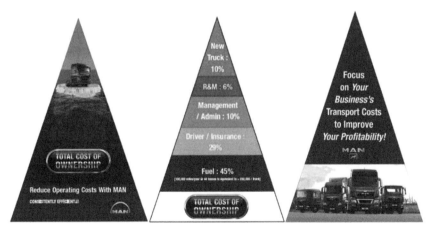

SOURCE MAN Truck and Bus UK Limited, 2019

FIGURE 11.6   Driver categories as tested

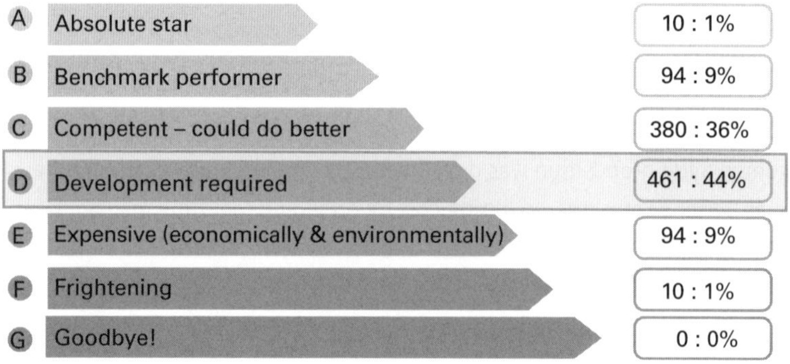

A	Absolute star	10 : 1%
B	Benchmark performer	94 : 9%
C	Competent – could do better	380 : 36%
D	Development required	461 : 44%
E	Expensive (economically & environmentally)	94 : 9%
F	Frightening	10 : 1%
G	Goodbye!	0 : 0%

SOURCE MAN Truck and Bus UK Limited, 2019

What was more important was that the ability to operate at benchmark performance levels would yield a 10 per cent reduction in fuel consumption that would in turn double the bottom line of the typical operator (see Figure 11.7).

Using the Energy Saver, A–G ratings the average driver performance was rated as a D. When the fuel consumption of a D driver was compared to that of a benchmark B driver the difference in consumption was 11 per cent.

This research led to the creation of a value proposition that highlighted the need to focus on the total cost of operation as opposed to the traditional bargaining on the price of the product. This sounds like a very simple message to communicate but it had serious implications for both the sales and service networks as it represented a need for significant change to the traditional way of working.

Delivery and communication of this new Trucknology concept was further developed with the aid of the internet and the introduction of a dedicated website that enabled operators to connect with both MAN and its dealer network.

Together with the development of the website, a new 'business solutions' approach to the market was introduced that enabled customers to track the performance of their vehicle in real time and for the service organization to arrange service schedules online and provide the customers with an electronic archive of all important legal documentation. This was a very significant development in service capability that further differentiated the brand from the competition.

A new franchise proposition, the 'UTP – uptime proposition' programme, focused on providing the customer with a guaranteed uptime – working time – and ensured that any vehicle called in for service would be back on the road within 24 hours. This development led to the creation of a further added-value service called 'Mobile 24',

FIGURE 11.7 Fuel consumption

A	Absolute star	83
B	Benchmark performer	89
C	Competent – could do better	94
D	Development required	100
E	Expensive (economically & environmentally)	109
F	Frightening	121
G	Goodbye!	130 (E.S.T)

SOURCE MAN Truck and Bus UK Limited, 2019

FIGURE 11.8 Transport management solutions – vehicle and driver performance

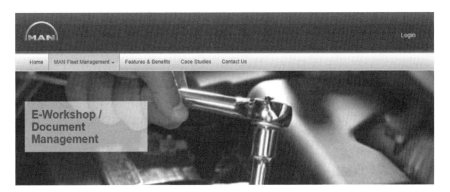

Keep your vehicle on the road for longer but ensuring maintenance is efficiently managed.

Downtime can be minimised even after your vehicle has arrived at the workshop for a routine safety inspection. With E-Workshop, the MAN technician plugs in the diagnostic tool to view the list of faults recorded on the vehicle.

If fixing any of those faults is safety-critical or likely to affect the efficient running of the vehicle, the workshop can quickly notify the operator who can take the decision to leave the vehicle with the dealer for longer while the faults are rectified, or schedule the work for another date.

Underpinned by a Document Management system, all maintenance records generated by technicians are stored for future reference or for use in demonstrating compliance.

SOURCE MAN Truck and Bus UK Limited, 2019

which managed all roadside breakdowns and again gave MAN a leading position in the supply of national service cover.

Three online solutions were developed with Trucknology Fleet Management:

1 Daily uptime report – detailing vehicle off the road (VOR) status.

2 E-workshop reports of all maintenance records – critical for compliance and improved fleet administration.

3 Real-time driver and vehicle performance monitoring fuel consumption, CO_2 emissions and carbon footprint, driver rating and performance.

A dealer workshop management and service scheduler was included as part of the systems development to enable both management reporting and workshop technician control.

This new Trucknology offer to customers soon started to show results. Operators with the typical 3–4 per cent return on sales (ROS) saw their bottom lines improve significantly as improved driver efficiency helped their operating performance.

Learning from business innovation

Changing a traditional business model that is standard practice in a conservative industry is extremely difficult and should not be undertaken lightly. The launch of new electronic, digital products, however, allows organizations to seriously consider their current routes to market and addresses the two key questions facing many company executives:

1 What are your target markets?

2 What are your sources of differential advantage?

In considering any radical business model change, the following five issues should be clearly understood:

1 Assess the state of company readiness:
   a. For the executives who have the 'Big Idea' for change, do not make the mistake of you. Change will be resisted, particularly by those areas of the organization that fear that their current positions and departments will be threatened.

2 Internal communication before external communication:
   a. In order to reduce the level of resistance to change it is important to develop clear, consistent internal communication before any external information is delivered to customers. The external market will only be convinced of the new value proposition if the customer facing-staff has total belief in the new way of working.

3 There are many examples of new product launch failure due to customers having been told one thing only for something else to be delivered:
   a. Establish a clear value proposition.
   b. The value proposition needs to be clearly understood and this has consequences for the internal organization and associated networks.

Product-led organizations sometimes struggle with the concept of lifetime value especially when this becomes the basis of differentiation. This issue may have consequences for training and skills development and requires an assessment of core competences and resource capacity.

4 Understand the risk

  a. Developing a new customer value proposition and changing the business model is not without risk. There is a risk that the new customer offer costs more to deliver than is first calculated.

  b. There is the risk that the process of delivery or execution is flawed. Early testing with valued key accounts can eliminate many errors and actually increase customer intimacy.

5 Establish and agree operating standards.

  a. Any value proposition carries with it roles and responsibilities.

  b. This is especially the case with advanced services that guarantee outcomes. It is therefore important to establish basic standards of operation and clearly communicate what the customer's role and responsibilities will be in ensuring the required outcome.

Become a service company that also makes products

The old business model of manufacturing products and providing average service throughout their working life is now outdated and cannot provide a sustainable competitive advantage. Today's winning companies provide class-leading service and also manufacture products.

The MAN Truck & Bus UK case study shows that a relatively small commercial vehicle importer can compete with the home market competitors at a time of enormous industry change.

Market share increased four-fold from 3 per cent to 12 per cent, turnover increased by a factor of 12, parts sales increased from £10 million to £100 million and with over 10,000 vehicles under contract a new future contract income of c.£250 million was created.

In addition, many truck operators are now operating more profitably and the dealer networks with a new service-based franchise proposition have seen the ROS change from 1 per cent to 6 per cent, albeit on smaller turnovers. The average dealer now has a service turnover of £4 million with a 6 per cent ROS (£240,000 pa) compared to a previous sales and service turnover of £12 million with a 1 per cent ROS (£120,000 pa).

A value proposition is therefore not just for the end customer but for all the stakeholders in the value chain and is proof that with the right internal communication, culture and leadership a struggling organization can compete at the highest level.

Adapting to an uncertain future

What we have witnessed over the last 50 years of truck and van manufacturing and distribution is the rise of owner operators to become significant logistics businesses and they have forward integrated into owning dealerships by turning their workshops into franchised service centres.

We have seen manufacturers also pursue extended enterprise activity by owning their own dealerships and completely managing direct customer relationships, and harnessing the power of digital communications to build intensive market intelligence databases in support of customer relationship management, repeat business and brand management.

Increasingly manufacturers have invested in product development and telematics that enable the activity of fleet management to be significantly influenced by the manufacturer, and tools that are available from OEMs have generated significant added-value service revenues tied to repair and maintenance contracts.

The impact of 'non-traditional investors'

In 2020, we are seeing the phenomenon of 'non-traditional investors' such as Amazon, Google, Intel, Dyson, Warren Buffett and Marc Benioff taking stakes in energy companies, nationwide truck stops, charging infrastructure businesses and very sophisticated freight management software systems that will be a big factor in how the shape of the truck and transport industry will evolve over the next 50 years.

Perhaps the most visible example of this new breed of investor/player on the automotive industry stage is Elon Musk and his company Tesla, details of which follow in a case study.

CASE STUDY
The Tesla approach to distributing and servicing BEVs

In a press statement in October 2012, Elon Musk, Chairman, Product Architect and CEO of Tesla Motors, explained the market representation strategy of his company and why it was different to the traditional automotive franchise model that had been in place for almost a century.

The Tesla model was to be a direct sales organization, effectively a vertically integrated model. This is very different to the traditional franchise dealership model where independent owners take responsibility for all the costs of showroom construction and occupancy costs, and inventory levels financed mainly through manufacturer finance company credit schemes.

Elon Musk considered there to be a fundamental conflict of interest between selling internal combustion-powered cars and selling battery electric vehicle product. Explaining the advantages of EVs would necessarily require the undermining of petrol- or diesel-powered cars, so therefore it followed that it suited Tesla to set up its own showroom staffed by product specialists to ensure this new vehicle platform would be communicated effectively.

Tesla Motors embarked on establishing a presence in high-visibility locations in major cities and saw their retail operation more as a gallery than a showroom. The gallery was staffed by product professionals who were highly trained as electric vehicle product specialists and were educated in how to discuss all models of electric vehicles, not just a Tesla.

They were not paid on a commission basis and did not operate any of the high-pressure sales techniques that were normal in conventional franchise systems.

Tesla Motors has been subject to a variety of lawsuits from various states who saw Tesla as being in violation of the rules that govern how auto manufacturers can sell and distribute their product. Vehicles have been sold in the same way since the 1900s; legislation controls how sales are to be transacted.

Insideevs notes:

Automotive franchise laws were put in place decades ago to prevent a manufacturer from unfairly opening stores in direct competition with an existing franchise dealer that had already invested time, money and effort to open and promote their business. That would, of course, be wrong, but Tesla does not have this issue (Insideevs, 2017).

It is further worth noting that these franchise laws do not exist outside the United States, where almost 75 per cent of luxury cars are sold.

Tesla aftersales and service strategy

At the beginning of 2012 Tesla had 10 stores, one gallery and nine service centres in the United States. At the end of 2012, the plan was to have 19 stores, three galleries and 26 service centres. By the beginning of 2013 the plan was to have more Tesla service centres in the United States than stores and galleries combined. Plans were in place to open service centres in numerous cities where stores did not exist. By the end of 2013 over 85 per cent of all Model S reservation holders in North America would be within 50 miles of a Tesla Service Centre; 92 per cent would be within 100 miles.

In 2018 Tesla had 200 locations in the world and 120 were outside of the United States. Sales had grown from 17,842 in 2013 to 368,186 in 2019 and cumulative production over the past decade was almost a million units (Shoolman, 2017).

However, in February 2019 Elon Musk announced that the company would be closing half of its retail outlets and would rely almost entirely on online sales, which again highlighted the innovative and disruptive nature of the Tesla business model. (Hawkins, 2019).

Tesla enters the commercial vehicle market

Tesla's biggest 2017 moment was the unveiling of their fully electric semi-truck. Investopedia writes: 'The truck features enhanced autopilot and boasts an energy consumption of less than 2kWh per mile. The Semi has been receiving pre-orders from various delivery companies, including UPS who ordered 125 trucks. Production on the Semi is expected to begin in 2019' (Zucchi, 2019).

Other Tesla products

Tesla's mission is 'to accelerate the advent of sustainable transport'. Tesla sells powertrain systems and components to other manufacturers. Tesla has also expanded into the retail sector with the Powerwall, a line of home batteries that are designed to connect to a solar energy system, in which Tesla also has an offering (Zucchi, 2019).

Is Tesla a tech company or a car company?

Tesla did not invent the electric car or even the luxury electric car. Investopedia states:

> What Tesla did invent was a successful business model for bringing compelling electric cars to the market. Part of the strategy was building a network of charging stations to solve one of the greatest obstacles facing the adoption of electric vehicles – refuelling on long trips. Tesla's unique business model, which includes control over all sales and service, is one of the reasons its stock has soared since its initial public offering (Zucchi, 2019).

Tesla to forward integrate as a Tier 1 supply company

Tesla will build its European Gigafactory in Germany after UK consideration was canned over Brexit uncertainty.

Speaking at an award ceremony hosted by German motoring publication *Auto Bild*, Tesla boss Elon Musk revealed plans to erect the factory near Berlin. He listed Germany's production of some of the best cars in the world, and German engineering, as big factors in locating their 'Gigafactory' in the country.

Tesla currently has large-scale 'Gigafactory' battery plans in the US locations of Reno, Nevada and Buffalo. A third plant is under construction in the Chinese city of Shanghai, making the Berlin plant its fourth globally. No opening date has yet been given.

Tesla's EV line-up looks set to expand rapidly over the next few years. It currently offers the Model 3 and Model S saloons, alongside the Model X SUV. Next year, the Model Y crossover is set for an introduction with the high-performance Roadster sports car due soon after (Holding, 2020).

The firm is also planning a pickup truck, along with an HGV – the 'Tesla Semi (Electrek, 2020).

The future of Tesla

Tesla's mission is focused on accelerating the world's transition to energy that is sustainable and zero emission. Tesla wants to completely change the way people think of buying cars. They want to centre it around efficiency as well as being 'eco-friendly'.

They realize the harm the emissions from cars are doing to the environment, and are making what most might call a successful effort at reducing it. After successfully making the electric car a viable thing, Tesla wanted to overcome the key industry challenge of long-distance travel by electric cars: 'range anxiety'.

Tesla wanted to ensure that charging and the distance a car can travel were to be no barrier to changing from petrol and diesel cars. The superchargers made that a reality. Tesla, in conjunction with its battery partner Panasonic, has embarked on becoming the largest US producer of batteries for electric vehicles with the building of its Gigafactory in Nevada. They plan to compete with China to be the leading provider of batteries for all forms of future battery electric-powered vehicles. Details of their plans are outlined in Chapter 6.

Future automotive industry structure

Conventional car and truck manufacturers are going to find their market positions challenged on multiple fronts over the next 20 years as a result of innovation delivered by the likes of Elon Musk and Tesla.

Suppliers of BEV components, specifically battery power packs and technology necessary to power autonomous driving, will gain major influence over the future size and shape of the market.

Ride-hailing companies and current tech giants like Google and Apple will compete to dominate the customer interface and data flows. Google maps currently integrates services for Uber and Lyft.

Summary

- Business model innovation in the 21st century needs to be more than new product development. The type of industrial revolution envisaged is going to be powered by forces that were unheard of by the likes of Rudolf Diesel, Michael Faraday, James Watt or Nikola Tesla.

- Over the last 50 years in the UK, over 30 British commercial vehicle manufacturers have gone out of business. The UK market is served by just five non-British truck manufacturers producing seven brands.

- New online marketing communication channels have been created that have disturbed the traditional means of communication with customers and have led to the development of new methods of both selling and payment.

- Tesla have their business model based on three fronts: selling their products direct to customers, providing servicing facilities, and charging infrastructure for its electric vehicles

- Future winners in the tier supplier market space will be those positioned in the design, development and manufacture of AV software, sensors, powertrain control units, thermal cooling systems and advanced navigation and in-car communication systems.

References

Electrek (2020) Tesla Semi. Retrieved from: https://electrek.co/guides/tesla-semi/ (archived at https://perma.cc/5HGY-7EXH)

Hawkins, A (2019) Tesla will close most of its stores and only sell cars online, *The Verge*. Retrieved from: https://www.theverge.com/2019/2/28/18245296/tesla-stores-closing-online-only-car-sales (archived at https://perma.cc/FX4Q-A5MH)

Holding, J (2020) New 2020 Tesla Model Y: specs, prices and on-sale date, *Auto Express*. Retrieved from: https://www.autoexpress.co.uk/tesla/model-y/96548/new-2020-tesla-model-y-electric-car-enters-production (archived at https://perma.cc/VLN4-VBPY)

Insideevs (2017) The Tesla direct sales vs franchised dealership battle is far from resolution. Retrieved from: https://insideevs.com/news/333376/the-tesla-direct-sales-vs-franchised-dealership-battle-is-far-from-resolution/ (archived at https://perma.cc/H3LV-REB4)

MAN Truck & Bus UK Limited (2019) Images. Swindon, Wiltshire, UK.

McDonald, M (2018) *On Value Propositions*, Kogan Page, London

Shoolman, A (2017) How many Tesla Service Centers are there? *Alex Shoolman*. Retrieved from: https://www.alexshoolman.com/blog/2017/08/19/how-many-tesla-service-centers-are-there/ (archived at https://perma.cc/98CA-9VK6)

Zucchi, K (2019) What makes Tesla's business model different? *Investopedia*. Retrieved from: https://www.investopedia.com/articles/active-trading/072115/what-makes-teslas-business-model-different.asp (archived at https://perma.cc/XTV7-NA9B)

12

Financing the future

This chapter will familiarize the reader with:

- The shift in the centre of gravity for the global automotive industry as it is moved from the United States and Western Europe to Asia and particularly China.
- Automotive industry consolidation 1980–2020.
- New investor community – impact of 'Fintech'.
- Smart and connected trucks drive digital freight management services.
- Future changes to the automotive 'franchise system' business model.
- CRM – customer relationship management in the future (MAN case study).
- The requirements for a new transport ecosystem for 'on-demand mobility' and self-driving taxi fleets.

Industry consolidation and growth over period 1970–2019

Since joining the European Union in 1974, existing UK OEMs have been party to massive consolidation in both the manufacturing side of the industry and the distribution and logistics sectors. The development of integrated supply chains and global partnerships in research and development and manufacturing capacity has been one of the most important growth engines for economic welfare in Europe. Both the passenger car and the commercial vehicle industries contribute tremendously to societal, environmental and economic welfare and growth in Europe:

- The automotive sector represents 7 per cent of the EU's GDP; tax contributions alone from 15 EU countries are around €410 billion, representing 6 per cent of total EU tax revenue (ACEA, nd).

- 5.4 million cars were exported in 2017 from the EU and the European automotive industry accounts for over 40 per cent of global automotive share value (ACEA, nd).

- Commercial vehicles transport 75 per cent of all land-carried goods and 90 per cent of freight value. An average return on sales of 7 per cent is robust but does not compare as favourably as some emerging technology and service businesses who deliver in excess of 20 per cent ROS (ACEA, nd).

While we can look back on nearly 40 years of growth from 1980 to 2020, the European industry is at a tipping point. A report by McKinsey on the future of the 'European automotive industry' predicts a disruptive path ahead for current OEMs and the emergence of new business models and supply chains that will demand that market-leading OEMs redefine their role in a newly created ecosystem because their technological leadership and expertise is at risk (Dekhne *et al*, 2019).

McKinsey reports that the success story of the European automotive industry is going to be challenged by the combination of two revolutionary forces that together are fundamentally changing the industry:

1 There is a momentum driving change way beyond the traditional players who have evolved over the last century, eg Ford vs Tesla.

2 The new players are from different regions, especially rooted in Asia, so we see a new automotive centre of gravity located in China. Annual production has grown from 87,000 vehicles in 1970 to 28 million in 2018.

Notable investments

A key driver of the challenge and change facing traditional OEMs is investment. This has come from tech companies and venture capital/private equity players from outside the industry and is making a significant impact. Existing members of the established automotive supply chain, large and small, are benefiting from these non-traditional types of investors in the industry.

BYD – CHINA'S LARGEST ELECTRIC VEHICLE MANUFACTURER

Warren Buffett – head of the Berkshire Hathaway investment organization – made a $250 million investment in Build Your Dream (BYD) in 2008, when it was a little-known Chinese manufacturer of electric vehicles and lithium-ion batteries. In 2017 that investment was valued at $1.8 billion as shares had risen from around $8 to $80 over the decade of shareholding (Lau, 2008).

Another little-known investment by Buffett's Berkshire Hathaway in 2017 was 'Pilot Flying', a major truck stop retail operation in the United States that has 5,000 diesel pumps and, more importantly, 70,000 parking slots. Buffett will no doubt be looking at the revenue opportunities downstream for both electricity charging and payments, and the installation, when required, of both electric and hydrogen refuelling facilities (Hammond and Buhayar, 2017).

Buffett's significant holding in General Motors (GM) also reflects his confidence in the future of electric cars. General Motors is spending $2.2 billion to refurbish an underused Detroit factory so it can build electric and self-driving vehicles, eventually employing 2,200 people (Nasdaq, 2012).

GM announced through *TechCrunch* on 27 January 2020 that its long-term commitment is to EV technology. GM is investing $2.2 billion in its Detroit-Hamtramck assembly plant and a further $800 million in supplier tooling and other projects. This is GM's first all-electric production plant (Korosec, 2020).

Since autumn 2018, GM has committed to investing more than $2.5 billion in Michigan to bring electric vehicles to market through investments at Orion Assembly, GM's battery lab in Warren, Brownstown and this 2020 direct investment in Detroit-Hamtramck. GM will build EVs and SUVs. GM's joint venture with LG Chem – which is investing $2.3 billion to manufacture battery cells in Lordstown, Ohio – will supply battery cells for the electric vehicles manufactured at Detroit-Hamtramck (General Motors, 2020).

ARRIVAL

We have also witnessed smaller operations like UK-based Arrival receive significant investment. Arrival is an Oxford-based electric truck manufacturer that currently employs 300 staff and is developing medium-sized urban delivery trucks for Ryder, the Royal Mail and DHL, to name just a few.

On 16 January 2020 it was announced by the *Guardian* that Arrival had secured an £85 million investment from Kia and Hyundai. This brings Arrival to a £3 billion valuation, meaning it has achieved 'unicorn' status, a new company valued at more than $1 billion (£770 million). This is a rare feat in British manufacturing (Jolly, 2020).

The founder of Arrival is a UK-based Russian oligarch who made his fortune in the telecommunications business and has developed a brand-new manufacturing business model for Arrival that would be alien to many existing commercial vehicle manufacturers. Arrival claims to be able to build a truck in four hours, with 80 per cent of its future component architecture, including the build by digital printing of lightweight bodies, managed in-house. This will enable the business to evolve into a major tier supplier to the industry in the future, and in the process it will most likely be subject to acquisition from the more forward-thinking OEMs.

CONVOY

Seattle-based Convoy raised investment capital from a long list of notable tech names that includes Microsoft's Bill Gates; as of 2019, the company had raised $400 million (Korosec, 2019).

Convoy said it plans to use this money to expand its on-demand shipping platform beyond the Seattle area where it has been refining it. Dan Lewis, Convoy's Chief Executive said in a statement, 'Convoy's mobile app and automated brokerage raise the bar for service reliability and reduce wasted miles – increasing revenue and improving operations for everyone involved (O'Brien, 2017a).

Perhaps just as notable as Convoy's ability to raise money is its ability to attract some of the biggest names in tech to plough money into truck technology. The 2017 investment round was led by Y Combinator's Continuity Fund, the venture capital arm of the famed Silicon Valley start-up incubator programme. Anu Hariharan, Partner, YC Continuity, in a statement on Convoy, commented: 'This service allows shippers to transform their supply chains, at the same time that it allows carriers to grow their businesses more quickly, on their own terms. In 10 years, we'll be astonished that this was ever done another way' (Loizos, 2017).

The roster of investors also includes Mosaic Ventures, former US Senator Bill Bradley and media mogul Barry Diller. Those names joined Convoy's other notable backers, including Greylock Partners, Salesforce Chief Executive Marc Benioff and Amazon founder Jeff Bezos via Bezos Expeditions.

The latest investment is an indication of how trucking tech is drawing a host of new investors who see an opportunity to disrupt the traditional shipping and logistics markets.

Venture capitalists have taken notice

Growing numbers of venture capital firms are pouring money into start-ups that promise to reinvent some – or all – of the massive global trucking ecosystem that remains the backbone of the world economy. The potential opportunities to disrupt this enormously complex industry have attracted investors that include corporate venture capitalists in the trucking industry and marquee names from Silicon Valley.

Smart and connected trucks drive digital freight management services

The advent of smarter and more connected trucks is drawing the attention of investors who see an opening to innovate. Once these venture capitalists grasp the size of the potential market for trucking services, their minds and cheque books open quickly. They see logistics and trucking technology as the key to disrupting numerous other businesses; that means even bigger investment opportunities and returns may be found down the road.

'A lot of the tasks that were previously done offline for trucks are now being digitized, and it's going to impact this industry tremendously,' said Paul Asel, a managing partner for Nokia Growth Partners. 'But if you start thinking through different industries that trucking impacts, it becomes even more significant. That's why I'm investing in this space (TTT Global, 2017).

According to CB Insights, a venture capital data firm, trucking-related start-ups raised $583 million across 33 deals in 2011 through July 2013. That figure doesn't include the $62 million raised by Seattle-based Convoy in September 2017. Overall, the sector was projected to raise more than $1 billion in 2017, well above the $763 million invested in 2016. That's about eight times the $132 million that was invested in 14 trucking start-ups in 2013.

CB Insights has been tracking transportation venture capital for several years, but broke trucking into its own category in 2016 because activity had become so significant (O'Brien, 2017b). 'People are realizing that trucking is a large opportunity,' analyst Kerry Wu noted. 'With the driving patterns on highways, the use cases for connected and autonomous technologies are much more evident than with passenger cars' (TTT Global, 2017).

There are venture capitalists from the traditional transport and automotive manufacturing sector, such as Volvo Group Venture Capital, who have invested in trucks for years. And there are incumbent tech truck companies such as telematics leader Omnitracs.

These players have embraced the idea that technology is changing too fast for them to do everything, so they're looking for outside partners who can innovate faster.

Trucks are 'smartphones on wheels'

Strategic investors are recognizing that new technologies are making the logistics industry more accessible to companies. 'Every truck is connected these days, and automotive has become more techy. These are smartphones on wheels,' said Per Adamsson, President of Volvo Group Venture Capital. 'And that opens it up for more companies to come into this space' (O'Brien, 2017b).

As well as Volvo, other companies from the tech industry are investing, such as Nokia and Intel. Indeed, one of the largest venture capitalists investments in a trucking company in 2017 was the $156 million raised for Chinese logistics provider Huochebang, according to CB Insights. That investment round was led by Baidu Capital, the venture arm of the internet giant (O'Brien, 2017b).

Silicon Valley investors also joined the fray. In 2016, venture capitalists firm Greylock Partners led a $16 million round of funding for Seattle-based Convoy. Simon Rothman and Reid Hoffman, co-founders of LinkedIn, both joined the Convoy board and said the firm saw enormous potential in Convoy's on-demand trucking service.

Sometimes, the interests of all the venture capital categories converge. That was the case in 2017 when Silicon Valley's Peloton Technology raised $60 million in a third round of funding for its truck platooning platform. Peloton's previous investors included Intel via its connected automobile fund, Japanese auto tech company Denso, and some notable Silicon Valley angel funds (O'Brien, 2017b).

The 2017 investment was led by Omnitracs and followed a partnership the two companies had previously announced to integrate their telematics and autonomous technologies. It also included Volvo and Nokia Growth Partners, among a total of 17 investors in the round.

A key driver creating interest from Fintech investors is the opportunity to address operational costs involved with logistics and distribution. Fuel cost and driver wages are two of the largest costs that can be improved due to the availability of technology embedded in the product and digital services that make the capture and analysis of performance data more accessible.

As we progress through the 21st century we are witnessing a significant change in the attitude and approach of the investment community to the logistics and distribution industry. The competitive advantage is gained through understanding two key factors about the business: it is time and information sensitive. Entrants into this space such as Peloton, Work Truck Solutions and Convoy have grasped the goal of securing marginal gains across many touchpoints along the supply and distribution chain occupied by third-party logistics providers and their retail customers.

Peloton co-founder Dr Josh Switkes said he had been in automotive tech for more than a decade before he gravitated to trucking in 2011. He realized the marginal gains from productivity improvements could be significant.

But it was a lonely journey when he began fundraising in 2013 and eventually persuaded a couple of Silicon Valley angel funds to back the company. 'Automotive investment was not a big thing in the valley,' he said. 'The conversation around vehicle automation was almost non-existent at that point.' There were some truck start-ups that had raised venture capital money, but they didn't do well.

'The VCs who were familiar with the truck industry weren't very excited about it,' Switkes said (O'Brien, 2017b).

Google went public with its autonomous vehicle programme. Intel launched a connected car investment fund, which evolved into a broader vehicular focus that included trucks. Uber and Tesla began making noise about their autonomous vehicle ambitions. Intel invested in Peloton's second round of funding. And in March 2017, Intel acquired Mobileye, the Israeli autonomous vehicle tech company, for $15.3 billion. The whirlwind of developments put a spotlight on vehicle tech, and shifted investors' attention to trucking (O'Brien, 2017b).

The truck industry was revolutionized from the turn of the century when effectively the analogue lorry of the last century became the digital truck of the 21st century. From 2000 we saw the development of on-board telemetry and electronic control units that revolutionized maintenance services. The 'Black Box' technology residing on the vehicle enables remote diagnosis and early warning 'Hot Alert' communications to fleet managers.

With increased regulation forcing preventative maintenance checks at regular intervals, the technology revolution inside vehicles that has enabled operators to better control services levels and product compliance has been the catalyst to attract investment from technology partners and venture capital groups.

'Last-mile' services to transform transport and logistics

For Paul Asel of Nokia Growth Partners, however, transportation goes beyond a question of telecom equipment. He sees a day when autonomous trucking enables a radical transformation of last-mile services for on-demand services by making it cheaper and more efficient. Goodbye bicycles, hello roving autonomous delivery vehicles. 'If we find business models that make sense now, they will make even more sense when autonomous trucks come into play,' Asel said. 'And we think the last mile is going to be a very, very big deal' (O'Brien, 2017b).

Autonomous vehicles already play a part in mining and port authority freight movement operations. Mining companies worldwide – particularly those in Chile, Australia and Canada – are making the transition from manned to unmanned truck fleets. Autonomous haul trucks are operated by a supervisory system and a central controller instead of a driver. They use predefined GPS courses to navigate haul roads and intersections, and to determine the locations, speeds and directions of other vehicles. Implementing autonomous haulage means more material can be moved efficiently and safely, creating a direct increase in productivity.

In July 2017, Autotech Ventures of Silicon Valley announced that it had closed a new $120 million fund, which it says was the first dedicated exclusively to automotive tech. The firm had already made six investments, with four focused on trucking (at time of writing, they have 25 investments). The founders want the firm to serve as a bridge between entrepreneurs and larger transportation companies. As such, a large portion of its fund came from vehicle manufacturers and trucking firms (O'Brien, 2017b).

Dealer systems for niche vehicles (O'Brien, 2017b)

In addition to the revolution happening in the logistics and distribution sector, we are witnessing a desire and motivation for manufacturer dealer operations to update their internal systems. One such example is the management of stock location for niche vehicles. In the period 2018–2020 we have seen the rental and short-term leasing of capital goods gain ground and it's important that dealers can respond to demand quickly. This is where systems provided by Work Truck Solutions have succeeded.

Work Truck Solutions, a company founded in 2012 by serial entrepreneur Kathryn Schifferle, was developed as a platform to serve the highly fragmented market for dealers that sell customized trucks for specific needs, ranging from fire trucks to ambulances to repair vehicles for specific industries. The inventory tracking system was so limited that figuring out which dealer had which type of work truck involved making dozens of calls. Schifferle noted that raising money early on was difficult. First investment arrived in 2014, led by Golden Seeds, a female-founder-focused fund. As of 2017, Work Trucks had signed up more than 650 dealers and reached the break-even point.

In 2016 Work Truck Solutions embarked on an expansion programme that saw the company enter new markets, and was successful in achieving a €5 million round of funding in June 2016.

'Work Trucks are a player in a market space that could develop into a $130 billion industry. It is at the centre of the 21st-century passion and obsession with data analytics and a focus on intensive analysis of customer behaviour, satisfaction levels and how to differentiate your brand through a

FIGURE 12.1   Investing in the future of trucks

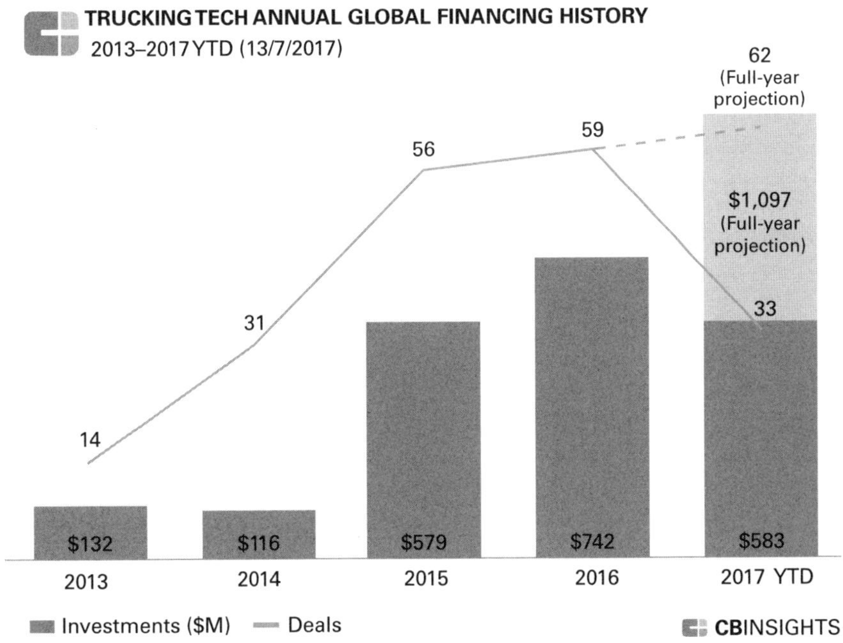

TRUCKING TECH ANNUAL GLOBAL FINANCING HISTORY
2013–2017 YTD (13/7/2017)

62 (Full-year projection)

$1,097 (Full-year projection)

59

56

33

31

14

$132	$116	$579	$742	$583
2013	2014	2015	2016	2017 YTD

■ Investments ($M) — Deals

CBINSIGHTS

SOURCE TTT Global, 2017

unique form of service.' This kind of differentiation was discussed in Chapter 11 with a focus on disruptive business models. However, the kind of investments we are witnessing in the commercial vehicle industry are going to be a major factor in how the market for trucks and vans will evolve, especially in the aftersales arena (Figure 12.1) (Loizos, 2017).

Future aftersales success factors

Figure 12.2 outlines how manufacturers will need to rethink some of the market representation and distribution activities they invest in and control. Revenue streams will be challenged with the substitution of electric powertrains for internal combustion engines.

There are over 2,000 moving parts in an ICE product, but in many cases less than 20 moving parts in a BEV product. Many components used in regular maintenance will be obsolete. No more filters, radiators, hoses, exhausts, water pumps, starter motors, alternators, gaskets to be replaced. Some forecasts envisage that the aftersales revenues currently enjoyed by truck dealers could be halved.

Many of the new entrants into the market, such as Nikola, Tesla and Arrival, are dealing directly with the end customer and have extended enterprise arrangements with their customers to use their depots for regular services.

A great example of an OEM that has successfully developed a vertically integrated enterprise for aftersales is MAN Truck & Bus UK. This service network could be described as the UK's commercial vehicle 'service factory of the future'.

The end of the 'franchise system' as we know it

Since the early 1900s, vehicle manufacturers have an established market representation strategy rooted in a 'franchise agreement' for franchised dealer sales and aftersales representation rather than direct sales and support. The franchise agreement is highly regulated in the United States by both State and Federal legislation, and currently it is not possible for manufacturers to sell direct to retail customers.

In Europe the block exemption regulations that started in the 1980s have sought to regulate unfair practices and focus on any anti-competitive action related to pricing and monopolistic supply arrangements.

FIGURE 12.2 'The service factory of the future'

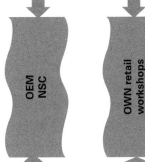

Global plan for parts management and warehouse/distribution strategy Including any 3PL contracted services

- Direct relationship with end customer for sales and aftersales
- Leadership in digital services. Telematics, maintenance & repair contracts, e-workshop management tools
- Control of vehicle population anaysis and calculation of aftersales potentials for use in network planning

OEM HQ

Management of local parts supply delivering world-class availability in support of 100% uptime goals

- Operation of dealer management systems, including parts inventory on a consignment basis
- Central control of facility management and occupancy costs

OEM NSC

Delivering TCO goals for every customer and high-quality R&M programmes to manage client O licence compliance

- Recruitment and retention of technical staff
- Utilization of CRM systems and development of CSI ratings with all customers
- Responsible for local operational profitability and ROS target achievement

OWN retail workshops

SOURCE Authors

However, since the availability of internet search engines and the increasing availability of high-speed broadband and digital media platforms, 70–80 per cent of the retail buyers will search manufacturers' websites to get all the information necessary to make an informed decision. It is also clear that the profitability of franchisees has increasingly been under pressure and in many cases does not deliver, as a minimum, the cost of capital (Srivastava *et al*, 2018).

The future of electric vehicles, where there is a significant price differential between ICE and BEV product, will put even more pressure on manufacturers to review their sales and aftersales strategies, especially where the maintenance revenues from servicing vehicles will see reductions in revenues in excess of 50–60 per cent. This is due to the reduced requirement to maintain parts that no longer form part of a vehicle's content, eg no oil change, filter replacement, hoses to check or replace, no exhaust, no engine or gearbox components, and braking and transmission components no longer are a key part of regular maintenance work (Srivastava *et al*, 2018).

Current players emerging in the electric and alternative energy space like Tesla and Nikola have already announced they will be selling direct to the end customer and making maintenance and servicing arrangements with the workshops and distribution depots of key accounts. Nikola, with the likes of Ryder, Amazon and Rivian, are good examples of this new market representation paradigm shift.

A SYSTEM APPROACH TO SELLING AND CUSTOMER RELATIONSHIP MANAGEMENT

When you see the emergence of start-up services like Convoy and Work Truck Solutions it is not difficult to see what a world of difference the future holds when compared to the heyday of the 1950s and 1960s when Ford and GM ruled the world and people like Joe Girard (Guinness World Record holder as 'world's best car salesman') were the stars of the GM sales teams.

The system he helped to develop and perfect at GM was the GO programme, which stands for 'Get Organized'. Compared to what we see today from the likes of Salesforce it was a very crude system involving sending postcards every month to celebrate, or make potential clients aware of, some specific event. Joe collected a random list of people and businesses that could be found in telephone or other local business directories and religiously sent these direct mail shots every month to potential customers.

It is a system that author Dennis Evans used when starting as a salesman for a Chevrolet Dealer in Pietermaritzburg South Africa in 1975. Not knowing anyone, following his migration to the country, he can still remember his first customer, a sugar beet farmer named Mr Mike Gibson, of Connemara Farm in Howick falls, northern Natal, who test drove and purchased a Chevrolet 1.5-tonne light utility vehicle pickup following interest created by the receipt of a postcard of the truck in the post.

In 2019, customer tracking tools embedded in systems like Salesforce are used instead of postcards. Automation and the emergence of artificial intelligence software systems like Work Truck Solutions and Convoy will be the catalysts to revolutionize the routes to market that truck and van manufacturers will undoubtedly pursue as we transition to not only the electrification of the industry but also the automation of transport and mobility.

CASE STUDY
MAN's approach to CRM – the guiding principles
From author's interview with Iain Russell, CRM manager, MAN Truck & Bus

An example of how customer relationship management (CRM) has been successfully introduced within a major commercial vehicle manufacturer is illustrated by how MAN Truck & Bus UK has embraced data analytics through its CRM strategy.

CRM in MAN consisted of customer databases (the mainstay of any good CRM tool) that were held in multiple locations, in multiple formats and contained inconsistent data. MAN took the decision a few years ago to standardize and centralize the collection and storage of customer-related data by using the Salesforce.com platform, a global leader in this market.

The thinking behind this move was the aim of having a single, consolidated, accurate, relevant and useful database of customers (the market) and also their areas of operation, the types of products and services they use and their needs and wants from a major vehicle manufacturer partner. MAN is working towards going even further with this platform by integrating 'configuration, price and quote' (CPQ) activities into the same platform – this leads us to the biggest benefit of an all-encompassing CRM platform.

How the Salesforce platform supports MAN's direct sales model

MAN's direct sales model is unique within the UK vehicle sales and manufacturing sector. MAN owns the direct working relationship with its customers without needing sales dealers and agents acting as an intermediary. However, for the direct sales model to have the most impact, the manufacturer (rather than the local dealer) has to create and maintain a strong relationship with the market, almost knowing what the customers want before they know themselves what they want, and this is where Salesforce comes in.

Salesforce has the ability to hold and display all kinds of historic data relating to individual and groups of customers. On an individual level, MAN can see a significant volume of trading history, down to the direct products and services that they have (trucks, vans, repair & maintenance) but also their acquisition methods (purchase, lease, hire, etc). By using this data MAN can anticipate a customer's needs and be very proactive in developing a relevant sales strategy. On a group level, MAN is able to extract and analyse data that allows it access to factual evidence of purchasing trends by customer classification (small, medium, large or retail, national key, international key, etc), area of operation (long haul, construction, distribution, etc) or product type (light, medium, heavy, etc). This enables MAN to strategically tailor market offerings to attract the widest (and most profitable) customer base. Since 2015, targeted campaigns have been created by analysing this data, as well as being able to identify areas of the market where weaknesses exist, and appropriate actions can be developed.

The long-term plan for configuration price quote (CPQ) will mean that a sales executive can use a single, integrated front-end system to look after customer data, log activity, generate vehicle configurations, quotes and, ultimately, place the orders directly to the factory – one system, one login, one consistent process.

What were the main barriers to adoption?

Maintaining data has never been the strong suit of a sales executive; they want to be out talking to customers and selling products and services. Sales teams need to be made aware that there is a downstream and long-term benefit to them maintaining and enriching the data held about customers. With an ageing sales force, IT literacy is not the greatest and some people do genuinely struggle with the technology – deals are no longer handwritten and getting to grips with user interfaces, mandatory fields and the sheer volume of data that it's possible to collect does scare some people.

How does a system like Salesforce add value to MAN's direct sales activity?

Consider something as simple as the size of the fleet of an individual operator – it always used to be knowledge held in the head of the sales executive concerned, but now this data can be stored and analysed by customer and segment, and the market understood in ways that were incredibly difficult before. The same can be said about the types of operation that a customer has – before, we 'knew' that a tractor unit would mainly be employed on long-haul work but now we know that they're hauling fridges, or furniture, or fuel, or something else – we can be so much more specific in understanding what the market does at a very granular level.

What are the business-critical data capture and analytics requirements that are key to CRM and the direct sales model in the future?

In a nutshell, anything that allows the manufacturer to group, classify and segment the market to generate and drive different ways of thinking about the market and enable innovative routes to market and products and services to be developed.

Being able to anticipate what an incipient customer requirement is and when they want it is an immensely powerful message to have and would transform the relationship from customer/supplier to one of true partnership and collaboration. It's not what you make, it's what you know that counts.

Automation and AI in the logistics industry

There are few sectors where investment in automation and artificial intelligence are more evident than in the logistics and distribution marketplace manufacturers need to serve. The history of logistics is also the history of automation and trends are putting automation at the top of many CEOs' agendas. Efficiencies are being driven by automating tasks such as picking and putting away in warehouses; AI will take over many repetitive activities undertaken in warehouse operations. McKinsey Global Institute estimates that fully automated high-bay warehouses with autonomous vehicles navigating the aisles will be commonplace by 2030 (Dekhne *et al*, 2019).

Managers with augmented-reality goggles will be able to 'see' the entire operation, helping to coordinate robots and people. Warehouse management systems will keep track of inventory in real time, ensuring it is matched to the ordering system. 3D systems will manufacture parts made to order. Manufacturers are going to have to be as innovative, productive and efficient as their customers.

THE AUTOMOTIVE REVOLUTION

World economies are changing rapidly. Developments in emerging markets, the accelerated rise of investment in new technologies, sustainability policies and marked changes in traditional consumer behaviour around ownership have changed the economic landscape forever. In particular the automotive business has been heavily affected by digitization, increasing automation and new business models.

The traditional top 10 OEMs (see Chapter 8) are all being profoundly affected by the growing momentum of these changes. Four technology-driven megatrends are disrupting the industry:

- autonomous driving;
- connectivity;
- electrification;
- shared mobility.

McKinsey estimate that securing a strong position across all four of the above areas would cost a single player an estimated $70 billion through 2030. They doubt that any individual OEM could shoulder this level of investment alone, which is why partnerships and targeted acquisitions offer an attractive strategy for staying ahead of competitors (Gao, Hensley and Zielke, 2014).

McKinsey state that investments in new mobility start-ups have increased significantly. Since 2010, investors have poured $220 billion into more than 1,100 companies across 10 technology clusters. Investors invested the first $100 billion of these funds by mid-2016 and the rest thereafter (Holland-Letz et al, 2019).

Not only are automotive products changing but production processes and players along the value chain are as well. The 2019 trade war conflict between the US and China, and the UK's departure from the EU in Europe, are forcing OEMs to seriously rethink their global ambitions and reassess regional value generation (Holland-Letz et al, 2019).

Diverging markets will open opportunities for new players, which will initially focus on a few selected steps along the value chain and target only specific, economically attractive market segments – and then expand from there. While Tesla, Google and Apple currently generate significant media interest, they represent just the tip of the iceberg. Many more new players are likely to enter the market, especially cash-rich, high-tech companies and start-ups. These new entrants from outside the industry are also wielding more influence with consumers and regulators (that is, generating interest around new mobility forms and lobbying for favourable regulation of new technologies). Similarly, some Chinese car manufacturers, with impressive sales growth recently, might leverage the ongoing disruptions to play an important role globally (Gao, Hensley and Zielke, 2014).

The content of automotive product is also changing with electronics and software playing a much more significant part of overall vehicle value, and requiring skills and knowledge that so far have not been among the core competences of automotive engineering.

Automotive semiconductor sales have increased 300 per cent over the last 20 years. Vehicle software content will see an annual growth rate of 11 per cent and make up 30 per cent of a vehicle's total cost. Electronics and electrical content will comprise 25 per cent of the total future vehicle cost. There are reports that have indicated that a modern high-end car has 100 million lines of code, 15 times more than a Boeing 787's avionics (Gao, Hensley and Zielke, 2014).

Summary

- The shift in the centre of gravity for the global automotive industry as it is moved from the United States and Western Europe to Asia and particularly China.

- The automotive sector represents 7 per cent of EU's GDP; tax contributions alone from 15 EU countries are around €410 billion, representing 6 per cent of total EU tax revenue (ACEA, nd).

- 5.4 million cars were exported in 2017 from the EU and the European automotive industry accounts for over 40 per cent of global automotive share value (ACEA, nd).

- In 2030, one car in ten sold could be a shared car, according to the McKinsey Urban Mobility 2030 Berlin case study (McKinsey, 2016).

- There are currently 61 Chinese brands selling electric vehicles – more than any other world market.

- Chinese government subsidies for electric vehicles reached €4.8 billion in 2017.

- The Chinese government plans to increase the number of public charging poles from 200,000 to 5 million by 2020.

- In the UK, Arrival, a Russian-backed new player in the electric transport market has attracted significant additional investments from South Korean OEM's Kia and Hyundai, and will emerge as a key future tier supplier to the emerging EV market.

- In the United States, Silicon Valley technology investors have found value in the emerging digital freight services sector with investments in Convoy, Peloton and Work Truck Solutions.

- The premium vehicle market share of traditional OEMs in the United States decreased by 15 per cent from 2013 to 2018.

- Tesla's market share in the same time increased from 1 to 6 per cent.

- The US has led in total disclosed investments into future mobility technologies since 2010 with around €69 billion, followed by China with around €40 billion. The two European countries in the top 10 are the United Kingdom with €2.3 billion and France with €1.5 billion (Holland-Letz et al, 2019).

- Investments in charging infrastructure through 2035 will need to total $130 billion. To put it into perspective, that amount is equivalent to 40 per cent of the 2017 German federal budget in. More than 38 million additional public charging spots will be needed globally to meet demand (Anderson et al, 2018).

- The future of the traditional automotive franchise model is threatened by new players implementing a 'direct sales' model and establishing control through a vertically integrated supply and demand channel.

- Commercial vehicle maintenance revenues from the van and light truck sector will diminish as ICE components are no longer part of the product, eg no exhausts, water pumps, hoses, air filters, oil filters, engine gaskets. This presents a significant threat to future OEM profits.

- CRM expertise to manage market representation activity will be a critical success factor in the future.

- The industry will need to finance large fleets of self-driving taxis. Capital amounting to $1.8 trillion will be needed to finance a total of 72 million self-driving taxis through to 2035. This creates a whole new world of financing opportunities for many different types of players, including cities and their public transportation authorities, car rental companies, OEMs and banks or institutional investors (Anderson et al, 2018).

References

ACEA (nd) Facts about the automobile industry. Retrieved from: https://www.acea.be/automobile-industry/facts-about-the-industry (archived at https://perma.cc/4JLV-86MV)

Anderson, M *et al* (2810) BCG Where to profit as tech transforms mobility, *BCG*. Retrieved from: https://www.bcg.com/en-gb/publications/2018/profit-tech-transforms-mobility.aspx (archived at https://perma.cc/5VK8-QRPN)

Dekhne, A *et al* (2019) Automation in logistics: big opportunity, bigger uncertainty, *McKinsey*. Retrieved from: https://www.mckinsey.com/industries/travel-transport-and-logistics/our-insights/automation-in-logistics-big-opportunity-bigger-uncertainty (archived at https://perma.cc/XA45-SSMQ)

Gao, P, Hensley, R and Zielke, A (2014) A road map to the future for the auto industry, *McKinsey*. Retrieved from: https://www.mckinsey.com/industries/automotive-and- assembly/our-insights/a-road-map-to-the-future-for-the-auto-industry (archived at https://perma.cc/7TAE-APFP)

General Motors (2020) Detroit-Hamtramck to be GM's first assembly plant 100 percent devoted to electric vehicles. Retrieved from: https://media.gm.com/media/us/en/gm/home.detail.html/content/Pages/news/us/en/2020/jan/0127-dham.html (archived at https://perma.cc/R7NE-3869)

Hammond, E and Buhayar, N (2017) Buffett's Berkshire Hathaway buys stake in Pilot Flying J, *Bloomberg*. Retrieved from: https://www.bloomberg.com/news/articles/2017-10-03/buffett-s-berkshire-hathaway-acquires-stake-in-pilot-flying-j (archived at https://perma.cc/T55W-Y4VP)

Holland-Letz, D *et al* (2019) Start me up: where mobility investments are going, *McKinsey*. Retrieved from: https://www.mckinsey.com/industries/automotive-and-assembly/our-insights/start-me-up-where-mobility-investments-are-going (archived at https://perma.cc/QZE9-D2HX)

Jolly, J (2020) UK electric van maker Arrival secures £85m from Kia and Hyundai. Retrieved from: https://www.theguardian.com/business/2020/jan/16/uk-electric-van-maker-arrival-secures-85m-from-kia-and-hyundai (archived at https://perma.cc/KRA8-2RWP)

Korosec, K (2019) Convoy raises $400 million to expand its on-demand trucking platform, *TechCrunch*. Retrieved from: https://techcrunch.com/2019/11/13/convoy-raises-400-million-to-expand-its-on-demand-trucking-platform/ (archived at https://perma.cc/X4GZ-YACC)

Korosec, K (2020) GM commits $3 billion to build electric and autonomous vehicles in Michigan, *TechCrunch*. Retrieved from: https://techcrunch.com/2020/01/27/gm-commits-3-billion-to-build-electric-and-autonomous-vehicles-in-michigan/ (archived at https://perma.cc/NCV2-RAVU)

Lau, J (2008) Buffett buys BYD stake, *Financial Times*. Retrieved from https://www.ft.com/content/235c9890-8de5-11dd-8089-0000779fd18c (archived at https://perma.cc/R5UG-LFTZ)

Loizos, C (2017) In a first deal of its kind, Convoy lands $62 million led by YC's Continuity Fund, *TechCrunch*. Retrieved from: https://techcrunch.com/2017/07/25/in-a-first-deal-of-its-kind-convoy-lands-62-million-led-by-ycs-continuity-fund/ (archived at https://perma.cc/FY22-HMQH)

McKinsey (2016) Urban mobility 2030: Berlin. Retrieved from: https://www.mckinsey.com/industries/automotive-and-assembly/our-insights/urban-mobility-2030-berlin (archived at https://perma.cc/3GE4-YDG9)

Nasdaq (2012) Warren Buffett's Berkshire Hathaway buys General Motors and Viacom, Adds WMT, WFC, IBM, DVA. Retrieved from: https://www.nasdaq.com/articles/warren-buffetts-berkshire-hathaway-buys-general-motors-and-viacom-adds-wmt-wfc-ibm-dva (archived at https://perma.cc/N72C-RSF4)

O'Brien, C (2017a) Bill Gates Joins $62 million funding round for trucking tech firm Convoy, *Trucks*. Retrieved from: https://www.trucks.com/2017/07/25/convoy-raises-62-million-financing-round/ (archived at https://perma.cc/93YE-8LWH)

O'Brien, C (2017b) Venture capitalists flock to truck technology startups, *Trucks*. Retrieved from: https://www.trucks.com/2017/07/31/venture-capitalists-flock-truck-technology-startups/ (archived at https://perma.cc/TY9N-SA6D)

Srivastava, R *et al* (2018) It's time for a new way to sell cars, *BCG*. Retrieved from: https://www.bcg.com/publications/2018/new-way-to-sell-cars.aspx (archived at https://perma.cc/SQK5-3MYE)

TTT Global (2017) Venture capitalists flock to truck technology start-ups. Retrieved from: https://www.tttglobal.co.uk/blog/read/148/venture-capitalists-flock-to-truck-technology-start-ups.html (archived at https://perma.cc/BW4C-65C5)

13

Journey milestones

This chapter will familiarize the reader with:

- The current position we all face with regard to the need for zero-emission vehicles (ZEVs).
- The central role of global warming in the future of trucks and transportation.
- The challenges faced by OEMs to meet future regulatory requirements and the ambitions of the Paris Agreement.
- Where rare earth materials are concentrated.
- The role of battery technology and alternative fuels for trucks and transportation.
- The potential impact of new investors in the ZEV market.

Climate change and global warming

The challenge of climate change and global warming remains central to the future of the automotive industry, trucks and transportation – the subject of this book. *The Road to Zero Emissions* is a journey we are all going to be taking when facing up to the reality of global warming and climate change. We can all contribute to ensuring that it's not just the future of a fossil fuel that is at stake but the future of the planet we inhabit.

A global framework to limit climate change is the central construct of the Paris Agreement. This seminal, legally binding agreement contains detailed global goals to avoid dangerous climate change by limiting global warming to well below 2°C and pursuing efforts to limit it to 1.5°C. It also aims to strengthen individual countries' ability to deal with the impacts of climate change and support them in their efforts.

According to Climate.gov, in September 2017 the level of carbon dioxide (CO_2) was higher than at any stage than in the last 800,000 years with a level of 400 parts per million. Climate.gov also states that it was more than 3 million years ago that atmospheric CO_2 was this high. The sea level at this time was at a level 15–25 metres (50–80 feet) higher than it is today (Lindsey, 2020).

Climate.gov reports further that human-made CO_2 in the atmosphere has increased significantly since the beginning of the industrial era, noting, 'Unless we do something to reduce the amount of CO_2 entering the atmosphere, the world will continue to experience the effects of climate change' (Lindsey, 2020).

Life on Earth is only possible because of the important role CO_2 plays in the atmosphere. CO_2 and other greenhouse gases prevent some of the heat generated by the sun and absorbed at the Earth's surface from simply escaping back into space. This maintains the Earth's temperature at a level sufficient for humans, plants and animals to survive (Global CCS Institute, nd).

The search for alternative fuels and shifting centres of power

OEMs are facing the challenge of building the best EV powertrain package. There is a material sourcing challenge we must face up to, in a business that is very dependent on the supply of rare earth materials (REMs). These REMs are currently controlled by a single country, China, whose current conflict with the United States over tariffs threatens the stability of supply chain development until agreements are reached.

The fight to control BEVs

As the global automotive industry responds to the climate change challenge and the demands from government and regulators who are introducing zero-emission zones prohibiting the use of non-compliant vehicles in city and urban environments, the future of electric vehicle manufacture will be determined by the geographic location of battery production. Currently, the concentration of electric vehicle manufacturing and battery technology know-how and production capacity resides in Asia.

Up to 2020, the EV battery situation in Europe has been something of a paradox; European carmakers have struggled to secure sufficient battery supply. Investments in battery manufacturing have thus far been heavily concentrated in Asia. Plans for 70 global gigafactories have been communicated, and 46 of them are located in China. China clearly has a well-developed industrial strategy to encourage these new plants. It is evident that Europe does not currently have a clear industrial strategy to entice gigafactory investment. This has led to a number of Europe's indigenous battery manufacturers also investing and establishing themselves in China. McKinsey notes: 'Netherlands-based Lithium Werks, which already has two plants in China, announced plans in September for another. The company says it prefers to build plants in China because the infrastructure is better, and it is easier to get the permits needed to build a factory' (Eddy, Pfeiffer and van de Staaij, 2019).

In 2020, the battery market represents a potential opportunity for European battery manufacturers and automotive companies, and for the European economy. China, Japan and Korea currently dominate the global battery market. In 2018, only 3 per cent of the world requirement for EV batteries was satisfied by companies operating outside of Asia, while European companies supplied only 1 per cent of batteries (Eddy, Pfeiffer and van de Staaij, 2019).

The UK must also seek to become a major player in this arena by establishing itself in the battery manufacturing market in order to protect the 800,000 direct and indirect jobs currently in the automotive industry. The Faraday Institution has detailed analysis of what UK job opportunities will be protected if investment in battery manufacturing is made – see Chapter 1.

In 2020, lithium-ion is understood to be the leading technology platform for electric vehicle batteries and has played a big role in driving uptake of passenger car electric vehicles. Its features have delivered high energy density and charge retention capacity alongside low maintenance requirements, but there are signs that this dominance is reaching its limitations.

Battery technology originated in Japan and was then further developed in South Korea, but the centre of the world's battery production for electric vehicles is shifting to China. China's cell production already has a larger share of global production than Japan, and China's global market share is rapidly approaching 70 per cent by 2020 (Eddy, Pfeiffer and van de Staaij, 2019).

E-mobility and power demand on national grids

There is the assumption that the growth in electric vehicles will also cause an increased demand. McKinsey, using Germany as an example, predicts that this increase is not likely to cause a substantial increase through 2030 – about

1 per cent to the total and an additional 5 gigawatts of generation capacity. However, this could grow to 4 per cent by 2050 and an additional 20 gigawatts.

As McKinsey propose that 'e-mobility will not drive a substantial increase in total electrical grid power demand in the near to midterm', new electricity generation capacity will not be needed during that period (Engel *et al*, 2018).

Nearly all market reports on the viability of battery electric for long-haul road transport, where heavy batteries would reduce payload and limit range, conclude that there will be limited growth for electric heavy-duty trucks. A carbon tax or tougher emissions standards could get operators to spend more on lower-emission technology, though such changes seem less likely in the United States than in Europe.

The future of trucking and transportation

Trucking exemplifies both the challenges and the stakes facing the commercial vehicle business. Trucks collectively emit almost as much CO_2 as passenger vehicles. There are far fewer commercial vehicles on the road than passenger cars; however, the travelling distance is far greater and the imposed weight on the roads dramatically higher. According to the International Energy Agency, road freight accounts for 35 per cent of transport-related greenhouse gas emissions and 7 per cent of total emissions (Green Car Congress, 2017).

There is a requirement for a comprehensive infrastructure policy, driven by the UK Government's clean air policies, that is capable of re-imagining automotive manufacturing plants as 'freight-ports'. Freight-ports would be regenerated industrial and distribution hubs, sited on the edge of clean air zones.

Heavy-duty trucks and hydrogen cell fuel technology

Conventional diesel-engined HD trucks have provided the backbone of the US heavy-duty vehicle sector. However, an array of zero-emission and near-zero-emission fuel technology platforms are beginning to emerge and gradually penetrate into commercial sales. These include HDVs powered by natural gas, battery electric, propane and hydrogen fuel cell technology (HFCT).

This is certainly a step in the right direction. It should be noted though that no zero-emission platform (battery electric or fuel cell) is proven in Class 8 heavy-duty trucking applications. HFCT is emerging as a promising solution and may offer a long-term zero-emission solution due to its benefits of driving range and refuelling time. Heavy-duty fuel cell vehicles (HDFCVs) can also provide great utility and applicability to fleets.

Fuel cell technology is becoming increasingly mature and optimized for HDV applications. Nikola Trucks has been making the headlines in both the United States and Europe in promoting the technology and plans to launch a range of hydrogen zero-emission vehicles in 2020–2022. In essence, hydrogen fuel presents the most promising and most challenging aspects of moving heavy-duty FCVs towards actual commercialization and broad use to displace diesel HDVs.

For heavy-duty fleets, fuel costs are paramount in determining total operational costs. The current cost of hydrogen fuel, which is currently much more expensive than diesel, is a significant barrier to commercialization of heavy-duty fuel cell vehicles.

In California, where hydrogen is available, the cost is approximately $10 to $15 per kilogram. (California Fuel Cell Partnership, nd). To achieve parity with current global diesel costs the cost per kilogram for hydrogen needs to be closer to $3 per kilogram. Diesel costs in 2019 are around $2.75 per gallon in the United States. The cost per gallon for diesel in the UK is £6, equivalent to €8 and $8. Therefore, the cost of diesel fuel in Europe is currently three times that of the United States. There is clearly an opportunity for the UK and Europe to be early adopters of hydrogen as a fuel for the future in medium and heavy trucks.

As we enter 2020, we find there is almost no hydrogen fuelling infrastructure designed to serve medium and heavy-duty FCVs. Hydrogen fuelling stations for passenger vehicles are not equipped to fuel heavy-duty FCVs; those that do exist are located on transit properties and are designed to refill fuel cell buses.

Jon Leonard at Act News suggests:

> It's likely that the initial approach to build out a hydrogen fuelling network for heavy-duty trucks will focus on a 'corridor' concept; this will take many years to orchestrate, and each station will cost roughly $3 million. To build out a national network of heavy-duty FCV fuelling stations, it will likely take decades and cost billions of dollars. Careful coordination will be needed with the pace of rolling out the heavy-duty FCVs that will utilize such stations (Leonard, 2018).

The road to zero emissions will not only challenge the status quo of the traditional automotive manufacturers but it will also force them to radically change their current business models and deliver innovation on a gigantic scale.

The future of trucks and transportation will give rise to the following:

- Adapting the truck to the demands of AI and the automation of logistics and distribution freight measurement.
- The end of the conventional automotive franchise system.
- Heavy trucks remain dependent on fossil fuels.
- Light trucks and vans will dominate electrification transition.
- Hydrogen will be fuel of the future for heavy transport.
- Impact on national grid minimal and offset by development of alternative fuels.
- Charging infrastructure becomes a new revenue stream for existing OEMs to consider to offset the reduction of ICE maintenance revenue streams.
- 'Freight-ports' offer the potential to develop a sustainable transport ecosystem in support of clean air and zero-emission zones.
- 'Freight-ports' offer the best opportunity to regenerate 'brown field' sites vacated by redundant ICE manufacturing plants such as Honda (Swindon), Ford (Dagenham and Bridgend), Nissan (Sunderland) and Vauxhall (Ellesmere Port) into energy innovation hubs.

A key driver of the challenge and change facing traditional OEMs is the new type of investor. Tech companies and venture capital/private equity players from outside the industry are making a significant impact. Large and small concerns are experiencing the force of this new breed of investor.

It is clear in 2020 that an increasing number of venture capital firms are investing money into automotive tech start-ups. These start-up companies are seeking to disrupt the existing automotive business models and reinvent them. These changes will impact the massive global trucking ecosystem that is the backbone of the world economy. The potential opportunities to disrupt this enormously complex industry have attracted investors that include corporate VCs in the trucking industry and marquee names from Silicon Valley.

References

California Fuel Cell Partnership (nd) Cost to refill. Retrieved from: https://cafcp. org/content/cost-refill (archived at https://perma.cc/4DAM-K8E7)

Eddy, J, Pfeiffer, A and van de Staaij, J (2019) Recharging economies: the EV-battery manufacturing outlook for Europe, *McKinsey*. Retrieved from: https://www.mckinsey.com/industries/oil-and-gas/our-insights/recharging-economies-the-ev-battery-manufacturing-outlook-for-europe (archived at https://perma.cc/TB9B-DE62)

Engel, H *et al* (2018) The potential impact of EVs on global energy systems, *McKinsey*. Retrieved from: https://www.mckinsey.com/industries/automotive-and-assembly/our-insights/the-potential-impact-of-electric-vehicles-on-global-energy-systems (archived at https://perma.cc/YX2S-EW9U)

Global CCS Institute (nd) The Climate Challenge. Retrieved from: https://www.globalccsinstitute.com/why-ccs/meeting-the-climate-challenge/ (archived at https://perma.cc/8J5Y-DNHX)

Green Car Congress (2017) IEA: improving efficiency of road-freight transport critical to reduce oil-demand growth; three areas of focus. Retrieved from: https://www.greencarcongress.com/2017/07/20170703-iea.html (archived at https://perma.cc/ZMT5-SR5V)

Leonard, J (2018) Hydrogen fuel cell future is promising for heavy-duty trucks, *ACT News*. Retrieved from: https://www.act-news.com/news/hydrogen-fuel-cell-vehicles/ (archived at https://perma.cc/K7UQ-YYF3)

Lindsey, R (2020) Climate change: atmospheric carbon dioxide, *Climate.gov*. Retrieved from: https://www.climate.gov/news-features/understanding-climate/climate-change-atmospheric-carbon-dioxide (archived at https://perma.cc/S6LL-KS9A)

14

The journey continues – 2050 and beyond

This chapter will familiarize the reader with:

- What the truck and transportation market structure could look like in 2050 and beyond.
- The need for gigafactories to supply batteries for BEVs.
- The required vision from the European OEMs.
- The anticipated changes in the automotive world order.
- The impact of technology giants on the automotive sector.

Future destinations

In Chapter 1 we described our message:

> The future of trucks and transport and the underlying forces of change will unleash a whole new industry powered by electricity and technology that will usher in an industrial and economic revolution the likes of which the world has yet to see.

In the course of researching this book, discussions took place with OEMs, Tier 1 suppliers, government agencies, trade bodies and consultancy practices. These bodies provided real facts and figures about the future of a global industry that employs millions of people. Along the way, we have discovered that the rise of electric vehicles, alternative energy products, automated vehicles and concepts of shared mobility, will dramatically change the sources of profitability in the automotive industry.

A transformed market structure

Boston Consulting Group in 2018 highlighted that the industry will need to invest over $2.4 trillion by 2035 and the future markets for growth will be dominated by some key areas (Andersen *et al*, 2018):

- electric vehicle and autonomous vehicle technology;
- cumulative investments in EV technology through to 2035 will total $45 billion, representing 1.7 per cent of OEM cumulative R&D budgets;
- recruitment – thousands of specialized engineers will need to be recruited.

BCG stated in August 2018 that a dramatic increase in battery production capacity is essential to meet the forecast demand for future EV sales. An investment of around $220 billion would be required in battery production plants by 2035 to meet the forecast demand. This investment would be equal to around 13 per cent of the forecast revenue of battery suppliers in this timeframe according to BCG (Andersen *et al*, 2018).

McKinsey forecasts that to meet battery demand in the 2020s, automotive OEMs, their suppliers and investors must start making progress now. McKinsey research supports the view that it takes five to seven years from planning a new gigafactory through to complete production capability (Eddy, Pfeiffer and van de Staaij, 2019).

The development timing of new gigafactories is crucial. Battery production and supply must match EV production volumes. If not, battery manufacturers face the choice between building smaller plants (which are less efficient because of not reaching the required economies of scale, typically around 8 to 15 gigawatt-hours per year for optimal scale effects), or facing the unattractive proposition of operating large production plants at low volumes due to lack of demand (Eddy, Pfeiffer and van de Staaij, 2019).

Large plants with a manufacturing output greater than 8 gigawatt-hours per year are as much as twice as productive per euro invested than investments in smaller facilities. An 8 gigawatt-hours-per-year plant requires an investment of around $120 million per gigawatt-hour per year in capacity. McKinsey expects there to be a demand of 1,200 gigawatt hours per year by 2040. This capacity level would require investment of around $150 billion in cell manufacturing across Europe. Additional investment in R&D and the value chain (such as in electrolytes and electrodes) would also be required (Eddy, Pfeiffer and van de Staaij, 2019).

McKinsey estimate that 60 gigafactories (equivalent to Tesla's 35 gigawatt-hour capacity factory in the United States) will need to be operational by 2040. This will also accelerate the race to secure the rare earth materials necessary for lithium-ion cells – a race currently being won by China (Eddy, Pfeiffer and van de Staaij, 2019).

2050 and beyond

To maintain their leadership position in the global automotive industry, European OEMs need a compelling vision for the European automotive industry in 2050. It is our vision that in 2050, the European automotive industry will be able to say that its industry leaders used the momentum to adapt to significant paradigm shifts along several dimensions:

- from a focus on hardware to software and mobility solutions;
- from stable value chains to a dynamic transport ecosystem with fluid industry boundaries;
- from a stable set of leading players to a changed set of market players with new entrants and industry dynamics from China, start-ups and digital giants;
- from a relatively stable global regulatory framework to increasing regulatory volatility and uncertainty;
- from serving the traditional form of personal car ownership with strong emotional ties to meeting the changing preferences of digital consumers, ie from ownership to renting/pay per use;
- from a static delivery system to a dynamic, integrated transport network optimized in real time. For cities, the development of freight-ports and the integration of long-haul diesel freight and last-mile electric urban delivery transport will symbolize the successful transition to a zero-emission transport system

The Road to Zero Emissions is filled with many different scenarios that will determine the future size and shape of the global automotive industry. The aim of this book is to detail not only what is going to impact existing OEMs that have dominated the industry for 50–100 years, but the likely new entrants that will be positioned to replace them or become seriously wealthy as a result of IPO and M&A activity.

Existing OEMs need to realize that while the industry will continue to grow, sources of profitability will change dramatically by 2050.

Traditional OEMs face the double challenge of needing to make investments in growth areas at the same time that margins in their core business are declining. Among the factors driving the contraction will be lower profitability of BEVs and hybrid vehicles and the cost of compliance with emission regulations.

The Road to Zero Emissions ultimate message

Be prepared for massive change in how we experience transport and mobility. In 2050, the idea of actually owning a car will seem as alien as putting a horse and cart in your garage.

Car and truck factories that were the symbols of the 20th century, and were the bedrock of major cities for a century, will be transformed as the beating heart of freight-ports, a product of innovative city planning and urban/city regeneration.

In 2020, 54 per cent of the world's population lives in urban areas, a proportion that is expected to increase to 66 per cent by 2050. Projections show that urbanization combined with the overall growth of the world's population could add another 2.5 billion people to urban populations by 2050, with close to 90 per cent of the increase concentrated in Asia and Africa (United Nations, 2014).

We are observing a trend away from car ownership and towards sharing products and services that will see more than 20 per cent of passenger miles driven in autonomous vehicles. It will probably be 10 to 20 years before autonomous vehicles and the high-speed 5G network – which are both needed to properly address the price of anarchy – are rolled out onto public roads.

How this shift takes shape will influence the way cities look and feel in the future, too. Autonomous cars have the potential to collapse travel times – and that opens up the opportunity to rethink how cities are planned (Mayfield and Punzo, 2019).

Last, but not least, the era of the automotive industry being a significant driver of global trade will see a future shaped by the possibility of digital colonization of economies and the industry settling for regional concentrations of commercial activity that will avoid the chaos of trade wars, tariffs and the spectre of military conflict.

The echo of the message on the monument to the glacier that no longer exists in Iceland is perhaps the most important to remember (Henley, 2019):

This monument is to acknowledge that we know what is happening and what needs to be done. Only you know if we did it.

The Road to Zero Emissions is your guide to what needs to be done: it's up to all of us now to go and do it.

References

Andersen, M *et al* (2018) Where to profit as tech transforms mobility. Retrieved from: https://www.bcg.com/en-gb/publications/2018/profit-tech-transforms-mobility.aspx (archived at https://perma.cc/5VK8-QRPN)

Eddy, J, Pfeiffer, A and van de Staaij, J (2019) Recharging economies: the EV-battery manufacturing outlook for Europe, *McKinsey*. Retrieved from: https://www.mckinsey.com/industries/oil-and-gas/our-insights/recharging-economies-the-ev-battery-manufacturing-outlook-for-europe (archived at https://perma.cc/TB9B-DE62)

Henley, J (2019) Icelandic memorial warns future: 'Only you know if we saved glaciers', *Guardian*. Retrieved from: https://www.theguardian.com/environment/2019/jul/22/memorial-to-mark-icelandic-glacier-lost-to-climate-crisis (archived at https://perma.cc/2E7T-WGQG)

Mayfield, M and Punzo, G (2019) Car ownership is on its way out. Could public transport go the same way? *City Metric*. Retrieved from: https://www.citymetric.com/transport/car-ownership-its-way-out-could-public-transport-go-same-way-4640 (archived at https://perma.cc/87MX-XL4Y)

United Nations (2014) World's population increasingly urban with more than half living in urban areas. Retrieved from: https://www.un.org/en/development/desa/news/population/world-urbanization-prospects-2014.html (archived at https://perma.cc/E67K-MBSX)

GLOSSARY

3PL	3rd party logistics
4PL	4th party logistics
AC	Alternating current
ACEA	The European Automobile Manufacturers' Association
ACEEE	American Council for an Energy-Efficient Economy
AdvHEV	Hybrid vehicle
AFID	Alternative Fuels Infrastructure Directive
AMT	Automated manual transmission
ANL	Argonne National Laboratory
ASEAN	Association of Southeast Asian Nations
ATA	American Trucking Association
ATRI	American Transportation Research Institute
AUR	Asset utilisation ratio
AWD	All-wheel drive
BET	Battery-electric truck
BEV	Battery-electric vehicle
BtL	Biomass-to-liquid
BTS	Bureau of Transportation Statistics
CAFE	Corporate average fuel economy – California EPA regulation
CARB	California Air Resources Board
CAT-ERS	Catenary-enabled trucks running on electric road systems
CEC	Commission of the European Communities
CFF	Clean fuel fleet
CI	Compression ignition (diesel engine)
CH_4	Methane
CNG	Compressed natural gas
CO_2	Carbon dioxide
CO	Carbon monoxide
COP	Conference of the Parties (UNFCCC): eg COP21 – Paris Climate Conference 2015
DC	Direct current
DFM	Digital freight matching
DfT	UK Department for Transport,
EBA	European Biogas Association
EC	European Commission
ECCJ	Energy Conservation Centre, Japan

EGR	Exhaust gas recirculation
EPA	US Environmental Protection Agency
ERS	Electric road system
EU 28	European Union – 28 member countries
Euro I – VI	European Engine Emission Standards
FCEV	Hydrogen fuel cell electric vehicle
FCV	Fuel cell vehicle
FQD	Fuel Quality Directive
FQP	Freight Quality Partnership
FR	Federal Register
FTA	Freight Transport Association
FWD	Front-wheel drive
GDP	Gross domestic product
GFA	Green Freight Asia
GFE	Green Freight Europe
GFP	Green Freight Programme
GHG	Greenhouse gas or gases
Gigafactory	A very large manufacturing facility (slang)
GIS	Geographic Information System
GPS	Global Positioning System
GVW	Gross vehicle weight
H2	Hydrogen (an energy carrier)
HC	Hydrocarbons
HDE	Heavy-duty engine
HCHO	Formaldehyde
HCV	High-capacity vehicle
HDT	Heavy-duty truck
HDV	Heavy-duty vehicle (includes both MFTs and HFTs)
HEV	Hybrid electric vehicle
HFT	Heavy freight truck
HGV	Heavy goods vehicle
HLDT	Heavy-duty light truck
HVIP	Hybrid and Zero Emission Truck and Bus Voucher Incentive Project
ICCT	International Council on Clean Transportation
ICE	Internal combustion engine
IEA	International Energy Agency
ILEV	Inherently low-emissions vehicle
ILUC	Indirect Land Use Change
ISO	International Standards Organization
LCV	Light commercial vehicle
LDT	Light duty truck
LEV	Low emission vehicle

LGV	Large goods vehicle (UK)
LHDE	Light heavy-duty engine
LLDT	Light light-duty truck
LNG	Liquefied natural gas
LPG	Liquefied petroleum gas
LRR	Low rolling resistance
LSP	Logistics service provider
LUC	Land use change
MDB	Multilateral Development Bank
MDV	Medium duty vehicle
MFT	Medium freight truck
MHDDE	Medium heavy-duty diesel engine
MIIT	Ministry of Industry and Information Technology
MoMo	Mobility model
MSW	Municipal solid waste
MTS	Modern truck scenario
MY	Model year (of vehicle)
NHTSA	National Highway Traffic Safety Administration
N_2O	Nitrous oxide
NO_x	Oxides of nitrogen
ECD	Organisation for Economic Co-operation and Development
OEM	Original equipment manufacturer (generally meaning manufacturer of a vehicle)
PBS	Performance-based standard
PC	Passenger car
PLDV	Passenger light-duty vehicle
PM	Particulate matter
PPP	Purchasing power parity
PPP	Public-private partnership
PSV	Public service vehicle
PTX	Private trading exchange
R&D	Research and development
RD&D	Research, development and demonstration
RFS2	Renewable fuel standard
RHA	Road Haulage Association
ROCE	Return on capital employed
ROS	Return on sales
RPE	Retail price equivalent
RPM	Revolutions per minute
RTS	Reference technology scenario
RWD	Rear-wheel drive
SMMT	Society of Motor Manufacturers and Traders

SMR	Small modular reactor
SO$_2$	Sulphur dioxide
SULEV	Super-ultra-low emission vehicle
TA	Transport Association
TCO	Total cost of ownership
THC	Total hydrocarbons
THCE	Total hydrocarbons equivalent
TPS	Tyre pressure system
TRR	Tyre rolling resistance
TTW	Tank-to-wheel
UCC	Urban consolidation centre
UCO	Used cooking oil
ULEV	Ultra-low-emission vehicle
UNFCCC	United Nations Framework Convention on Climate Change
US DOE	US Department of Energy
US EPA	US Environmental Protection Agency
USD	US Dollar
V2I	Vehicle-to-infrastructure
V2V	Vehicle-to-vehicle
WHR	Waste heat recovery
WHVC	World harmonised vehicle cycle
WTT	Well-to-tank
WTW	Well-to-wheel (total lifecycle emissions)
ZEV	Zero emission vehicle

UNITS OF MEASURE

°C	A specific temperature on the Celsius scale
°F	A specific temperature on the Fahrenheit scale
cc	Cubic centimetre
CO2e	Carbon dioxide equivalent units (based on 100-year global warming potential)
BCM	Billion cubic metres (usually of natural gas)
bhp	Brake horsepower: used as the standard measurement of power as it takes frictional losses into account
EJ	Exajoules
gCO2/km	Grammes of carbon dioxide per kilometre
g/bhp-hr	Grammes per brake horsepower per hour
g/km	Grammes per kilometre
g/kN	Grammes per kilonewton
g/kW-hr	Grammes per kilowatt-hour
g/mi	Grammes per mile
gpm	Grammes per mile
GJ	Gigajoule
GWh	Gigawatt Hour: a unit of energy representing one billion (1,000,000,000) watt hours and is equivalent to one million kilowatt hours. Gigawatt hours are often used as a measure of the output of large electricity power stations. A kilowatt hour is equivalent to a steady power of one kilowatt running for one hour and is equivalent to 3.6 million joules or 3.6 megajoules
Gt	Gigatonne
GtCO2	Gigatonne of carbon dioxide
Gtoe	Gigatonnes of oil-equivalent
hp	Horsepower
kg	Kilogramme
km	Kilometre
km/hr	Kilometre per hour
kN	Kilonewton
kwh	Kilowatt hour
lbs	Pounds (measure of weight)
lde	Litre of diesel-equivalent l/100 km
m	Metre
mb/d	Million barrels per day (generally of oil)

MJ	Megajoule
Mp	Megapascal
Mph	Miles per hour
Mt	Megatonne
MtCOe.	Metric tonnes of carbon dioxide equivalent
MT	Metric tonne (generally US)
MW-hrs	Megawatt hours
P	Rated power of engine family in kilowatts
t	Metric tonne (European or SI)
tkm	Tonne kilometre
vkm	Vehicle kilometre
Wh/L	Watt hour per litre

INDEX

NB: page numbers in *italic* indicate figures or tables